I LOVE YOU—BUT NOT YOUR ADDICTION:
Stuff You Need to Know for Family and Friends

By

D1527165

NAN REYNOLDS

Published in the United States by Beach Front Publishing

Virginia Beach, Virginia

I Love You — But Not Your Addiction:

Stuff You Need to Know for Family and Friends

First Edition, January 2019

ISBN: 9781795426343

Dedication

To Mary Spencer – Volunteer and friend extraordinaire
To Al Turoski – Teacher and heart.
To Stephanie Abbott Leary who waited for me and started it all.

Table of Contents

ACKNOWLEDGMENTS

My first and deepest gratitude to all of the families and friends who have attended the family education and have struggled, listened, learned, cried, laughed, grown, made mistakes and forgiven selves and others.

Thanks to Charlotte who wrote the letter and made the phone call.

To Sherie Duncan with her amazing skills and tenacity as she typed the manuscript and transformed it into presentable.

To my editor, Liane Larocque, for her encouragement and kind abilities and deep knowledge. And to her side kick Toby who licks her face and keeps her smiling.

This book would not have been possible without Liane and her support and skill.

Without her, I would have thrown my computer into the ocean.

To Tommy Loyola –my computer Hero.

To the artist of the Boxing Ring—Eric Moore and Sis Wenger for her passion for the kids and her lifetime work on their behalf.

To my four children from whom I continue to learn and always love.

To the lifetime friends in Michigan. Kellie Pingilley and Sharon Putinta and all of the team mates at Brighton Hospital for so many years. A special thanks to the 'angels' who worked so hard on the workshops we did. A special nod to Walter who so tirelessly supported the effort.

A smile and a hug to Jeff Jay who has had my back for years. It has been fun.

And my more recent appreciations to Claire Ricewasser who has been so encouraging and a great teacher of all things Al-Anon.

And, finally, to Kay Sudduth for all of the prodding and suggesting and sharing of wisdom, questions and bacon.

"We are all in the same boat on a stormy sea and we owe each other a terrible loyalty".   G.K. Chesterson

A Letter from Charlotte

Twenty-six years ago, I begrudgingly sat in the basement of XXXXXX Hospital waiting for the family group to begin. My boyfriend, well really, I was desperately trying to pretend he wasn't my boyfriend, having finished an inpatient stint, was now in outpatient treatment for cocaine addiction. For several months, we had separated. I had left him because his addiction had become unbearable for me. Our nine-year relationship had been a revolving door. We would be together during his "recoveries," then his addiction would creep back in, I would leave, he would "get better," I would return, repeat, repeat, and repeat. This time I had said it was for good. I even found myself a new man. This guy put me on a pedestal, wanted to buy a house for me and presented me with an engagement ring that I wasn't ready to accept. He convinced me to wear it and think about it. But I went to bed that night with the ring on my finger and woke up the next morning with it clenched in my fist. I knew this could not be a good sign.

I didn't have the best history of engagement rings. Just that past December, my boyfriend was at the height of his addiction. He knew I was close to leaving again. He also knew how very much I had wanted to get married when things had been good between us. So, he bought a beautiful diamond ring for me. I had never seen him so nervous as when he presented that ring and asked me to marry him. I had never been more brokenhearted (or so brave) when I had to say, "No." From that day on his addiction escalated.

Sometime around mid-afternoon on Christmas Eve, Jerry said he was going Christmas shopping. His family and my two daughters and their families were coming for dinner Christmas Day. I was preparing the entire meal. It was outside my realm of thought to ask anyone to bring anything or to ask him to help me. Hours went by, and he didn't return. By 9:00 p.m., I knew with every hair on my head, every nerve in my body and every heavy thump of my heart that he had encountered a snow storm and it was not the kind that would melt anytime soon. I took a hot shower, drank some wine, and tried everything I could think of to calm myself. I had been through this so many times before. There would be no sleep, just hour upon hour of anger, tears, loneliness, and desperation. My mind could not believe that he would do this on Christmas. He must be dead or injured.

When he dragged himself in at 8:30 a.m. on Christmas morning, his eyes were round dead pools. He reeked of body order and cocaine. He was still so high that his tongue was too thick to talk and, as my screams of rage, humiliation and exhaustion rained down on him, he walked past me to the bedroom and fell into bed. Several hours later, the family came, dinner was consumed, gifts were opened, I smiled through it all, and nobody knew. The compliments and praise I so desperately needed for all the effort I had put into everything did little to soothe the wounds in my soul. I left him shortly after that.

So, the evening after I woke with another man's engagement ring clenched in my fist, lo and behold, my quasi-ex-boyfriend showed up at the door. He looked terrific, better than he had in years. He was animated and happy but also, contrite. He said to me, "Char, you always said that if I went into treatment, you would be there to support me. I am not asking you to do that. I am in treatment, but I am here because I have learned that you need help, too." As I was about to shut the door in his face, he continued, "XXXXXXHospital has a Friends and Family group that meets on Wednesday nights. I won't be part of that group. You don't have to talk to me or be with me. It is about you learning how we got to this place."

I replied, "It's too late. I am done," and I closed the door.

A friend called me a few days later and told me that she had been talking to Jerry. She talked about how well he was doing and that this time she thought he had changed. Jerry had told her about the family group and, since she was having difficulty with her husband's drinking, she wanted to go and check it out. She asked me to go with her. So, that is how I found myself in that room all those years ago.

There were about twenty of us, men and women, young and middle-aged, sitting in a large circle when a boisterous woman with a hearty laugh came in, took a seat and introduced herself as Nan. That is all I remember about that first family group. Even though I don't know what was said or how things transpired, I know that that meeting, that hour and a half, was the beginning of a lifelong process that would change my life and everything about it for the better. That change did not come quickly. It did not come without pain. It did not happen without commitment and hard work. It did not come without failure.

Eventually, Jerry and I started going to meetings together on Wednesday nights. He went to AA/NA, and I went to the family group. Nan had been involved in his treatment and knew him well, or perhaps I should say, "she had his number." Jerry did not pressure me to move back in with him, but I did break it off with the other guy, and things were great between the two of us again. He was working his program, making amends to those he had hurt and almost literally preaching sobriety to everyone he encountered. It was euphoric. So, when Nan told me that she was pretty sure Jerry wasn't going to stay sober, I was certain that she was wrong.

After a few months into this routine, an old friend of Jerry's who he had not seen in a few years called me. He asked me why I hadn't contacted him when Jerry got so severely involved with drugs. He wanted to help, and he was going to start spending time with Jerry.

Within a few short weeks, something about Jerry changed. As it turned out, this well-meaning friend introduced Jerry to crack cocaine. This time Jerry descended into a world of drug abuse to the degree that he was unrecognizable to me.

Heartbroken and alone, I continued with the family meetings. This time I did not seek out male companionship. I knew now that I was broken and until I fixed what was broken in me, any relationship I entered into was doomed to fail. I needed to learn to love and heal myself. In the meetings, I learned so much about how my own dysfunctional family life had set the course for my co-dependent tendencies. I was the middle child in a family with five children. An interactive play that was put on in one of our sessions depicted the roles of children by their birth position within a family. It brought me to tears. As a child, I had been the invisible one, and I became the peacemaker who was a bridge between the youngest and the oldest. I craved the attention of my overbearing father whose cruel words and judgment robbed me of my self-esteem. I saw my child self-depicted on that stage, a scarf covering her head while chaos reigned around her, silently screaming, "I am here, please see me, please love me." Jerry had been a mirror of my father.

I wish I could say that those two years I spent in the family program cured all my quirks and I left the program completely in control of my life and full of self-confidence and self-worth. In reality, I left the program with a toolbox. It was up to me to put those tools to use or to lock them away. I have done both because an alcoholic or a person with an addiction is a person with an addiction for life, but a co-dependent is a co-dependent for as long as there is someone else's life to control. People who just NEEDED my help surrounded me! Even though my life was messed up, I knew the answers to everyone else's problems, even more so since I now had my toolbox.

Jerry eventually dug himself out of the hell he had entered. He once again went to outpatient rehab. This time there was no euphoric transformation. He just seemed normal. I eventually moved back in with him because somewhere in all of the work I had done on myself, I had decided that I was not willing to give up on him. I was learning about boundaries. I had my toolbox. I was getting better at recognizing my role in his addiction, my control, my passive aggressiveness and I learned about true commitment.

Remember that engagement ring? Well, we started talking about that again and, while he was at work one day. I dug it out of his drawer. I wanted to see how it felt to put it on my hand. I wanted to be sure that if he gave it to me again and I agreed to wear it, I was not going to wake up with it clenched in my fist. I opened the case and just stared at the ring for several minutes. It never made it to my finger. I closed the box and returned it to his drawer. It was several days before I could talk to him about it. When I finally did, I asked him what happened to my ring. With tears in his eyes, he admitted to me that, before he went back to rehab, he had pawned the diamond for drug money and had it replaced with a fake stone. Undeterred by the three engagement ring curse, we took the gold band from the ring along with some scraps of gold from each of my sisters and had it made into a ring with blue tanzanite we had bought on a cruise set on top of some baguette diamonds that formed a "J." So now, we had the band with something old, and something borrowed the blue tanzanite and the new baguettes. That should do it. This one will work; don't you think?

Well, it didn't. A year later, I found myself moving out again. I had begun detecting the signs of crack usage six months earlier. I talked openly to Jerry about it. I didn't criticize or belittle him. I told him I loved him and always would. I also told him that I was moving because I was broken, not because of him or anything he had done. This move was not his fault. By this time, I had more than fifteen years of co-dependency training. I had read books, gone to meetings and watched films. I thought I knew it all until a deep yearning caused me to start going to church about a year before this. What I had painfully discovered is that my judgmental little self had climbed a ladder of self-righteous recovery without ever addressing the very first rung and I had fallen all the way back down that ladder to the missing foundation. This time, when I moved, I bought a house, which solidified the commitment to my recovery and made it seem much more permanent to Jerry. For a while, he slid into occasional crack use. He was standoffish with me, and I just let go and let God. I never took that ring off my finger. It represented my commitment to both of us. It took us eight years of hard work to get our relationship back again.

As a child, I grew up in a church where we sang "Jesus Loves Me," but we learned about a vengeful and judgmental God whose standards one could never achieve. The guilt-based religion fostered a child in me filled with self-loathing and worthlessness. At eighteen years old, I was pregnant and married. I left the church behind. What I didn't realize is the cane of judgment I had been beaten with left with me. I had beaten myself with that cane for all those years. I believe now that every time I hit myself into a cave of worthlessness and self-loathing, every strike of that cane was a strike on the nails of the cross. Jesus wept for me. Jesus longed for me to build my foundation on his pure love and forgiveness. Until I could do the work of forgiveness, first of myself and second who damaged the child within me, there was no foundation and no first rung for the ladder to climb out of my despair.

As I worked through this process with the amazing Grace of God, the tools in the toolbox Nan had helped me gather all those years ago took on new purposes in rebuilding my life. I examined my experiences with my father and defined it by decades.

- Childhood-Fear and abandonment
- Teens-Rebellion
- Twenties-Hatred and blame
- Thirties-Indifference
- Forties-Acceptance
- Fifties-Forgiveness and healing

One of the first things I did after moving away from Jerry was to take my father to Alaska for his 85th birthday. Over the next ten years, I traveled with him to many places, spent time listening to the stories of his childhood, his military service and his adventures and his failures. He had been working since he was eight years old. My dad is a great storyteller. He was always the main character and usually the hero in these stories. In listening, I realized that his storytelling was his cry for attention, love, acceptance, and approval. I saw how wounded the child within him was and even envisioned the child in me cradling and comforting the child in him. We would take long drives with his hand over mine on the console between us. He sometimes wept over his declining health and his dependency on others because he could no longer drive. But, in all honesty, I was impressed that he accepted his weaknesses for the most part and humbly accepted our help.

My total acceptance and forgiveness of my dad were the most significant step in forgiving myself for the destructive things I did in the depths of my co-dependency. I recognized that the pattern of my life with Jerry had followed the pattern of my life with Dad. I asked Jerry to forgive me for my part of his addiction. Five years ago, I moved back in with Jerry.

My father passed away this past December. About a week before he passed, he called my brothers and sisters together. He told all of us that he was so very proud of us. But he said that our mother deserved all the credit for that. He said that he had not been a good father to us. He didn't know how to be one. As the babies kept coming, he felt his dreams were stifled, and the weight of keeping food on the table overwhelmed him. The fear of failing and the guilt of selfishness robbed him of being the father that he wished he were. I was so proud of him. I also knew that, when he died, I would have no regrets. I was so profoundly grateful for the then years we had together.

Three months after Dad died, my brother was diagnosed with terminal cancer. He was my closest brother and my business partner. We have worked together every day for more than thirty-six years. I was closer to him than any of my siblings. He was my champion and cheerleader. He had a huge heart. The two of us had shared our lowest lows and our highest highs. He died in July.

This has been one of the most challenging years of my life. Through it all, Jerry has been my rock. He held me when I cried; he comforted me when I raged. Jerry didn't expect anything from me. He didn't try to fix it. He was just totally, one hundred percent there for me. The gratitude that I felt for everything and everyone who had brought us to this place filled my heart.

The beginning of my healing started in that room twenty-six years ago. I wondered how Nan would feel about Jerry and me never giving up on each other. She had told me so often that we were caught in the windshield wiper effect. One moves away, the other chases and vice versa. Throughout the years Jerry and I spoke of Nan. Jerry always fondly referred to her as the drill sergeant. Through the grief and the family chaos of this last year, I have had to dig deep into that toolbox that Nan helped me assemble. The family program at XXXXXX Hospital was one of those "God things." When I walked away from the church I grew up in, the cane of destruction was not the only thing that left me. Jesus came, too. When I look back over all those years, I see where he showed up. I know that he had planned long before whatever crisis happened. When I finally surrendered the power to him, everything else fell into place. Had I listened more carefully in that room all those years ago, I would have had the foundation I needed to make the tools work, surrendering the power.

The last important thing that I learned was to listen to the small voice inside you that carries the voice of God. If you think you should call someone or send them a card, then do it. You may not know the reason why. Nan had been on my mind a lot lately. I decided to search for her on the internet. When I finally found her, she told me she had been writing a book about the Family Program. She wanted to share everything she had learned and experienced in the decades of being a champion for this cause. She also said that she had been in a slump recently, wondering if it was worth it and who would care. My call to her came at a time she needed it, and she asked if I would write this letter.

Believe in the "God things" take heed of the messages. You never know whose life you may affect. Having the opportunity to give back to Nan, is a wondrous gift. If I play a minimal role in keeping these valuable and much-needed programs available-how fantastic, that would be!

Comments from the "War Zone"

A sampling from many family members who have experienced the struggle.

This is a wonderful and much needed book to publish and to share.

-Becky

I had no idea what healthy support and good information looked like. Healthy for me and for my husband. The lessons served me well throughout my life. I learned the value of connection and helped me realize that I did not have to be alone.

-Anetia

I learned the great benefit of learning that "NO" is a full sentence. I learned that neither my husband or I could 'fix' our son. The family information has helped me keep most (well, some) of my sanity!

-Jane

The trouble that families have in living with someone's addiction is we enter the war unarmed. No matter what we try the addiction always wins. Until we get armed with stuff that really works for us, we continue to fight a losing battle. And if that is not a war zone, I do not know what is! This book is great armor. The knowledge changed and saved my life.

-Mary

The information here offers a priceless and safe place to open our minds while understanding too well the confusing pain, sadness and occasional joy that accompany the presence of addiction in our family.

-Kathy

The addiction of a loved son was tearing my family apart and destroying me to the core. The family information has taught me critical life skills to understand and how to recognize and deal with this overwhelming disease. Loving an addict from a distance, learning how to communicate and recognizing enabling behaviors are critical. The key to family survival is knowledge, peer support, healthy communication and guidance. Sometimes the new awareness was not what I wanted to hear or learn, but it was what I needed to understand.

-Christopher

I have benefited greatly from all of this knowledge. Our son has both addiction and a mental illness challenging him and us. This book pays special attention to the needs of the non-addicted family members and friends who have been deeply affected. Take it from a veteran of the War Zone—this woman knows what she is talking about.

-Dr. Robert

When I learned our son had addiction and mental health issues, my world turned upside down. This book has offered knowledge, resources, advice, comfort and encouragement. Attending a support group has also kept me in check and on track.

-Joyce

INTRODUCTION

The road to addiction (or harmful use) is a trip through the fire swamp. Full of surprises, horrors, sinkholes and twists. So, also, is the trip through the recovery process for both the person with an addiction and anyone else who cares for them. Help is available today for many people with addictions who chose to get out of the swamp and maintain sobriety. Not so for many thousands of family members. If a family is fortunate, they will hear about and attend Al-Anon or Nar-Anon and find wisdom for themselves. They do not, however, receive some necessary education that a substantial family and friends program would offer.

I think of a family program as a place to get your car serviced before you start your trip. It is an education that is similar to the content of the driver's manual that holds new information for you. Some of the pages are about repair-some about the operation and some about maintenance. Some help you identify the problem.

So, it is for us, the family and friends of a person with an addiction. The content of the family program is preparation for the long journey. It is like filling the gas tank before you get on the highway. It can help us avoid some pot-holes and unnecessary side trips. A GPS so to speak.

This information will offer these things:

- It is a menu of 21 chapters of interest to family and friends to introduce you to the possible content of a family program.

- Is not intended to be a list of do's and don'ts.

- It will encourage new topics for consideration and to help develop a new perspective on the situation for selves.

- It will help family and friends have more tools in their toolbox.

- It encourages the family to recognize the need for their education and growth.

- Is intended to encourage the family to take the focus off of the person with an addiction.

- It will help recognize and honor the family and support their need to heal.

- It will help the family support system become more effective and knowledgeable, which will, in turn, also help the person with an addiction. Someone once said: The only thing worse than living with a person in active addiction is to live with an untreated family member.

William White said, "We all have a need to try and make sense of things." This book may help.

Chapter 1: Attitudes

Attitude is everything—some feel they are more important than facts. Some feel they can make or break a day. We have a choice over our attitudes. It is the one thing we do have the power to change. It is said that life is 10% what happens to me and 90% how I react to it. In one group, I always asked the family to shout out what their attitude was towards a person with an addiction, or addiction itself. The list that spread over the board began to make the point. There are several attitudes about both. Some extensive research by Bill White and Ernie Kurtz revealed that, since 500 BC, attitudes about "drunkards" were found in a myriad of writings. It showed, as it does today, that there was a strong opinion about seeing the problem as mental health, or disease, or viewing it as a choice, or as 'immoral and weak' behavior. Is it in need of punishment or treatment?

When asked to shout out what attitude (not feeling) they have, the answers were: When I think of someone who is drunk or addicted, I think they are sick, disgusting, morally weak, repulsive, frightening, pitiful, irresponsible, ugly, bad, flawed, distant, dangerous, stupid, lost in the sauce, a loser. I also asked what attitude or judgment they held about the family in general or parents of a person with an addiction: Most responded that they felt there was something hidden and profoundly wrong in that family, the family was to be blamed, and the house was to be avoided. (Consider that about 15-20% of the households on your street are dealing with this problem—mostly hidden).

When asked what first impression they acquired, or where it came from, the answers were usually a childhood memory, or perception or an expressed familial attitude. My own came from watching *The Lost Weekend* movie years ago. Ray Milland was an alcoholic who had delusions of mice coming out of the wall with blood running down. He was hallucinating, but my young mind was terrified, and an attitude was set.

Let me ask you to imagine a scene: You are standing at your curb and looking toward two homes. On the right lives an alcoholic father who is generally pleasant, helpful and a 'good guy.' He falls asleep on the couch early every night and misses the family interactions. The house on the left also has an alcoholic father. He is loud, the yard is unkempt, his children and wife are withdrawn and look unhappy, and he occasionally parks the car in your yard.

Let me ask you—who needs help? We so often judge the severity of this disease by the behavior of the person with an addiction. How many times have I heard someone say "but, he's such a nice guy!" The truth is that both men have a progressive, chronic, and fatal disease that needs to be treated. A male patient once got upset that his family was in the family program. He yelled at me that he was a great father—after all; he paid for all of their colleges. I am sure it would have been too painful, even though necessary, for him to hear directly from them about their relationships. This disease seems to be elusive to identification and truth. It is often our innocent and uneducated attitudes that feed into the continuation of the denial. We need to see beyond the behavior.

I remember the time my husband came home and headed straight for the cupboard above the refrigerator to get to the Vodka. I took it very personally and got upset that he had not greeted all of us first. Today I would completely understand his need to beeline it to the alcohol to get his shaky nerves under control. Today I would arrange an Intervention. Today I would have stopped enabling and disabling behaviors and attitudes. I once apologized to him for failing him in so many ways because I did not see what I now could see and know what I now know. Attitudes often change a great deal with education.

What follows is a test about attitudes: Answers to follow (peek if you must).

The original source of this 'test' is unknown.

"THE TEST"

1.	Some social drinkers consume far more alcohol than even advanced alcoholics do.	T	F
2.	Tranquilizing drugs, such as Librium or Valium are often valuable in maintaining the recovering person with an addiction through the first year of sobriety.	T	F
3.	The family member of a person with an addiction may become as disturbed as the person with an addiction.	T	F
4.	An alcoholic with over ten years sobriety may safely take an occasional social drink.	T	F
5.	Chemical dependency is considered a symptom of an underlying personality or mental disorder.	T	F
6.	The family member with knowledge and understanding of chemical dependency will have the ability to keep the person with an addiction on the road to recovery.	T	F
7.	The first step in helping a person with an addiction dependent person is determining the underlying reasons for using.	T	F
8.	The spouse and/or parents of the addicted person are often a primary cause of the problem.	T	F
9.	The addicted person is as blameless for their condition as the person with diabetes but is responsible for their recovery.	T	F
10.	In the person with an addiction's family, most family members have unknowingly provided the environment for the person with an addiction to continue "using."	T	F

11.	Becoming unconscious from excessive drinking is called a blackout.	T	F
12.	"Involuntary" treatment of a person with an addiction has been shown to be effective.	T	F
13.	The ability to confine drinking to weekends suggests that a person is probably not an alcoholic.	T	F
14.	A person who never consumes anything stronger than beer is probably not an alcoholic.	T	F
15.	No one fully knows the causes of chemical dependency.	T	F
16.	A chemically dependent person who is maintaining sobriety has no greater number of serious emotional problems than other people in general.	T	F
17.	Alcoholics tend to abuse any other chemical substances given them, which produce a sedative effect.	T	F
18.	It is usually wise to conceal liquor when entertaining a recovering alcoholic in your home.	T	F
19.	Once the person with an addiction begins the recovery process, it is usually not necessary for other family members to grow, since the major problem has been resolved.	T	F
20.	In essence, chemical dependency boils down to a simple question of willpower.	T	F
21.	A person in treatment for alcoholism can safely use 'pot' during recovery.	T	F
22.	This "test" was tons of fun.	T	F

Answers and Explanations of 1-21

1. True. It is true that there are some people who may be harmfully involved but still choose to consume more. An alcoholic may truly wish to have only 2 drinks and may continue on into the night and not quite know why. That is why the dishonesty begins. They have to explain to themselves what they cannot. The body is in charge, not the choice.

2. False. Another name is Sedative-ism. The brain does not distinguish between drugs—beer, Valium, Librium—all the same in this sedative class of drugs. Recovering people need to avoid all mood and mind-altering drugs. Some say the brain has been hijacked.

3. True. Who could live with such craziness and not become a bit off plumb? We adapt to the impossible and get really bent out of shape in that effort.

4. False. The brain does not care how long it has been or how old you are—there are many stories of people with addictions who relapsed after many, many sober years in the false hope that it had all gone away. Nope.

5. False. Chemical dependency may co-exist with another primary problem, such as a mental disorder, but many people with addictions, once detoxed, find that the symptoms of 'mental disease', like depression, disappear. It is not a symptom of personality disorder. It is its own entity and may develop as a means to manage some other problem.

6. False. The family, regardless of how knowledgeable, will never have the power to control someone else's outcomes. Don't we wish!

7. False. The first step is to put out the fire. When a house is on fire, we do not stand at the curb and wonder how it started. Nor do we attempt to assess the damage and begin repair until the smoke is gone. How many hours have we spent discussing and arguing about how and why the person with an addiction is using drugs?? No person with an addiction ever had a goal of becoming addicted.

8. False. Good grief! Some of the finest parenting is no guarantee that your child will not become involved with drugs. It is a great distraction for families to sit around and blame each other and parents and life's difficulties. There are many reasons that one might feel bad and we surely do hand out hurt to each other. But—that does not cause addiction. We simply do not have the power to create addiction in another person. Bad feelings—yes. Addiction—no.

9. True. A very true statement. People who slip into addiction did not have that on their bucket list. Most cannot tell you how, why or when it all got away from them. But recovery is totally theirs to achieve.

10. True. Unknowingly is the main word here. We just simply do not see what we need to and do not understand that love does not equate enabling the problem. We are innocently ignorant.

11. False. Becoming unconscious is passing out. A blackout is an alcoholic-induced amnesia. A blackout is very different and the cause of much family confusion and argument. You can be fully awake and be functioning in a blackout

and people around are unaware that a blackout is in the process. It is an alcohol-induced state of functioning in which you simply do not remember any of the events. Think of a tape recorder running without any tape in the machine. Promises are made and the person with an addiction truly does not remember. Imagine the arguments and think of the disappointments that children have over picnics and movie plans that were promised and denied. Black outs can last for moments or days. Many cannot remember driving home and would fearfully walk around the car the next day—checking for dents or blood. Some have awakened next to strangers. Some had conducted business meetings and had no later recall. It is also said that if you lost your wallet in a blackout you could only recall where you left it while in your next blackout. This is called an en-bloc blackout. How strange is the brain??

12. True. Many people with addictions had said that their brain cleared during a treatment that some judge had mandated, and they could finally benefit from the experience. Very few knock on a treatment door for the right reason. Some want a respite from the horrors of the addicted life. Some want to get away from dealers. Some want to reduce their tolerance levels. Most do not come as volunteers. BUT— amazingly, many are grateful after a few days or weeks when their denial reduces, and they can remember how it used to be for them and can see what could yet be.

13. False. Not one. Not ever. Many try to return to use by having 'just one'. That might work for a short while, but relapse is on its way. What makes us think that we can outsmart the body and brain? It is very similar to a diabetic indulging in sweets and thinking nothing will happen to their insulin regulation.

14. False. Beer is probably the biggest killer of all. It takes longer, because of the water volume, but its continual abuse pays a high price.

15. True.

16. True. Once the brain has recovered, it is hard to tell the players.

17. True.

18. False. This seems too infantilizing and silly. Why not just have a conversation with the recovering guest and ask what would be comfortable for them. People with addictions are in charge of learning to say NO to the world full of drugs. They can learn to be graceful about this and use some humor—or be honest. I had a recovering friend who, when asked what she would like to drink, would answer: "I'll have a Mai Tai, please. But if you are out of fresh gardenias, I will just have a Coke." If you are in residence with a recovering person, it is best to discuss this issue and be honest. My own feeling is that, for a year at least, in the interest of being supportive, any recovering person needs to come home to a safe place at the end of the driveway. It is to be on guard against the unguarded moment—like the trigger of opening the fridge to see a cold beer there.

19. False. It is suggested that family attend the meetings themselves for an extended period. You would be surprised at the questions, dilemmas, and situations that need to be addressed after the early 'pink cloud' days of initial recovery. You sometimes find those deeper problems arise after that 'major' problem of addiction are faced. The 12-Step programs are useful in all of life's affairs. Do not go

with the person to their meeting unless it is an OPEN meeting where all are welcome.

20. Double false. It is neither simple nor willpower.

21. False. This is a national debate at present. I can say that people in the treatment center needed help in withdrawal from their marijuana use. (blackouts are seen here, also). For a recovering person to continue to seek a mood and brain-altering substance often alters their thinking and lowers resistance to other drug use. What is the point of recovery if you just switch horses? You cannot be on the clear-headed and emotionally honest journey of recovery if you are numbing yourself and your feelings and hindering the ability to grow.

22. Whatever. I hope so.

Chapter 2: Chemical Dependency is Not

A Moral Weakness

Some still call addiction a sin. It is not and never has been. People say, "Well, you have a choice," and that reveals a sad lack of understanding. The fact that even the person with an addiction cannot explain their usage and their return to the drug even in the face of deep resolve to abstain is cause to question the repeated accusations of moral weakness. People of all range of morality can become addicted. The more the person has high morals, the more guilt and shame they feel as they repeatedly heed the need to use and do not understand why.

No amount of being yelled at, threatened, or shamed can budge the return to oblivion. This is not about morality. It is much more severe.

Ponder this thought for a while: Some Southern Baptists are genetically predisposed to become alcoholic but will not ever have a problem because their religion asks that they do not drink. In this case, their morality/values/religion kept them from this problem, which does not mean that the problem is a sin.

A Bad Habit

Many people are harmfully involved in drug (alcohol is the most available drug) users who may have periods of life where their continuous and ritual usage could be seen as a habit. They, however, do eventually age-out of such heavy use due to factors such as maturity, marriage, children, or employment. They may have created much carnage in their lives but are at some point able merely to quit. They have had the choice all along and have just chosen to stop.

These are not people with addictions. People with addictions eventually lose choice. No one knows the first time this happened—especially the people with addictions themselves. They wanted to stop after work for 'just two beers' and got home at 10:00 p.m. after far more. You know the chaos this creates at home. Excuses, yelling, anger, confusion—the wall of separation grows higher and higher. Trust takes a hit.

A Mental Illness

Chemical dependency is not a mental illness. It, however, may co-exist with another primary diagnosis of mental health of some sort.

I like to think of cream in a cup of coffee. You cannot taste the coffee or get a clear assessment of it until the cream is removed.

My first professor in Addiction Studies said that you could not get an accurate picture of mental health issues until the drugs are removed from the system for several months. He also stated that sometimes the Bigger and Truer problems begin to surface two years after a person with an addiction starts recovery! George Vaillant is his 75-year study of 200 men, and their alcoholism states that alcoholism was generally the cause of co-occurring depression, anxiety, and bad behavior, not the result!

So much of the behavior of chemical addiction mocks the behaviors of mental health. For instance, depression and mood swings and paranoia. Etc. I remember one alcoholic man in treatment who was depressed, and the doctor ordered a psychiatric evaluation. Well, things were slow, and he had to wait almost ten days to have this service. Surprise! He felt great by then. The test was canceled. Alcohol is a depressant.

Today both of these difficulties are referred to as Dual-diagnosis. Both need to be addressed and monitored for months. The brain takes a while to wake up and recover. The brain may also need some temporary legal and non-addictive medication to supplement necessary support while it begins to function again.

Some people truly have both issues. A good book on this subject is *AT WIT'S END* by Jeff Jay and Jerry Boriskin. I also recommend seeking the help of a doctor who belongs to and is certified by the American Society of Addiction Medicine.

A Sign of Weak Character

This seems to be a cousin to the belief that addiction is a moral weakness.

Do you even think about how much people with active addictions do achieve in their lives?

while maintaining their high standards?

However, it must be hard to maintain qualities of good character while you are sedated, hung-over, quietly desperate, driven, preoccupied, and feeling horrible much of the time. Their whole being begins the fine art of distraction—full of lies and manipulations. It becomes necessary to hide all truth and get to the next drink, drug, or location. Addiction is the only game in town.

They slowly distance from "how they used to be."

It is inconceivable to me that they are ever able to keep and remember a promise or behave in an honorable way. Their attempts at this are so sad.

I remember one man who was coach of his son's football team. He arrived at the field highly hung-over and probably still a bit off plumb. He tried so hard to coach but took a few timeouts to go behind a fence and throw-up. Trying so hard to be desperately there, as promised. Trying so hard to be honorable.

Anne Lamott, in her recovery, said, "I was deteriorating faster than I could lower my standards."

A Result of Life's Pressures

My Gosh! A thousand excuses.

- ❖ My husband does not help out enough
- ❖ My dad never came to any of my games
- ❖ My sister is so mean to me
- ❖ My wife avoids me at night
- ❖ My mother never was loving
- ❖ My mother never protected me
- ❖ It is raining
- ❖ You never clean out the litter box
- ❖ My dog died or my dog just had 15 puppies
- ❖ My boss does not appreciate me
- ❖ We need more rain
- ❖ I lost my daughter
- ❖ My wife left me
- ❖ My husband is having an affair
- ❖ I am so bored
- ❖ I am getting old
- ❖ Everyone drinks
- ❖ The dryer broke
- ❖ I miss my father
- ❖ I hate my father
- ❖ I never see my grandkids/my grandkids get on my nerves
- ❖ I feel hopeless
- ❖ I am so broke

On and on and on.

The ONLY reason a person with an addiction uses is that they are ADDICTED! SIMPLE.

You need to understand that the person with an addiction needs to find reasons and excuses to justify the use. That is because they do not understand their disease. One thing for sure—it has absolutely nothing to do with family or friends. We may hurt each other or let each other down, but that is NOT a reason for addiction. It is a reason to feel hurt, angry, or sad and may need some hoped-for healing, but it is not a reason for addiction. Many people deal with the pressures of life with no thought of turning to a mind-altering solution. Addiction has a life of its own.

A Temporary Loss of Control

Every person with an addiction would wish for this. Hoping and hoping that 'this time will be different.' A.A. wisdom says that one drink is too many and one hundred is not enough. Addiction seems to trump all aces or attempts to make it manageable. It is chronic, progressive, and fatal. When you have to "control" something, it is a problem. Do you control your *broccoli intake?*

Temptation waits in every bar, at every bus stop, every alley, and every party— waiting for 'temporary' usage. Some in recovery say that went to their old bars stools and tried to have just two bottles of beer. It worked—for a short time and attempts at controlled drinking in the long, or short, term end in either abstinence or a return to alcoholism (Vaillant). Achieving long-term sobriety usually involves a less harmful, substitution dependency, a new set of relationships, some sources of hope and inspiration, and experiencing negative consequences of drinking (Vaillant). Remember, once you let that Chucky guy on your bus (see Grief chapter) if you are the person with an addiction, he will resume his seat behind the wheel. Eventually.

It *is* a Biopsychosocial Disease

There is no doubt that the social scene you are in may be an influence or the state of your mood— but the primary influence is that genetic predisposition in your family tree. The more people with addictions you have hanging around on your branches, the higher your chances of inheriting the tendency towards this disease.

Actuary tables once showed that children of alcoholics who had a meaningful education about their family disease were far less likely to develop the problem. They attributed this to their education and knew they were a higher risk and became acquainted with some facts of this disease:

➤ Having a higher tolerance than their friends was a red flag!

➤ Experiencing a blackout was an early sign!

Not all of the children, by any means, would develop the problem but it was an effective deterrent, as the possibility exists.

➤ They were highly aware of their relationship to sedatives. (Beer).

I repeat:

IT IS ITS OWN ENTITY AS A TOXIC BRAIN DISEASE.

Ten major health organizations support the disease model.

Chapter 3: Feelings

I have to laugh whenever I think about writing this. I keep hearing an orchestra break forth in the song Feelings written by Morris Albert in 1974. You either loved it or hated it.

Imagine yourself as a bug with antennas. As we move through our days, our feelings can act like feelers to the situation we are in at the moment. They can detect what is safe and what is uncomfortable. Is it pleasurable or painful? They are our reaction to the world around us. We need to recognize them.

Feelings are also the language of intimacy and recovery. Emotional honesty is the key to intimacy. Feelings are real, and they are our truth. They are not debatable. We, however, do need to develop the ability to examine them. It is part of getting to know yourself. Most of us have one or more "buttons" that can be pushed that came from childhood and indeed may not be relevant to whatever pushed that button today. For example, if you were ignored or shut out as a child, then you might feel that way today in numerous situations where you are, indeed, NOT being ignored or shut out. You may take it personally when the present state does not warrant the feeling. It does not mean that you are not feeling shut out, it only means that you need to examine the moment and emotion and see if it is valid or is it just that old childhood button in you.

Many people will experience blame and guilt when it is merely an uprising of one of their childhood passions and not valid for the moment happening today. Trace the origin of your emotion—where did it begin? Is it an old tape playing in your mind?

One of the hardest to achieve—and most rewarding—is that glorious moment when you QUIT TAKING IT PERSONALLY THAT WHICH IS PERSONALLY HAPPENING. Remember to keep your Q-TIP handy. Much of the time, when things feel personal, and you feel affected, the source of the unfavorable exchange lies in the giver of it. There are, of course, situations when the moment is genuinely personal, and your feeling is valid, but there are far more times when the feeling is not valid for the current event.

There are many ways that we block ourselves from our feelings. We can deny, ignore, minimize, distort, disguise, rationalize, lie about, and distract. They can be so painful and overwhelming that we tend to freeze them. Being numb is normal for most family members who have lived with addiction or any other oppressive situation as a child or adult. Like a tray of ice cubes, however, it is not possible to freeze a chosen few. That ability to freeze your feelings, however, is necessary and normal in a war zone. Living with addiction is similar. Dr. George Vaillant states in his book, *The Natural History of Alcoholism* that stress of living with the person with the addiction is second only to the stress of the Holocaust. Claudia Black's recent book., UNSPOKEN LEGACY, is an exhaustive study of the trauma and stress of addiction in the family with a great focus on the possibilities of healing and recovery

It was not unusual for someone in the family group during treatment to begin to have endless anger and tears. Like a dam breaking. Like holding your breath for months until it finally felt safe to breach the dam. You begin to break the rules of no talking and no feeling in the family. It might feel like ice cubes tumbling out of the ice maker in the refrigerator door—all in a free fall covering the floor.

Much of the pain for the family is released as anger (when turned outward) or guilt (when turned inward). Another wise quote: "Of the Seven Deadly Sins, anger is possibly the most fun. To lick your wounds, to smack your lips over grievances long past—to savor to the last toothsome morsel both the pain you are given and the pain you are giving back—in many ways is a feast fit for a king. The chief drawback is that what you are wolfing down is yourself. The skeleton at the feast is you."[1]

Another image that is useful when thinking about your feelings is to imagine a piano with all 88 keys. High notes and low notes and all in between. Some people prefer to live only on the high notes, are fearful, and prefer avoidance of the low notes. To be fully alive and human makes a more complete and lovelier tune with all 88 keys in play. It is more honest. The negative feelings in life are part of it. We seem to fear them and fail to understand that we can manage them when we face them. The way out of them is through them—not a detour.

It is a large part of family recovery to defrost all of the feelings, understand them, and move on. The body has amazing ways to heal itself. You may need some professional help with this. Honoring our feelings, naming them, understanding the source, talking about it, crying, and moving on into today is wise and rewarding.

Think about this. If you are not allowing your feelings and are stuffing them inside of you— where do they go?? To your heart, blood pressure, intestines, muscles? Maybe they reside in your attitudes and outlook on life.

What has become clear to me is, as I said earlier, that loving someone with an addiction is very much like having a root canal. The pain is great, and the experience is often brutally felt. A major difference between the person with an addiction and the family is that the person with an addiction is numbed with a chemical and the 'other' is not. Some research had shown that feeling memory,

---

[1] (Buechner, et al. 1993)

over time, is obliterated if the event occurred when the person was using mind-altering substances. On the other hand, the non-using family registers the event at a ten on the feelings Richter Scale and the passage of time never does erase this feeling memory. So— think about this. Years can go by.

For the person with an addiction, the memory of events, if remembered at all, does not carry with it the memory of those old feelings that occurred at the very time of the event. Not so for the family. For them, every time an old memory surfaces, the old feelings that the event was wrapped in surging forth and onto the surface again. Thus—recovery for the family requires that they are able to field the feelings and put them into perspective quickly. The feelings arrive as a flashback—not just a memory. They are instantly upon you. They are always passengers on the memory train.

I believe that this non-Novocain factor is one of the most difficult challenges of family recovery. The person with an addiction faces a hard journey into recovery in the conquest of the past shame and guilt. They do not, however, have to contend with the ever-lurking pesky feeling memories that occurred at the time of the event. I repeat that the person with an addiction has a tsunami of negative feelings when facing their past behaviors—that is what A.A. is so helpful in resolving. This is not the same as the instant feelings that arrive at the very time of the incident. The family registers these. Families need some education about this part of their recovery. "I cannot ever forget" is often heard from them. This is true. It is the feelings that pop up and come knocking at unpredictable times. The best direction for families is to talk about those feelings, understand them, sort out what is rational at the moment.

Family members had shared many stories of their strong reactions when their recovering person came home beyond the expected time. The person with an addiction came through the door with innocent attitudes and reasonable explanations and runs into a volley of anger and lecture and suspicion. The family had flashed back to the feelings of the past when the person with an addiction came home late. I remember another recovering man who had a flat tire and called from a roadside phone. His wife heard background noise and was sure he was in a bar. He was flabbergasted at her reaction. She was in a flashback.

Family members have shared many stories of leaping out of bed at 3:00 a.m. when the phone rings. Panic, fear, wide-eyed. It is a wrong number. Their recovering person is peacefully asleep. Family members had shared many stories, even years into the recovery, that tell of shock and flashbacks during some innocent event that rubber-bands you back to the terror of a prior event when the addiction was active.

Post-Traumatic Stress Disorder is seen in families. In World War I, it was called Shell Shock. It is still common for returning veterans. In later wars, the return home was facilitated more quickly than prior times. Flying home versus a return by ship. What was lost was the time when the men and women could share and talk and cry and process their awful memories and feelings. Today, the flight home is silent. And the price was high as each goes their way in silence and isolation. What is true today is an abundance of what is called PTSD.

Some family and friends' treatment is focused on helping families deal with the aftershocks of the trauma of living with addiction in a loved one. As I alluded to in the car accident, it seems unreasonable to ask much of the family in that back seat when they are so wounded. Surely, they can attend Al-Anon and other support groups, but their own hearts and minds need primary focus. Feelings need to be expressed, grief needs to be processed, shame and guilt need to be alleviated, boundaries need to be set, and isolation needs to end. The price and toll on those who love an addicted person are high. The trauma can be in many forms: The finding of your son passed out in the backyard or bedroom. The unexpected outburst of physical harm. The call from the police. The shock of looking under their bed and finding drugs. The realization that you have been believing so many lies. The threat on your life from them or the drug world. The loss of control of your life. Any emotional moment or hours. The slipping away from your own authentic life. The call from the emergency room. Trauma can be dramatic or subtle. One time or chronic. It all leads to our shutting down into 'numb' and, usually, anger.

The passage of time can be a part of the healing, but it is not enough. We need to recognize our own 'shell shock' and need to help to recover. Some of us will say, "I'm fine" and find that, months later, we still are numb and isolated and joyless. So, let us identify some feelings. I am looking at a list of 357 of them. Think of the 88 keys on the piano. Some positive and some negative. The main feeling groups are:

- ❖ Love, Affection, and Concern
- ❖ Elation and Joy
- ❖ Potency
- ❖ Depression
- ❖ Distress
- ❖ Fear and Anxiety
- ❖ Impotency and Inadequacy
- ❖ Anger, Hostility and Cruelty

Here is another list to help you identify what you feel:
- ❖ Sad and Lonely
- ❖ Angry and Confused
- ❖ Guilty and Overwhelmed
- ❖ Bitter and Rejected

- ❖ Helpless and Afraid
- ❖ Worried and Disappointed
- ❖ Blamed and Resentful
- ❖ Jealous and Inadequate

- ❖ Vindictive and Depressed

- ❖ Lost and Pooped
- ❖ Abandoned and Betrayed
- ❖ Sorrowful and Bitter
- ❖ So/So and Relieved
- ❖ Insecure and Unloved
- ❖ Encouraged and Happy
- ❖ Grateful and Joyful
- ❖ Hopeless and Sad
- ❖ Miserable and Hurt
- ❖ Meek and Grieved
- ❖ Disgusted and Unsure
- ❖ Relieved and Embarrassed

It was helpful to sit in a group with many others who share all of this. Just the laughter that began to be heard was a start toward healing. I would always ask everyone, at the close of the meeting, "And—how are you?" Their answer was always: "Fine" My response was always: "You lie!" More laughter.

Another group exercise that you can imagine and do by yourself or with other family members: Give each person a paper plate and crayon. On one side draw the MASK of how you like to look to others and, on the backside, draw a face of the underlying feelings of how you feel. Then share this with yourself or others. It is a fun way to start to get emotionally honest and closer to self and others. No doubt you use several masks daily, but usually, there is one that is your most frequent gift to the world. I discovered that a man who always looked angry was just a hurt person and kept his distance with the glare. His angry face was his childhood decision that prevented intimacy with others but felt safe to him.

One Final Thought About Feelings

We often confuse FACTS, OPINIONS, and FEELINGS.

FACTS are not debatable. Like salt and pepper. They are not open to judgment. They simply ARE.

When we are with others, we are comfortable sharing safe facts about ourselves. (First name). We are a little more hesitant to share risky facts (Age, address). They are rather non-emotional.

OPINIONS are only shared information and are very debatable. They are what one thinks about something. Some people never have an opinion but love to criticize yours. Like the person who never has an opinion about what movie to see or restaurant to frequent BUT—they never like the one you suggest! Did you ever think that, rather than argue about an opinion, you could merely clap your hands and say, 'thank you'? Opinions are interesting and part of making us who we are individually. There is no power on earth as strong as a made-up mind. By the way, when you say, "I feel you are too lazy," it is an opinion, not a feeling. Just using the 'feel' word does not make it a feeling.

FEELINGS are the language of intimacy and really 'getting to know you.' They are a part of moving away from living in the problem to living in the solution.

And a final word about ANGER; I urge you to find a copy of the short story called *A Hole in the Fence* (An old parable). It is a moral tale about a man who taught his young son about his anger and what it did to others. The boy had a fierce temper. The father bought a bag of nails and asked the boy to hammer a nail into their fence every time he got angry with someone. Over the days, the number of nails decreased. The boy found it difficult to do this task and so he began to control his anger. Finally, the day came when no nails needed to be nailed. The father then asked his son to remove the nails. Some of the nails were stuck, but most were removed. He then asked his son to look at the fence and describe what he saw. The son replied, "a fence with holes." The father said that this is what the hearts of those he had wounded looked like. You could apologize, but the holes would always remain. Some still had the unrecoverable nails in place. The scars would always be there. The boy learned that verbal abuse, although forgiven, would always leave a mark.

Chapter 4: Grief

Why Ponder Grief

Grief is a complex and honorable emotion. It is a normal and confusing cluster of ordinary human emotions arising as a reaction to loss. Understanding the process of grief is necessary for our recovery. If you live, you grieve. Unresolved grief feels like standing in bubblegum. Stuck. Besides seeing reality and taking self-responsibility, the task of coming to terms with our losses is a major step toward maturity and successful living. One survey of active and vital people at age 90 and beyond found that all of them indicated that they had been able to do their grief work well. (Not their words but all indicated that they had been able to come to terms with their losses in life and to move on and connect to new directions).

We usually think of death when we consider grief. This fear, of course, is the primary and most gripping fear and also what fuels our enabling behaviors (discussed later). What this discussion will show is all of the other great losses families experience when someone they love becomes addicted. There are less obvious and smaller daily losses. It is like a million little funerals. This discussion is not intended to make things even worse for you, but to help you get clarity on why the situation is diminishing. It will help you put a name on it.

I think that grief is what really "is wrong with" families. A family's mental health and level of functioning vary greatly, of course, but if you add addiction to their home, it all becomes less functional in any desirable way. The family can go from good to worse or bad to worse. But what is the commonality in any family is the loss occurring and the grief reactions to those losses. Grieving is the only way to heal grief. It is avoided at a high cost. Loss needs to be recognized and validated. Many feel that it takes three to five years to complete the grief journey in the loss of a person if, indeed, you are allowing the journey. Smaller losses may take less time.

There is also anticipatory grief. This is when the loss can be anticipated and processed over time before the actual loss occurs. It is the slow letting go of the person or thing that is slipping away. I am thinking of a man whose wife had several years of alcoholism and the resultant health issues and treatments and hospitalizations. As she edged toward death, her family experienced repeated trauma, stress, and desperation. At the time of her death, that family had already experienced so much of the grief process that the final loss, although deeply sad, was not devastating. This is normal. They no longer were losing their life energy to anger, bargaining, and depression. When you consider it, life is a series of hello and goodbye, connect, and disconnect. When it is such a natural and predictable part of every life, why are we so ill-prepared or uneducated about it?

Let me chat about what grief is. As someone said, grief is to be lived through and cannot be 'cured.'

Just What is Grief
The process of grief occurs when we are separated from something of value to us. The body registers the pain and discomfort. If we lose an un-valued thing, the body goes on its merry way. Who cares? No big deal. No loss here.

Grief is physical. Two of the main signs are hurt and anger. But who among us, when angry, stops and thinks: "Oh, I am feeling a loss here?" No—we yell or act out our anger. And who among us has an understanding that tears and heartache are signs of specific loss? No—we cry or whine or get depressed. Did I mention that I have a PhD in whining?

Probably the best tool in my toolbox was the discovery of the grief process. It is not that the understanding was a detour, salve, or eraser. It was merely a way to get a handle on what on earth was going on with me. Once I knew how to precisely pinpoint the loss, it helped me clarify and come to terms with it. I could manage it and it no longer managed me in some vague way. Today, I know that when the signs of grief come over me, it is like a turkey pop-up button and time for me to identify and honor whatever loss is trying to get my attention. These valued losses may be seen or unseen, gigantic or minuscule.

An Example

It was years after a divorce, and I was happily pushing the grocery cart down the cookie aisle. Then—fig newtons!! My eyes burst forth, and I was powerless to divert the wave of grief that seemingly came from nowhere. I abandoned the cart and sat in my car. It came to me that I had always put fig newtons in the shopping cart to take home—his favorite cookie. That was another clue to the unresolved loss of being able to love and care for someone who was now gone. It is strange and wonderful how identifying and being able to understand what my eyes were telling me led me to a resolution of that loss. No problem with fig newtons today, except eating too many.

Grief has been compared to an ocean wave. At first, it is a massive crash on the shore, a tsunami. As time passes, the waves reduce in size and power. Eventually, they are simple, gentle swirls over the sand. And, sometimes, a huge wave reappears and knocks you over, but it is a single event. Grief is messy.

Grief Takes Time

I have also read that grief is like a huge yellow cat asleep and curled up in a chair. That cat sometimes wakes up and leaps upon you as you walk by. There are pockets of pain for ages, and we cannot prepare for their attack. We can only recognize the reason. Grief can come in on several trains. A song, an odor, a date, a familiar place. It can also arrive on some other train track. All I know is that understanding the grief process helps. It gives you a handle on how you are and only you are in charge of that.

Al-Anon has a book called, *Open our Hearts-Transforming our Losses*.

More Comments on Grief

How we deal with grief—the separation phenomena—may have both a cultural or parental influence.

We can learn from childhood to block, dishonor, divert, and distract our bodies' natural response to separation from a valued thing/person. Our body may have more sense and emotional honesty than we may allow. Grief is the pain that heals itself if we get out of the way. But—we do not believe this, and many of us run tapes in our heads that we learned long ago. Think a moment about how your parents handled their pain. You are fortunate if they were not shy or inhibited about showing their grief, many of us, however, had other messages:

Have you heard:

- Be a man—or I will give you something to cry about. Men do not cry
- Girls do not look pretty when crying
- Get a grip—be strong
- You just want sympathy
- I hate tears
- Keep your dignity
- Etc.—Fill in your own.
- Or—cultural tapes that stop the flow.

I had a British heritage and had to have a lot of therapy to learn not to be British with feeling expression (or lack of). Where on earth did this come from? Many strong men cry, and many women do not care if their nose runs with their mascara.

Now let me talk about learning from your pet. Do you have a dog or cat?? What do they do when you leave the house? What do they do when you return home? They are always grieved when you go and will act accordingly. They seem to sense when you are ready to leave the house and will sulk, or look pitiful, scratch at the window, or worse. And—homecoming is all joy. Except for some cats that will retaliate before they deem to cuddle you ever again. Paybacks. Animals do not run the tapes in their heads to stop their feelings. I learned by watching mine. They definitely were not British. Their hearts were on their sleeves (sort of).

One more story to illustrate: This is a myth, but worth remembering. When lions go on a hunt, they put the oldest male lion in the center of the clearing. He has no teeth, no claws, and no clear vision. What he does still possess is a huge and loud roar. So—eventually the prey enters the clearing and the old guy blasts the prey with a world-class roar. The prey, of course, then runs into the brush around the clearing. And what is waiting there? The real danger. The killers. The lionesses. The moral is: Go for the Roar!!!

A challenge for you: When the pain of loss comes across your heart, lean into it. Go for the roar. Do not fear it. The hurt will dissipate. Cry. Feel the hurt. You will live. The body is trying to heal. Trust it.

We too often, fearful of the pain, run into the brush. In this brush are all of the ways we try to outrun, distract, and hide from discomfort. All of our addictions can serve this purpose. They are all not in our best interest and surely not helpful in the healing process. Shopping-eating-sexing-excessive focus on another-gambling-technical usage-any excessive appetite-volunteerism-busyness.

I love when I can cry, identify the loss, look it in the eye, go for the roar, begin to diminish its power over me. It helps me reach the goal of acceptance of the loss so I can close the door on it. What I love is not the pain, of course, but the knowledge that the only way to heal grief is to get through it. Once healed, you eventually can reattach and connect to other places and directions. Completing the business of grief and goodbye will free you to take your full self to new stages of your life. You will be amazed at how true this is. Trust the bodily process.

The grief process itself: From the work of Dr. Elisabeth Kubler-Ross. On Death and Dying 1969. It should be said that other researchers in the years that followed have disagreed with her work. It is my personal experience that she was spot-on. Knowing her stages has helped me understand where I am on the journey. This clarity has helped me move forward or at least know that I am not lost. These five stages are easily understood and remembered. This book includes a list of her five stages, which I will explore further. There are multiple books on grief at every bookstore. This is a brief presentation.

It also needs to be said that what follows your arrival at acceptance (step 5) is future living without interference from old grief issues. One is then free to reconstruct and move on. It is akin to shutting one door and opening the next.

"Though no one can go back and make a
brand new start, anyone can start from now
and make a brand new ending."

-Carl Brad

An example of a loss: Let's use the loss of trust because it is so common and so painful. Follow the stages of grief with this discussion of the loss of TRUST.

This loss is universally true if you are in a relationship with someone who is addicted. That person is truly no longer present— they have been beamed up into a toxic brain situation and the only focus for them is to connect to their chemical of choice. But we do not see this immediately and the exit of trust from the relationship begins to develop. When you think about it, trust is founded on being trustworthy. Keeping promises, showing up, doing what you say you are going to do. Addiction interferes. It is one of the most painful losses and hard to rebuild. See if you can relate to the grief process in the loss of TRUST:

Five Stages of Grief
- ✓ Denial
- ✓ Anger
- ✓ Bargaining
- ✓ Depression
- ✓ Acceptance

Stage One: Denial

This sort of denial is hard to explain. It is not the denial of a wrongdoing. If you are in a state of denial, you are not aware of it. Please read the chapter on denial.

It is hard now to realize that I truly did believe all of the excuses. All of the times I called his employer to make excuses because I thought he was in bed due to a sinus problem. (more like a fifth of vodka). Who knew? I was looking at and living with a full-blown alcoholic, and it never crossed my mind. Even during all of the nurse training, there was no information on addiction. In denial, you do not see what you see and do not know what you know. Denial can be very comforting—and very dangerous.

- We are in denial about just what the problem is.
- We are in denial about just how we are.
- We are in denial about how we have been affected.
- We are in denial about problems with our own life.
- We are in denial that we need help.
- We are in denial that, even though nothing is my fault, there are some changes I need to make.

Sometimes, we are just too close to see the broad picture. The behaviors of anger were still not understood as a reaction to the growing loss of trust. We have a hard time saying that we do not trust the loved one. It feels so disloyal and against our values. There was no full consciousness that loss of trust was in process. All was reaction.

Can you accept the fact that you trust the person but not the addiction? Of course, one first has to see that you are up against addiction now housed in the addict.

A typical remark from fathers of a person with an addiction is, "Well, I drank when I was a kid, and I outgrew it." Another example of denial: have you ever seen that graphic art where there is a design you must stare at and through until another picture appears? Well, once your eyes have adjusted to the hidden picture, you have a hard time not seeing it.

Or—remember when, in elementary school, there were books with pictures with ten hidden figures and you had to find them. Once you found the carrot, rabbit or teacup, it is hard to un-see them. This is the same feeling you get when the curtain of denial lifts and you see clearly. At last!

The acceptance of this loss of trust is not an indictment or mean or unloving. It is simply reality. It is a fact, and we often, in our hurt state, become angry.

Stage Two: Anger

Living with a chronic feeling of anger can spread from slightly annoyed to full-blown rage. You have a sense of something leaving the relationship, but still not clear that trust is flying out the window daily. In hindsight, you can remember that there was distinctly a loss of loveliness in the air and the communication and the daily tasks of living. You can remember that your heart hurt—and yet, still unable to put your finger on the reason. Trust was no longer in residence.

We take it all so personally. One main reason for our anger is that, in our attempt to trust, we allow ourselves to be used. Are you angry with yourself for this? Our anger displays as whining, lecturing, yelling, threats, violence and broken dishes in response to broken promises and hearts. This addiction thing is brutal on the heart. Your energy goes toward trying a million "fixes" with both behaviors and feelings all to resuscitate trust. It is akin to arranging the deck chairs on the *Titanic*. All of our bargaining behaviors, however, do keep us busy and postpone the dreadful truth of our powerlessness.

For example: have you ever spied on your person with an addiction? That is a bargaining step to verify whether you can trust your doubts or not and to check up on the whereabouts of the person with an addiction.

Stage Three: Bargaining

These are all of the tremendous mental and physical efforts to try to keep trust alive and back home. We can be very tenacious and creative with these.

- They are all of the blaming and "if only (s)."
- They are most of our enabling behaviors and attitudes and feelings.
- "He will be okay once he graduates."
- "He will be okay once he meets the right girl."
- "She will be okay if she gets a job."
- "It was his mother's fault."
- Maybe if I do…
- Or if I do…
- I need to keep the kids quiet…
- God should...
- If only he/she...
- ETC…

We do so want to trust this person. And, you can trust the person, just not the addiction! What you are pitted against is their denial, delusion, and compulsion and there is no room for trust. The person with an addiction cannot trust himself or herself. They also have no real idea of this. They may believe what they say, but their chemical breaks promises. We can spend years, money, health, and sanity trying to keep trust alive. There seems to be an endless list of bargaining ideas and efforts to keep trust from leaving. All useless. All to no avail. Not effective. Trust is most painfully out of the building. On to the next grief stage.

Stage Four: Depression

This is a very sad time. All of our efforts to convince someone to get clean and sober have failed. We are worn out with all of the energy we have expended trying to hang onto trust in the relationship. Perhaps we even stop the recriminations. I like this stage because it means we might be quiet, stop all of the running around, and start to think about ourselves. We throw in the towel. It is a time to self-monitor and police ourselves.

- We finally might see that trust has gone.

- We finally might be ready for some help for self.

- We finally realize that trust has been kidnapped and we allow ourselves the reality of this sad truth.

This is the time to "Go For the Roar" and let you feel the full grief of this loss of trust. You might even consider putting your feelings on paper or sharing with someone. Write a letter to trust. This is the time to "let go" all of the effort to keep trust alive and to allow yourself the pain and hurt.

Most of us do not know that there is a stage 5 and, like the journey and the faulty GPS, we circle and keep returning to stage 1-4. We can become mired in the mud of hurt, anger, bargaining, and depression. Around and around and around. It reminds me of the time I kept circling around and around the Washington Monument in D.C. to find the exit to head south.

The main problem with this is that the anger can kill us. So can depression. Blood pressure, headaches, physical illness, ulcers, GI problems, and dental issues are not unusual. It is important to realize that you can now move to stage 5 in this process. People ask how to get to stage 5. Go For The Roar-Let it Go-Be Done with it, for now, farewell to trust at this time. Feel the pain of the loss of trust and move on. Families need to learn to deal with pain and their powerlessness.

Stage Five: Acceptance/The Destination

Acceptance does not mean that this loss is okay with you. It does not mean you do not miss trust with the person with an addiction. It merely means that you accept the reality of the loss. It is a present reality. Period. No more denial. No more bargaining effort. Just the sad acceptance that addiction takes trust and holds it hostage.

You are now free to integrate this into your view of the situation, and it helps us reframe. Your energy can now go into stage 6.

Stage 6: Reconstruction

You can set new goals and new connections. Your well-being can return. You may still feel sad, but sadness is not as debilitating as anger and depression. You can put sadness in your pocket and go on to your own authentic life. Someone said, "I do not want to have a sad life. I want to have a happy life with some sadness in it."

Before we leave this exploration of the loss of trust, I want to share some thoughts on trust. It is probably the most crucial part of any relationship. In its absence, all else seems like junk. And, like the hummingbird, it flies backward and is so fragile.

Another quote: "Trust leaves like a racehorse and comes back like a snail." (Unknown n.d.)[2] So, my suggestion is that you should not discuss the trust issue for at least one year with the recovering person. They want your trust, and you so want to trust them. But a wiser response would be: "I do so want to trust you. It is a great loss for me and us. I do trust you, but I do not trust the addiction and all of its power. Can we live well together, each following our recovery plan for one year before we talk about trust?"

---

[2] Unknown

It is also a truth that the person with an addiction does no longer trust us—we have also deceived, spied, and withheld ourselves. Understandable, but not a relationship-builder. We have also failed the person with an addiction in our innocent ignorance about the disease of addiction. Another quote: "When I knew better, I could do better." (Unknown n.d.)[3]

Usually, we are in the same war without any defense or training or weapons. How we do flounder about without family education.

This has been an example of the loss of trust. The following pages will help you identify several other losses due to addiction. You can follow the stages of grief through each loss.

There are three areas of loss: (See grid)

1. Material: Our stuff. Measurable and Visible things

2. Intrapersonal: Things inside of me and about me

3. Interpersonal: Things between us

Our losses: (See what you can identify and add your own)

➢ The presence of the person:
   It is the presence of the absence (even if they are sitting next to you)
➢ The familiar:
   We miss so much of what has been valuable in our day, like—talking. It feels like we are not in Kansas anymore, Toto.
➢ The Quality of Life:
   Addiction is like a cancer of the family. We adapt and adapt until we are really out of shape in every way.
➢ Communication:

---

[3] Unknown

Relationships turn into case management. Talking is fraught with control and anger or silence.

➤ Confidence:
You wonder if you ever got anything right or ever will again. One group member said that he felt the loss of 'being right' as he increased his knowledge of addiction.

➤ Expression of Feelings:
We walk on eggshells in order not to upset the person with an addiction for fear they will use.

➤ Trust:
(Already discussed): We become detectives and accusers.

➤ Peace of Mind:
There is always an awareness of impending or feared event. Worry is the activity of the day.

➤ Serenity:
We are unconsciously or consciously distracted.

➤ My Mind:
Who among us has not acted nuts at times? Like a husband who stood outside in the mud and shrubs in the rain to watch his wife in their bedroom to see if she was drinking. Really?

➤ Control:
Here is a formula for you: Love + Terror = Control. Enough said. We try to steer their bus at every opportunity.

➤ Values:
Ask if you have ever acted like you never dreamed you would or could? An affair? Hit a child? Told lies?

➤ Privacy:
Parents feel this loss when their adolescent enters some form of help. Also, a felt loss when our person with an addiction parks their car on the neighbor's lawn.

➤ Support:
We back away from help. Others can tire of our telling our story. We are no longer fun people.

- ➢ Innocence:

  Who knew? Very often, families felt shocked and amazed and terrorized in the world of addiction. It is so alien and frightening to many families. It can introduce us to the world of ugly.

- ➢ Dreams:

  Most of us have an idea of what it would be like for our children, our marriage, or childhood. Our lives go off the rails when addiction enters. Even siblings feel cheated of their wished-for relationship with an addicted sibling.

  Another quote: "Life is what happens when you are making other plans." (Suanders 1957)[4]

- ➢ Self-esteem:

  Even if your self-esteem is excellent, this experience can diminish you. It inevitably attacks you if you are taking it personally. We feel as if we have failed. (See section on the Q-Tip)

- ➢ Respect for self/other:

  When we view this as an issue of choice, we lose respect when the behaviors of addiction rear their heads. Again, families judge the person with an addiction. Families also can react in undesirable ways to all of the stress.

- ➢ Focus:

  How many speeding tickets do you think a family member collects? Or bungled tasks due to such an exhausting distraction? We sometimes look in a mirror and wonder who that is anymore.

- ➢ Feeling valued:

  Addiction values only the next high. You cannot expect to get love or approval from someone who no longer has it to give. It is no longer accessible.

- ➢ Touch/Affection:

---

[4] Allan Saunders; Publishers Syndicate; 1957

There is such growing anger, hurt, and pile of resentments and bad memories. This is not conducive to genuine affection.

➢ Plans:

Oooppps. A detour into another world. Did you want to take a class, a vacation, plan a retirement? A myriad of broken plans. Planning a picnic or even dinner is hard.

➢ Old Connections:

We spend a lot of time remembering how we connected in healthy ways before addiction. Alcohol has been known as a solvent of many things, and we comfort ourselves with the memories of happier days.

➢ The Possibilities:

This is one of the most profound losses. It covers an array of territories. When you think about it, addiction is so very predictable (contrary to recovery) and what one can predict is that the main possibility is now that things will only get worse and the plans you had for the relationship or future have run aground.

I think of parents who drove north to Michigan to attend their daughter's college graduation. What they found was their daughter fully alcoholic and not in school for several months. Think of the shock.

➢ Time:

Families often state that they are angry about the loss of time. This is also how they feel about going to meetings and the recovery efforts for themselves. All I can add to this is that you will learn, grow, and gain some wisdom. Is that a waste of time?

➢ Money/Credit:

Need I even comment on this one? What can be guaranteed is that this loss is gone, gone, gone, spend no more time in anger. Kiss it sadly goodbye.

➢ Job:

Many family members are so distracted at work that they perform poorly. It is known that family members, like the person with an addiction, often call in 'sick' on Mondays. They are exhausted.

➢ Health/Sleep/Energy:
George Vaillant did a long and extensive study on alcoholism and stated that the stress of living with a person with an addiction was second only to the stress of the Holocaust.

➢ Joy:
Anger, hurt, depression, exhaustion, stress, all seem to rob one of joy.

➢ Friends/Family:
Friends often back away. They feel they do not want to interfere, or they feel uncomfortable in the often-embarrassing time together. The family may feel the same. Lucky are you if you are surrounded by friends and family who do understand and are supportive.

➢ Openness:
Keeping the secrets and walking on eggshells is common, shame keeps us silent.

➢ The 'Used To(s)":
We used to: Talk, laugh, go to church, eat dinner together, go for walks, have sex, hug, watch TV. Where have they all gone?

➢ Routine:
Much of life consists of routine and predictability. It all saves time and is comforting and unique to each of us. Addiction rocks the boat. Addiction capsizes the boat, and many routines become up-ended.

➢ Own Authentic Life:
"The problem in her life was not that he left, it was that she never showed up." One can try to please, fix, and cover up to the point of eclipsing self and putting your own life on

hold. I remember a man who lived on a lake but had not been in his boat for seven years because he was afraid his alcoholic wife would topple over the edge.

➤ Predictability:
The only thing you can count on is for life to be predictably unpredictable. Addiction has a way of interfering and is full of other plans for you.

➤ Childhood:
So much is written on this. Children of people with addictions are born to loss and often do not even know there was an alternative. Even the fun things can turn quickly into a bad memory. The slogan for adult children of alcoholics is, "It is never too late for a happy childhood."

➤ Rituals:
It is said that maintaining rituals in family life is a stable, healthy thread into adulthood. Addiction is not interested in them and depression can destroy the desire to keep rituals in place. They get dropped and minimized.
It is important to know that there are losses in recovery, also.

➤ The Familiar:
So many families ask "What should I do when they come home (now in recovery)? The Betty Conyers book, *Everything Changes*, is an excellent source to help you learn about the tough first year of recovery and understand further the roller-coaster life of loving a person with an addiction.
On the changes in the first year, it is like taking a 90-degree turn into a new universe. It cannot be said enough that attendance at AL-ANON or NAR-ANON is so helpful to families. As the river turns the bend, it takes a lot of sandbags and new perspectives.

➤ Chaos: (Some people miss this—it is now too quiet)

Unbelievably, some people miss the action. It is like living near Central Park and taking a vacation in the woods. You cannot sleep. Not enough noise. Some feel that the home is now empty. One young girl once said that she liked it better before recovery because at least everyone was around and now they were at 'those meetings.'

➤ Lifestyle Changes:
This is difficult. Everyone gets nervous about what it will be like when recovery begins. No alcohol in the house? Can I really be honest with them? How do I get off the eggshells? What can we talk about? How should I act? What can I do? This is such a substantial reason to attend your 12-step meeting and listen and listen and ask and listen.

➤ Esteem and Identity from Feeling Needed:
Parents of adult people with addictions have a hard time not hovering. How do you become the parent of an adult child? You are indeed still the parent, but no longer parenting.
Caretakers often feel as if they have received a blue slip. Discharged from duty. They can resent that their person with an addiction spends so much time in meetings or on the phone with 'those other recovering people.'
We now can slowly learn how to be in a healthy relationship based on mutual needs.

➤ Familiar Role in Family:
Family members adapt to the stress of being in a relationship with an addicted parent or sibling. Think of a crib mobile. You add weight (a problem) to any part of the mobile; it will swing around and find a balance. It will be tilted, but it will stop swinging around. The family does the same thing to try to find a balance, even if it is on a tilt. When the problem is removed, the mobile swings again to

find balance. So, it is when there are so many changes as people grow and recover.

Can you now say that with the loss of so much of the above that you are "fine"? I can again lovingly say to you–are you sure?

You can use the grid on the next page to list your losses.

GRIEF GRID

LOSSES	MATERIAL	INTRA-PERSONAL "ME"	INTER-PERSONAL "US"
IN ACTIVE CHEMICAL DEPENDENCE			
IN RECOVERY			

It is important to mention that the person with an addiction also experiences enormous loss. A big part of their program is to understand that the addiction has exacted quite a price and they have grief work to do. Their principal loss in recovery, however, is the loss of their chemical and all the pleasurable things it has meant to them and how they have constructed their life and thinking around it. Many will say that it made them feel normal until it didn't.

It is another point worth mentioning that regardless of the path of the person with an addiction (success or failure at recovery) a significant other can regain all of the intrapersonal losses. To regain the interpersonal losses requires two people. It is also true that some losses may never return—such as money—which makes it vital that you sadly accept the fact that is gone, never to be recovered. But it is best to be sad and not locked into endless bargaining and anger about it. Kiss it goodbye. Save your blood pressure. Because of your expectations about how it will be once the addiction is treated, many family members have thought that everything will return 'as before' and are impatient with changes. Try to remove your expectations and be free to receive the gifts of recovery. For example, if you looked forward to your person with an addiction being home and involved with the family every night, you need to accept the fact that they may now be at a meeting. The gift of this is when they are now finally at home; they are drug-free and more present.

So, where are we? Here are some questions for you.

1. What is a loss for you (Take one at a time)?

2. Look at the stages and try to find where you are. It is possible that you may go either direction on the chart. It is normal to go back and forth in this process.

3. What bargaining have you done not to let go of your identified loss? Example: Loss of my health. I have started vitamins and exercise.

4. What will be a growth step for me? When will I feel better? Example: Loss of my self-esteem. I will no longer let anyone climb up their ladder of self-esteem on my rungs!

5. What is acceptable for me? How will I know? Example: Loss of my values. I will feel sad about this and return to my value system.

There is another example to help you grasp the concept of letting go—this one is true.

It is about monkeys. When trappers want to catch an ape or monkey, they construct a cage with very narrow slats and place monkey food in the cage. The locked cage is set in the jungle, and the trappers wait for monkeys to approach the cage, reach in, and grab the food. The narrow slats make it impossible for the monkey to withdraw their full paws and the thing about monkeys is that they never drop a food source. (I can relate). They are now trapped by their own doing and quickly caught.

What is it that makes it so hard for us to let go of that which is trapping us? If we continue to grasp the loss item, we get both paws stuck. We then drag thru life hanging onto the losses and dragging the whole mess with us. It is hard to reach into today when you are holding onto the past losses. It is impossible to enter into the future with your paws so full and so stuck.

What is required for the dropping is the grieving! Release the loss, be sad about it and free your hands for today. This disconnect will feel both like a loss and a relief. Strange as it may seem, to stay angry about a loss does feel like a connection to the person with an addiction. Those monkeys liked the security of hanging onto bananas.

There are a lot of "Dis's" when you let go: You might feel:

- Disengaged
- Disenchanted
- Disoriented
- Disidentified
- Discombobulated
- Disconnected

This new reality may make you flounder toward a new direction. AL-NON helps us stabilize into a more solid connection with the future.

We do need to come to terms with our losses. If not, we may remain miserable as we take our unresolved selves into future relationships. Sharon Wegscheider stated that we either fixate or transcend and Huxley said the choice is always ours.

If I had another lifetime, it would be to try to reach all the thousands of people who are no longer in the situation of a relationship with an active person with an addiction and these people are still angry and depressed and blaming their person with an addiction. They may have fleeting moments or perception about recovery for themselves but have no opportunity or direction for help.

For those who seek recovery, may you see the reality of what is. May you begin to enjoy the challenge of looking at yourself, may you accept your limitations, may you know you are never powerless for yourself and may you feel free of the decisions others make for themselves.

I have saved the best for last. I want you all to meet Chucky. Chucky is the doll first seen in the movie, *Child's Play*. He has been part of every grief lecture. I wish you could see him in person. The two Chucky dolls I have are part of every group. (In between meetings, they reside in the trunk of my car and I surely hope there is never an occasion when a policeman needs to lift the trunk!). They sit in the chair in the middle of the room. They lay on the table in the center of the group. They hang from the wall. They are a constant reminder of what we are up against. It reminds family members and gives them a visual of the enemy. It helps family members take the blame off their loved one and onto addiction. Chucky is the addiction. Chucky is all drugs (alcohol being the most prevalent drug). He represents the toxic brain syndrome. He represents the kidnapper. He is a terrorist.

Families and friends often ask the person with an addiction: "Why don't you just quit!!!???" or "How did you let this happen to you?" The person with an addiction really cannot answer these questions.

They are often as clueless as the family. They also are often in denial of their truth.

So, how does it happen? How does addiction (Chucky) eclipse a person? There was a saying: The man takes the drink-The drink takes the drink-The drink takes the man. (Japanese proverb).

Try to visualize what you are now reading. Chucky at first appears cute, friendly, and innocent. No harm was done. One day, he knocks at the door or rings the bell of the future person with an addiction. The door opens. Your person answers. Like an engaging

salesperson, Chucky asks your person if they would like to play. Looks like fun. He gets invited in. They play, laugh, and grow fond of each other. In fact, it all went so well that Chucky got invited back for yet another play date. And so it goes, sometimes for several weeks and sometimes for years. Your person is in charge and makes it clear to Chucky that the fun has to stop at 5 p.m. because of other commitments. So—Chucky leaves at 5 p.m. (This is the social use, and the choice remains with the user).

But—one day something different happens! No one can recall just what day it was and there were many explanations given about the fact that, for the very first time, Chucky did not agree to go home at 5 p.m. He argued, and they settled at

"WHO'S DRIVING YOUR BUS?"

5:15 p.m. No big deal, right? More time elapsed and Chucky

began to be there longer and longer. He is the one calling the shots every time. He left the playdate later and later and later. Chucky was now driving the bus. The choice was no longer with the person with an addiction. Several ploys and plots were used to try to regain control, but Chucky remained entirely in charge of the wheel.

Addiction is chronic, progressive, and fatal.

Chucky is no longer adorable. He has become the terrorist. He has no regard whatsoever for the person with an addiction or anyone else. There is an attached picture of Chucky driving the bus. It was drawn years ago by a young man in a state juvenile facility. I do not know his name. He surely captured the feeling of triumph in Chucky and fear in the person with an addiction.

It is true that Chucky also drives the family's bus. Not only that, but I envision the family reaching out their bus window to try to control Chucky's wheel as both buses careen down the road. One vision for families is to get your hand on your own wheel. If you are lucky, Chucky and passengers finally find their way to some help. This is not what Chucky plans, but it is an excellent detour for the addicted person and everyone else.

Treatment will help your person with an addiction get Chucky off of their bus. This is called Detox. They will offer much talk therapy and medication if deemed necessary for withdrawal. Treatment is not recovery—it is only a start. Hopefully, a long aftercare plan and the recovering community provides an entirely new bus route complete with a GPS to a new life.

In this unusual disease, it is vital for all to understand brain chemistry and change internal attitudes and join a recovering community. Would it not be nice if we could apply a cast or do surgery? Nothing so simple. Treatment will talk about ways to keep Chucky off of your bus.

One thing that bothers me is to hear about the significant relapse rate for addiction. As in many diseases, relapse is not unusual. Also, as in many diseases, it would be advised to carefully follow the suggestions and directions that would reduce the relapse rate! Example: How often do people with diabetes stray off the recommended diet? Relapse rates for addiction, diabetes, and asthma are similar.

Anyway, let us imagine that your person is now ready to re-enter their life. Someone once declared: "Recovery is easy, you just have to change everything." Your person with an addiction now has their hands on their bus wheel. There are two neighborhoods to choose between. There is no such thing as a neutral decision from now on. It is a choice for an unfamiliar neighborhood full of excellent opportunities for recovery, or it is a return to the familiar old neighborhood where triggers abound.

There is a lot of loss for the person with an addiction in recovery. The dangerous thought is to sit at the bar with my old buddies and friends and drink coffee or soda. Chucky is in that bar and is delighted to see them. He will wait. Chucky is everywhere and he is patient.

Let us think that your recovering person with an addiction is now nervously attending meetings. New people, new thoughts, new attitudes, new feelings. On the way to the meeting, they see a figure in the distance who is waving at them to pull over. Guess who?

What is Chucky saying? Try these:

- Hi. I have missed you.
- You are not much fun anymore.
- Wanna play?

- I promise that I will not hurt you again. I will go home at 5 p.m.
- And—the big one. Please let me get on your bus with you. I will sit in the back. You can keep your eye on me. I promise. I promise. I only want to ride a few blocks.

It is tempting. One of Chucky's feet on the bus step is the first beer, joint, hit, or pill. Once you let Chucky on your bus, he may sit in the back for a while but, eventually, when you look in the rear-view mirror, he has moved slowly up the aisle with his eye on the steering wheel. That is how it happens.

Relapse always has a risk of death. It can also serve as an opportunity to learn that you need to stop doing what you did and to start doing what you do not want to. A chance to keep learning. Of course, not much will lead to successful recovery unless you want it. A relapse is not a failure—it is a chance to reassess.

Chucky has created great grief for everyone. Nothing is harder for families than to feel powerless to keep Chucky off of anyone else's bus. A significant man in my life once commented to me: "When will you get it? My life cannot be what you figured out!" Then he nicely added, "Of course, I am open to suggestions." The best we can do, and the most rewarding is to make sure that Chucky no longer has his hands on our wheel

Some one-liners about grief:

1. I will come to understand my pain and find a value for it in my life.
2. Mark Twain: "When you are angry count to 4. When very angry, swear."
3. Sooner or later, we must give up all hope of a better yesterday.

4. Shakespeare: "Ah! The heartache and the thousand natural shocks flesh is heir to"
5. Misery is to be overcome—not to be used as a marinade.
6. When the horse is dead – get off.
7. The condition of being human is to deal with things that do not last.
8. There is no problem so big and complicated that it cannot be run away from. (my brother)
9. Freedom is having nothing left to lose.
10. Does your adjustment to life require suffering?
11. We, knowing not ourselves, oft beg our own harm!

Some final lovely thoughts:

- I am grateful for all that I have had
- I am grateful for all that I have lost
- I am grateful for all that remains to me.

Chapter 5: Enabling

I am certain that no one wakes up and thinks of their addict and says, "Oh, good. This is a day I can help make you sicker!" The truth is that most of us have never heard of the word at the top of this page. At the School of Social work, the word had a positive connotation. A social worker could help you find connections or a phone number or any number of needed directions. They enabled progress and well-being. However, when you enter the arena and discussion of chemical dependency, the very word becomes an indictment. I clearly remember my first Al-Anon meeting when the greeter at the door proclaimed, "Welcome to Al-Anon, honey. You are the enabler, and you are sicker than your husband." I no doubt thanked her (in my days of Nicing On the Fake), but I wanted to leave immediately. I was confused. Why was she smiling and loving while seemingly accusing me of something? It felt like one of those fuzzy-prickly moments. Whatever did she mean? All I knew was that I was pooped, confused, desperate and lost. And, by the way, my husband was the "sick" one—was he not the one wrapped around the toilet bowl?

There is a Winnie-the-Pooh quote that always reminds me of how clueless we are: "Here is Edward the Bear—coming downstairs now—Bump, Bump, Bump on the back of his head behind Christopher Robin. It is, as far as he knew, the only way of coming downstairs, but sometimes he felt that there really is another way, if only he could stop bumping for a moment to think of it."

This chapter is to invite you to stop bumping for awhile and think. It is impossible not to be drawn into the drama. We get lonely, desolate and lose vitality as we develop serious living problems of our own. We live in constant reaction to whatever the latest crisis is. We are slowly eclipsed by someone else's behaviors as we go bumping our way down the stairs.

There is another saying, "If you want to keep your eye on the devil, you invite him to the pow-wow."[5] So let us do just that.

Walking around and eyeballing this concept of enabling is a tough but rewarding journey. Knowledge about enabling is enlightening and empowering and very effective for your life (and for the addicts). Just what are we enabling? Most people would answer that we are enabling the addict to use their drug choice. That is only partially true. We actually have no power whatsoever over the choices of others. But, what IS true is that we are enabling the situation to continue without EFFECTIVE confrontation. We are pitted against someone's addiction; we are up against denial, delusion, and compulsion. Theirs.

It is not the person who is the adversary, it is their chronic-progressive and fatal disease. And denial is the linchpin of it all. You are pitted against Chucky (see Grief chapter). We are also delusional and in denial if we think we can find any effective maneuver in enabling actions, feelings or ideas. We just keep slamming into our limitations. More on this later.

Suzanne Farham wrote, " Even when a need exists and we are well qualified to meet it, we are not necessarily called to respond to it.--To be doing what is good can be the greatest obstacle to doing something even better."[6]

We are often referred to as "sick." I only agree with this if, indeed, there is some physical manifestation of our stress. Otherwise, why make a pathology out of something we were taught to do? I prefer to think of friends and families as a little bit off plumb. Parents, church, country, school all teach us to be helpful, kind, compassionate and to involve ourselves when someone is in trouble. You take soup to a friend with a cold. You run errands for

---

[5] Unknown
[6] Suzanne Farnham, et al, Listening Hearts Ministries

a waylaid neighbor. This is all good and nice. The problem is that the way we involve ourselves with an active addict is often disabling and harmful. We need to learn the effective involvements and responses. We need to learn A REVERSE LOGIC!

You are up against a toxic brain. Our many efforts to "fix" the addict are only our attempted solutions to a problem. These Home Remedies work if someone has a broken leg or cold, or surgery—but in the case of trying to "get an addict clean," they are only chances for us to become a part of the problem. Who knew?? When I knew better, I could do better. It is a strange thought to know we are not the solution and we are not the problem—but we can slip into becoming part of the problem with well-intentioned and ineffective efforts. When someone you love slips into addiction, the whole thing is a jolt to our expectations of how the relationship should be. What parent ever brought their child home from the nursery and anticipated a future of addiction for them? How many walk down the aisle and know they are wedding Chucky? (Remember that Chucky is all addictions).

Why is it necessary to understand how we fall into the sink hold of involvement? It has to do with a rational brain and a toxic one. The rational brain and thinking are no match for toxic thinking. In most cases of other diseases, the "patient" realizes there is a problem and agrees to cooperate with offered support and help. In chemical dependency, however, the person thinks they are "fine". A.A. states it is the only disease in the world that makes you think you are fine. And, as the disease progresses, so does the denial, delusion, and compulsion. These defense systems slowly eclipse the progressively addicted brain. I recall one wife who, exasperated, took a picture of her husband as he had passed out in the driveway. His head lay just behind a tire. She was certain that it would convince him of his need for help. When shown the picture, he simply answered, "That's not me."

We may see that there is a problem, or, at least, we can look at the consequences and the reason for the consequences. The addict might ask us to help remedy the results (like bailing them out of jail), but they still do not see the reason for the consequences. There is always some excuse or explanation or minimization. Like: "My car is on the neighbor's lawn because it was too dark to see the driveway last night." In the meantime (sometimes for years) we keep "helping" and follow a vicious slide into crazy living for ourselves. The addict keeps setting fires and does not really relate to the cause of all the flames and ashes. We keep trying to extinguish the fire, and we keep thinking the addict will see the problem. They do not. So, our enabling continues or escalates, as does all of the heat and carnage.

We keep expecting rational thinking and awareness from the addict who soon has a too much toxic brain and too much smoke in their eyes. We need to get out of the way and stop expecting rationality from the diseased brain. For instance, how many 'lectures' have you brilliantly delivered. 301? Or 906? Our great wisdom and sage advice have landed in the land of La-La. Many family members are amazed when their addict gets sober for about two weeks, and they seem to be returning to themselves. Family members state that they had forgotten "how she really was." It is like addiction has beamed them up, and they are now dropped back into the cornfield and are detoxing. Many professionals feel the brain will recover for at least a year or longer.

Some Terms of Enabling
Reverse Logic

The truth is that doing less is doing more. Ex: What if you do not pay their bills if they are spending their resources on drugs? This is really hard to do at times, especially if you are trying to protect small grandchildren. When you stop doing this, it suddenly puts you outside of your value system. You no longer feel nice or like a good caring person. It feels so unloving and ugly. What you will eventually see and feel is that it is the strongest love in the world to see a bigger picture and refuse to be part of their problem.

What is really a reverse logic is that you eventually know that you need to be a Pain Allower. You need to allow the addict to feel the consequences. If you attend any Open A.A. or N.A. meeting and hear a speaker, you will hear how they "hit bottom," and it was the pain that was their alarm clock.

One wife of young children related how she did not arrange to pay the utility bill in the winter. Instead, she wrapped the children in their snowsuits inside the home. When her husband got home, he did take notice of the situation. He went to treatment. How brave was she? He was grateful later for her wisdom and courage.

Pain is the wake-up call to action for all of us. Have you ever had a mild toothache? First the aspirin, then the drugstore for some product, finally, the dentist. Pain is what you want to allow to happen—because it is the best hope for action. See what I mean by Reverse Logic?

Of course, if the addict is in a truly life-threatening situation, we take life-saving measures. Detachment is not abandonment.

Finally, you are back in your value system when you know that you are caring enough to do an effective thing. You are putting what they need ahead of what you need by trying one more "FIX AND RESCUE."

I think it is important to not think of our actions and feelings and attitudes as good or bad. Just think of what is the most EFFECTIVE thing you can do when pitted against Chucky. Friends and family may disapprove of you and think you are cruel and mean and heartless. They simply do not understand the reason for your decision. It is quite alright to let other people be wrong.

Get your support from Al-Anon.

A HUMAN DILEMMA

There are a million of these. What do you do when your addict calls for a ride home? What do you do when their boss calls the house and inquires of their whereabouts? What do you do when your grandchildren are upset with their mom or dad's drug use?

Look at the dilemma of Students Against Drunk Driving:

We tell our kids not to drink, but we then say they should call us if they are drunk and need a ride. Look at the dilemma of an adult child who steals from you and you hesitate to file a report. Who wishes to involve them in the law?

There is so much that is common in all of us in this situation—like getting a cat out of a tree. We all know the feeling, but we have different cats and different trees and all sorts of other variables.

There is a mountain of wisdom to be had from others. You will find it in the support groups such as Al-Anon. Go and listen and discern what is best for you to do. Get support. You will be amazed at the experience and fresh ideas of others.

What is Effective

Generally, what is effective is not to protect the addict from the consequences. The exception to this, of course, is if the person is in a truly life-threatening situation. What is effective is to be SUPPORTIVE, NOT CUSTODIAL. A good picture of this is to think that they are running a race and you can be on the sideline with cheers and water. You cannot run their race.

This is best done if it is done from a base of love and support and firm position. Stop being reactive and start learning to respond.

Remember your Q-TIP (Quit Taking It Personally). It will feel personal, but has nothing to do with you. You are just in the boxing ring, and their behavior is not about you and is no measure of your worth as a person. By the way, good parenting is wonderful, but a guarantee of nothing. Plenty of good parents have addicted kids. Plenty of not-so-good parents have kids who do not use any

substances. Educate yourself on addiction and develop an attitude that goes with the fact. (See Boxing Ring).

It is true that there are many enabling systems in life. The courts, the medical field, the law, the neighbors, and friends, for instance. Education about addiction is painfully lacking. However, the only area we can be effective in is our own life, and in the direct relationship we have with the addict. It is easy to complain that the police or doctor did not take appropriate action, but that is a waste of our energy. Focus on what you alone can do not to enable. Someone once pointed out that there are two kinds of business: Mine and Not Mine.

Innocent Ignorance
Most of us are ignorant about all of this. Although so many people grew up with addiction in the house, or are currently in that situation, we have never had much help in recognizing or responding to it all. So, I think we are innocently ignorant. And, we are teachable. And, we get better.

I had no class on all of this in Nursing School and very little good information in the Social Work curriculum. Maybe you are lucky enough to have attended a Family Program somewhere or found some good literature about the family and addiction. Mostly, it is a seat-of-the-pants experience. Actually, I think the world could use some Al-Anon. Lots of meetings.

Options and Choices: Not Having a Sense of Choice

"You are more likely to get your way if you have more than one way." Most of us have habits and routines and automatic ways of dealing with life and its daily issues. It never really occurred to me that there were choices. Years ago, I was running around town doing several 'clean up' and enabling things for those I loved. Finally, I sought some professional help. Dr. Bob listened patiently to me in the first session as I rattled breathlessly all of the things I MUST-GOTTA-SHOULD-HAD to do. He finally said two words: OR NOT. I paid the huge fee and made another appointment. Same thing. I rattled on, and he sat calmly and responded to my I HAVE TO DO THIS list with the OR NOT. Another huge fee. I was becoming disturbed that the return for my check was just two words. But—I decided to give it one more try. You know the outcome. I decided to never return after that third session. About one mile down the street on my way to yet another task for someone else–I heard the words! "OR NOT." I had a choice! The idea that I was entitled not to be a part of something that was not my problem had just never occurred to me. Choice. Such freedom. The car almost turned itself around. And it was also a life turn around.

There is an exercise: The NINE dots. It is about Choice and Options. See if you can connect all nine dots with four straight lines without lifting your pen from the paper. The answer is on the next page. Don't peek.

The Dot Paradigm Activity About Choice

Can you connect all of these dots with four straight lines without lifting   your   pencil?

The Dot Paradigm Activity

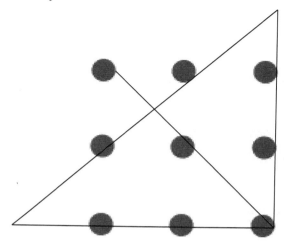

Solution to Can you connect all of these dots with four straight lines without lifting your pencil?

Comments on the 9 Dots

You notice that the answer creates two planes that allow for more choice and options. Most of us just keep drawing the lines back and forth to the dots and do not think of the facts that the answer lies in options. It breaks the predictability habit.

Detachment

This is a most misunderstood word. And anyone who felt abandoned as a child is reactive to it. It does not mean abandonment or lack of love. You will hear "you need to let go" often at the meetings, but it does not mean that you walk away. It means you need to 'let go' of trying to control the outcomes of another person by continuing all of the enabling efforts. Al-Anon refers to it as "loving detachment," and that state of mind and heart is truly the goal of Al-Anon. I can remain loving in tone and attitude toward the addict while I refuse to be part of their problem. It is to care about—not care for.

There is a quote from the Ya-Ya Sisterhood story that says it best. The oldest daughter had spent a childhood trying to fix everyone in her family who suffered from the mother's drinking. She grew up and gave up and went North to her career. Years later, she returned home, still full of anger that nothing she had done had helped anyone. The family reunion was held, and she noticed that not much had changed. But her heart did. She suddenly felt what detachment really is and finally knew her truth. As she returned North, she thought to herself: 'I cannot save you from your darkness, but I shall not close you out of my heart.' Her anger dissipated and love filled the space.

Another useful quote: "I do not detach from YOU, but I do detach from the agony of involvement in your problem."[7]

More Thoughts on Enabling

It is important to know that you can stop all enabling and your addict may continue to use their drugs of choice. You can also continue to enable in full gear, and your addict might choose to recover. So, why do we care about enabling if it does not guarantee someone else's outcome? Because you will feel better about not being part of their problem. You do not want to contribute to their decline. And it will be better for your health and stress. And you might ask yourself this question: <u>What will become of me if I do not quit this?</u> I think of that circus act where someone is keeping several plates twirling on the top of several tall sticks. It is a busy task and exhausting. Maybe we should just let the plates hit the ground, take a seat, have a hotdog, and see what happens. We can then turn our efforts toward a more effective relationship with addiction.

> **D**-on't
> **E**-ven

---

[7] Wells, Rebecca; Little Altars Everywhere; HarperCollins, NY, NY: 1992

- ➤ **T**-hink
- ➤ **A**-bout
- ➤ **C**-hanging
- ➤ **H**-im/er

One final question for you to ponder: What will be your first sign that you are making progress in reducing your enabling behaviors?

So, it is with new thoughts about this thing called Enabling. 'SOMETIMES THE HARDEST THINGS TO DO ARE THE THINGS WE MUST STOP DOING."

The Glorious List of Our Enabling

These can appear in many forms such as

- ➤ Behaviors
- ➤ Attitudes
- ➤ Feelings

Have some fun with this. Circle what you are great at doing. Then, circle all that you have tried. These are all fueled by an underlying need of our own. Think of a swimming duck and how calm it looks above the water and how busy it is below the surface.

These are the most common Enabling Opportunities I have heard over the years. You can probably add some of your own: They are all of our efforts to "fix" and "rescue" and "control" the addicted person. They are the Home Remedies.

Infantilize

We view them through our tone of voice and expectations of them as still infants, or much younger than they are. We 'baby' them. We lower our expectations. We do this to adults and teens. Another quote for mothers: Mothers are not for leaning on—they are for making leaning unnecessary. And: Prepare the child for the path, not the path for the child. And this parenting attitude can start very early. We over function as they under function. Are you doing for someone what they need to be doing for themselves?? Do you think of them as capable? Can you let them try and fail and then try once more? Such is the stuff of good self-esteem. I cannot believe that anyone can give someone else good self-esteem. Do you finish their sentences? Pay their insurance? Arrange their social life? Make excuses? Make their bed? Take them food? Remember the guideline of being supportive and not custodial. Do we enable or dis-able?

Chronic Anger

We are often in a constant state of everything from slightly annoyed to full rage. Mostly this is the result of allowing ourselves to be USED. It is also handing excuses to the addict on a silver platter. We are wrapped up in our foul mood, and the addict is out the door feeling justified in their use. A word for spouses: Do not allow someone's addiction to be a bitch-maker. It will harm you and your health. Again, go to Al-Anon and learn to have boundaries, how to say NO, and how to self-care. No one can use us without our permission. Anger becomes the Dance of Addiction. We are no longer in a relationship, but we have slipped into case management of something we have no power over—the behavior of someone else.

This anger often sounds like whining, sniveling, complaining, chronic unhappiness. I was the Queen of Pouting and Sniveling (anger through a small hole). This anger is one stage of grieving for all of the losses. Our heart hurts.

Letting Ourselves be Used: Let me count the ways.

Every hand in the audience was raised when I asked: Have you felt used? Well, only we are responsible for that. Almost all of our anger is because we are being rational in the face of addiction and expect a rational relationship. Ha! We are responsible for what we agree to. Remember that you have a choice. You can learn to say

NO to anything, and you do not need to be angry to do so. Nothing is so confusing as saying NO while kissing someone on the nose. (Snoopy)

You do not need approval. If of course, your refusal will cause harm to you, you need to look at options that are more permanent. Being a People-Pleaser pleases no one. Eventually, there is resentment, distance, and dishonesty. It is a short-term relief for a long-term issue.

Rush in with the Answers

I call it "Fools Rush In." The hardest people to get to stop this are the highly intelligent and high achievers. They are full of great ideas, wonderful advice, and great wisdom. SO WHAT!!! It is far more effective to listen well and encourage the other to conclude what is needed. A good friend of mine (In A.A.) once pointed out, "My life can't be what you figured out!" Wow. (He also added that he would be open to suggestions). I was trying to convince him of what movie we should watch and why. I wanted it to be *Jungle Book*, and he was hoping for John Wayne. Guess which one we watched?

Another example of this: A son was graduating from a treatment facility and was having a family discussion about his aftercare. The mom eagerly offered to drive him to his 12-Step meeting. Was that not supportive? No. It was too custodial. The wiser solution was for parents to offer to drive for two weeks and then expect their son to arrange his rides. He had the lost license and, he had the problem. It was healthy for him to take responsibility for his situation and find a solution. The result? He found a ride after two meetings. Actually, a lot of recovery talk goes on in the parking lots and hamburger places after meetings. And—what young man wants his mother to be waiting at the curb until the meeting adjourns? He needed to connect with other recovering people and the parents needed to get out of the chauffeuring business. Another benefit of this was the fact that it helped him increase his self-esteem to be his problem solver. Growing Up.

Making Excuses and Covering Up

I remember calling his boss and saying that he did not feel well. He was "in bed and had a terrible sinus problem." Amazing how the sinuses cleared up after treatment for his alcoholism. There are millions of examples of this. I often hear parents of a young adult or teen excuse serious issues with "He's only a kid," "It is only beer," "He was tired," or "She is with the wrong crowd," or equally dangerous beliefs. We have our denial to deal with, do we not?

Feeling Guilty and Ashamed and Not Talking About It

To make any sense of it all, we often take the blame onto ourselves. Little children always do this to idolize their parents. The thinking is this: If it is my fault, then I can change it. The truth is this: It is NOT your fault. Never was, never will be. Addiction has a life of its own.

If you had messages as a child that the reason your mom had a headache or dad did not come home or to your ballgame was because of something you did or said or did not do, the seeds are planted for a lifetime of thinking things are your fault.

The View from the Floor—and a decision you made when you had no ability to sort truth and discern a situation—often stay with us for a lifetime if not unearthed and re-educated. Combine this with the well-known rules of the family dealing with addiction: Do not talk, trust, or feel. A recipe for Enabling has been born.

I have to add that we often fail as parents in many ways, and maybe you even had a difficult time of it as a child. Many are damaged and many develop strengths. All are survivors. To be hurt is not the reason for addiction. It is the reason to feel bad. Some addicts had great childhoods; some did not. Many people who had pain as a child are not addicts. Some who had smooth sailing as a child are now addicted. There is no one commonality.

Many parents today tend to blame themselves or each other. I remember two fathers in the family group, sitting side by side. One felt guilty that his son was in treatment because he had been an active alcoholic and not present enough for his son. The man next to him said that he thought he was responsible for his son's problem because he had been too involved in everything his son did. The real culprit is that addiction is a brain disease and usually there is a genetic predisposition. I like to blame the great, great, great-grandparents.

What I love about this recovery world is that there is such wonderful opportunity to heal painful relationships and ourselves.

I Will Just Ignore the Situation

This 'fix' brings short-term relief and long-term pain. It is so very human when we feel overwhelmed and inadequate and fearful merely to put ourselves into a state of chosen denial. (This is not the same as the type of denial when we do not see what we see and do not know what we know). It is like taking a mini-vacation from the problem. The problem with that is that the problem does not take vacations. One woman shared that she would "step over the body and go play Bingo."

We can convince ourselves that it is all just a temporary situation. We can tell ourselves that there must be some reason for the body on the floor. We can talk ourselves into numbing our feelings. But no surprise that when we get back home, that pesky problem is still present, and nothing will change if nothing changes. We can try to be entirely independent, but our heart is usually still on-call.

Ove-Functioning

A therapist once remarked, "Did you know that over functioning is as much of dysfunction as under functioning?" Yikes! And here we have the delusion that we are "helping." No doubt, we have their answers—if only they would listen! No doubt, we are right—if only they would follow the brilliant suggestions. No doubt, we are experienced and wise—if they would somehow see that truth. And, no doubt, we get angrier and angrier. And we get increasingly sucked into trying to do the impossible. We do not understand how powerless we are. Ask what you are now doing for that person that they used to do for themselves (or never did but should).

It is as if we are eclipsed by their increasing failure to function as we pick up the task of keeping them afloat. Have you become addicted to someone else's possibilities? Are you using your talents for someone else? Can you see how we would typically have it in our value system to help someone, but with addiction, it becomes disabling for them?

Be a Drinking/Drug Buddy

People often think that by joining the addicted person:

- I can control what happens
- The addict will not be the driver
- We will have some shared times
- He/She will love me more
- I won't have another evening home alone. Waiting.

Whatever!

Years ago, I ran an aftercare group for 12 wives of men who had been in treatment. All had been through the mill. We met for three years and then disbanded. A year after that, they arranged a reunion. To my surprise, about six of the dozen had since realized that they also had a problem. It was interesting to hear that their addiction had been less problematic than the drama of their spouse, so they had not realized what was happening to them. As their spouse entered recovery, it was only when they tried not to drink at all for at least a year; they realized how very important their drinking was to them. You never really know how much you love something until you STOP using it.

Having Poor Boundaries

How many times do we draw that red line in the sand and then move it back repeatedly? The very first time we do not do as we said we would, we have lost all credibility. Al-Anon suggests you be very, very careful before drawing that line. I think that in over 30 years of talking to families, only one or two people followed through the first time. Hats off to them. We surely mean it when we draw that line, but time seems to soften all resolve, and we do not keep our word. So, why should anyone believe us?

Be a Drug Runner

The thinking is that 'if I get the alcohol/drugs at least he/she will not be on the road. They might kill someone, and I could not live with that'. What a dilemma. And, sometimes, how dangerous for you. You surely put yourself in harm's way in this world of drugs. I remember one father who climbed over fences and walked through alleys looking for his son. And, he had a pacemaker. And it is common to "just buy the beer" because it will mean that there will be no argument later. Peace at any price.

No House Rules

It seems fair to be clear about your expectations. So many of us have House Wishes, not House Rules. This is especially true for adolescents or young adults back living with you. You cannot, of course, have rules with a spouse. But you can decide what is acceptable for you and what is not—and be prepared to take your next step if this is not honored.

The house rules need to be clear, consistent, and constant. There is a section in this book on suggestions for some Home Contracts. It is good to put it in writing with everyone's signature. When you think about it, having real rules is an end to confusion and argument. The point is to make it clear what they are and then follow through. When you stay at the Holiday Inn, they might have a sign of rules by their pool. Ex: DO NOT THROW GLASS IN THE POOL. If I choose to throw glass, then that had been my decision to check out of the hotel. The responsibility is on me. Clear and simple.

This same concept can be very effective. It can be done lovingly and with mutual discussion and input. But you, as parents, are paying the mortgage, it is your home, and you set the rules. Parents need not take the position of 'throwing him/her out.' It is better to put the responsibility on the son or daughter who has signed a contract and will now decide his or her fate about residence with you. If they choose not to follow the Rules of the Inn, then they have chosen themselves to move on out.

A quote: You know how upset the kids get when the parents break the rules they have set!

I Pretend and Minimize

I may see the truth, but it is too painful to talk about or feel. So, I pretend that "He has a bad headache, or sinus trouble, or a long day, or "She is exhausted, or mad at her friend, or misses her brother." Any excuse will do. It is overwhelming to recognize and deal with addiction with someone you love. What pain and what powerlessness. What shame. What can I do? Addiction upsets all routine and the whole apple cart. So, I find lesser reasons or keep my head in the sand. I do not know that I can seek help. I do not know that it is not my fault. The bottom line for families and friends is to deal with their pain and their powerlessness. And, seek support and the facts of addiction.

I Blame, Endure, Deny, Hide, Justify my Feelings:

Just more of the Pretend, Minimize, Distract, and Avoid defenses we use.

I Take it Personally

This is such a burden. The fact that this whole mess has nothing to do with you. You cannot create or cause addiction in anyone. Period. We can hurt each other, let each other down, and inflict great pain on one another. That does NOT create addiction. It DOES create a pile of pain and resentment and confusion and depression.

Please find a Q-TIP somewhere, or several, and place them at various places in your day. It is a fun reminder that you need to Quit Taking It Personally. It feels very personal, but it is no reflection on your worth as a person. The bad news is that IF you had caused it, you might be able to fix it. Now, since it has nothing to do with you, you need to face your powerlessness.

I cannot tell you the number of stories I have heard from women whose drinking spouses convinced them to quit their jobs and stay home so they would not feel lonely. So, they did. Guess what? The wives were now at home, watching the addict on the couch and still drinking.

Bailiff

How many of us have rushed out to bail someone out of jail? People will criticize you if you do not. It did not occur to us that prison might be a transformative experience. There are worse things (like a coffin). It could well motivate someone into reality and a determination to not let this happen again. All I know is that going back to a nice clean bed and good food does not do much to break their denial. Many addicts will testify to the incarcerated time as a real awakening. Some jails even offer recovery programs.

Chauffeuring

Are you a taxi? Or, worse, is your name on the title of the car they are driving? There are bicycles and buses. I can remember one young wife who bundled up two small children at 4 a.m. so they could take their dad to work. Finally, she asked him to find another person to ride with or someone he could pay. He did. Why is it that we automatically cover the bases? There are other choices, and most recovering people agree with the idea that you made the mess, so you need to take responsibility for the cleanup. A word about car titles—get them out of your name. You are liable.

High Tolerance for Inappropriate Behavior

Some of this develops in the breeding ground of a childhood that calls upon us to survive. So, we adapt. It becomes a natural and smart reaction to an unnatural situation. The problem comes when we get older and are still using the childhood survival skills. We get ourselves really out of shape adapting to someone else's issue.

It does not occur to us that the bad behavior is someone else's task to change. We keep adapting. This is the perfect match for addiction. If you had to tip-toe around a situation that was tense, you would probably continue that way of living. And, you may be attracted to situations that still feel like 'old home week' as you continue to ply your skills at survival. The glorious goal of any growth and therapy is to become aware of your part of the dance and change your choices.

A Look at What Really Empowers Enabling Behaviors
This is like the feet of the duck. It is the "What's in it for me" list or the W.I.I.F.M. The truth is that the underlying engine that powers enabling is really a want or need of our own! It is natural to have needs and wants. Nothing wrong with that. However, when they are part of enabling someone else's addiction, we need to be able to identify them and think of how to get that need of ours met without enabling addiction in someone we love.

Some of our Needs/Wants (are the feet of the duck):

- Safety
- Connectedness
- Peace of Mind
- Reduced Stress
- Pain Reduction
- Role Identity and Fulfillment
- A Release of Feelings
- Approval
- Self-Esteem
- Lack of Shame/Guilt
- Powerfulness
- Control
- Maintaining a Routine in our Life
- To be Loved/Appreciated/Valued
- A Sense of Security

The point is this: In all of our enabling attitudes, feelings, or actions, one of our needs/wants is beneath it all.

Here are a few examples:

- I bailed him out of jail to get his approval or avoid stress or to maintain a sense of safety.

- I covered up his drinking by making excuses, which gave me a sense of security because he would not be fired.
- I drank with her so that we could feel connected. It was better than her going out with friends to drink.
- I lied for him because that is what a good wife does and to keep the children from knowing what was really going on. That would be too painful.
- I bring the alcohol home so that he will not drive drunk to get it. I do that for my peace of mind. What if he killed someone?
- I never follow through my threats. It keeps the peace, and nothing needs to change. It would be too disruptive to leave.
- I could never kick out my kid. What parent could do that?? That is not what parents do.
- I could never talk about this to anyone. I would feel so embarrassed, guilty, and ashamed.
- If I keep everything looking good, no one will know. Someone once said that her silverware drawer was in perfect order. (When you cannot control the big things, you can control the small ones).

Can you add some of your own? Can you see how very understandable it is for use to enable? Can you even imagine that you could maintain your self-esteem and peace of mind even in the face of living with an addicted person? You are not, I repeat, the problem, but we do slide into becoming part of the problem with our well-intentioned "helping." In general, the common motivation for our enabling is one of two things: To reduce our pain or to maintain the routine in our lives. The truth is that this is a delusion and short-lived.

In the case of spouses (or other adult living arrangements), it is entirely possible to remain in the relationship even if the addict continues the usage. The only time that leaving the situation is imperative is when there is a real danger to you. Run do not walk.

Other than that, many people will ask why we do not simply leave the situation (parent of minors, of course, cannot). There are many valid reasons why we stay. I think of us as living in a birdcage. You can go to Al-Anon and other supportive and educational meetings and learn to live more peacefully. You look at options and can even open the door to your cage. That does not mean you will choose to fly away. But you can find options if you must. That does not mean you will choose that path, but at least you have a choice. You may well choose to stay in your decorated cage with the door open. Many do. It is quite OK to love an addict. You may stay for financial necessity, or for moral value. The important thing here is this: If you choose to stay, you need to accept the reality that this is your choice and stop being harsh with the addict. They will continue to do what addicts do. You have chosen to stay. The one thing you cannot expect is a healthy relationship. This is not possible with a person so altered and missing in their life.

I know a woman who left her alcoholic husband years ago and then their young son developed cancer. After long months, she decided she could not deal with this alone and returned to the marriage. Today, she still lives with that same drinking husband. She gets frustrated, but mostly has constructed her own authentic life and is loving toward him. She does not take it all personally; she fills her life with other healthy people and relatives and remains respectful of his choice to drink. Sometimes, we cannot have everything. She feels her life is not perfect, but good enough. What is important for us is to feel not trapped. What matters is to feel you have a choice or option.

Another memory of mine is of an elderly gentleman who finally had his wife in a treatment center. He listened intently to the Enabling lecture and raised his hand to say that the only way he could see that he was enabling her was his very presence in the home. I remember thinking that it was a shame he had not received help years earlier. He had not been aware of possible choices for that household.

Keep in mind, there are two situations we enable:

1. We enable the addict to keep using without an effective confrontation.

2. In recovery, we enable the addict not to grow, mature or master his or her own life.

Think of the butterfly and the struggle for freedom. There is a story of a man who tried to help the butterfly emerge from the chrysalis. He very carefully cut the wrap away so that the caterpillar could ease out. The caterpillar died. The man did not know that the struggle was necessary to grow and stretch wings. The struggle was what removed the powder from the wings so that they would expand and carry it away.

So often, we are thrilled when the loved one starts a recovery that we rush in with all of their answers. Or, we clean out their garage or pay their bills, or over-function in some way. This is a disservice to them. The addict now has to climb up their ladder of mastery and self-esteem. Please do not think they can do that on your rungs! It is called self-esteem, not YOU-esteem. If they ask you for help, of course, you can be supportive. Just do not be custodial.

Example: A son/daughter wants you to call creditors or pay their bills for them. It is far better if you help them make the calls or show them how to budget, write checks, etc. Think of

97

the Peace Corp who did not give grain for bread, but taught people how to plant it for themselves.

Step by little step, the person needs to re-enter life on life's terms and master one small victory after another. Remember, be supportive and not custodial. Do not do for someone what they need to learn to do for themselves. Start at any age. Sit on your hands and your great talents and watch as they struggle and achieve.

Good

I remember one competent mother, spent years preparing the path for her son. She thought through every one of his challenges and gave fabulous directions. He, of course, just numbed out and followed. And used marijuana and alcohol. Once he was clean, residing in a recovery house in a distant state, he called his mother to report that he was on his way to work. It was raining. She asked if he had an umbrella! Much to her credit, she even laughed at herself. He was 27 by now. She had a colossal family relapse! Some habits are hard to break. Fortunately, he laughed, too. He remains in recovery, and she is now dealing with her issues of anxiety and control.

I repeat, sometimes the hardest things we have to do are the things we have to stop doing. A frequent question: What is the difference between being supportive and being enabling? The simplest response is: Is your help in the direction of their recovery or does it feed into a continuation of the addiction. You need to keep your goal and wish clear. If they are still in active usage, you want them to stop. If they are in recovery, you want a child to grow up and master their life. If they are a spouse or other adult friend, you want to be in a healthier and mutually accountable relationship.

Is your decision to be 'helpful' in the way of your goal or wish? Does your decision or action interfere with what a person needs to be doing for themselves? You cannot give anyone that gift. It is gained through self-effort. As the man said: Someone else's life cannot be what you figured out (you may be full of good ideas for someone else, and maybe they will benefit from your suggestions. Usually, however, we grow from our own mistakes and pain).

If your action alleviates a natural consequence for them, it is enabling. I repeat the quote from Susan Farham: "Even when a need exists and we are well qualified to meet it, we are not necessarily called to respond to it. To be doing what is good can be the greatest obstacle to doing something even better."

Remember that pain is a great motivator. Adult addicts have experienced more loss than adolescents and become more easily motivated to change. However, whether dealing with adolescents or adults, we need to be a pain-allower. It is the greatest love of all because it puts your need to find comfort in enabling as secondary to that which might be effective in reducing their denial.

The final section of this Enabling chapter is to leave you with a list of things that are more effective. (Suitable for framing and putting on the refrigerator door for frequent visitation). I shall repeat some of the one-liners that are easy to recall:

1. Go to Al-Anon or another support group
2. Get books on the subject, and read them
3. Get off the eggshells
4. Share feelings
5. Ask their opinion and listen to learn, not argue
6. Remove your expectations, and try to see the person for who they are, not who you want them to be
7. Work on your resentments – Stop being used
8. Take responsibility for your responses

9. Improve patience with self and others
10. Let go of a sense of permanence and outcomes
11. Use the "N" vitamin (NO)
12. Do not rush in with answers to their problems
13. Stop infantilizing
14. Be a pain-allower
15. Be open to new ideas
16. Remember: support only recovery, not addictions
17. Be supportive, not custodial
18. When all else fails, get a roll of decorative duct tape and keep it handy. Apply a six-inch strip over your mouth when tempted to be reactive, angry or any other useless lecture or advice or outburst. Keep this especially next to your phone.
19. Best of all: Read the Love First Organization website about what an intervention is. Arrange one if you can.

Chapter 6: Those Meetings, Change, and a Man Named Ernie

The 12-Step Meetings

I went to my first Al-Anon meeting because someone at the treatment center said I should go. In those days, most of the attendees were women. Today, there are many men in attendance and an occasional special group such as parents only. Everyone was so nice, and we always went out to eat with many of the other people after the meeting. I loved the clams. I also loved the fact that it was great to have a "date" with my husband when he did not drink. I loved not having to drive the car home. I loved the feeling of sharing this experience with him. What was missing was the fact that I had no real idea what Al-Anon was all about–for years, really. My periodic attendance matched his periodic relapses.

It is because of this that I feel that some understanding of these programs would have been helpful from the start—to build respect for their purpose, acquire some small knowledge of their history, and gain some glimmer of what attendance might birth. Alcoholics Anonymous is the granddaddy of them all. The other myriad of 12-Step support programs is based on the same 12-Steps, traditions, and concepts that are the core of A.A. (There are over 200 different types of support groups today).

My favorite is Messies Anonymous. I called them once for some information, and they could not find their pamphlet to send. But, more about the Granddaddy. A.A. has a philosophy that the more sophisticated a situation is, the more we need to keep it simple. They have incredible slogans that you might see on some car bumper stickers. Like, KEEP IT SIMPLE, STUPID OR 'KISS,' I AM A FRIEND OF BILL W., or ONE DAY AT A TIME.

A.A. was started by Bill Wilson and Dr. Bob Smith in 1935. There is an enjoyable old film that tells the story of their journey from despair to recovery. (*My Name is Bill W*) with James Wood and James Garner (1989). Another excellent video is *Bill W. –* a documentary about the Co-Founder of Alcoholics Anonymous.

A.A. is now in at least 115 countries and has three guiding principles:

❖ Recovery

❖ Unity

❖ Service

There are open meetings when anyone can attend, and closed meetings for those whose only entry ticket is a sincere desire to stop drinking and any other drug use.

There is a long beginning to the A.A. history. In December 1934, Bill was hospitalized once more in New York. During this time, he experienced a "white light" spiritual experience and his despair lifted. Some claim the 12-Steps were revealed to him. He had tried for years to help himself and other alcoholics get sober. He had attended the Oxford Group since the 30's and tried to remain sober by following their principles. He eventually left that group and founded A.A. with Dr. Bob Smith. In the simplest of explanations, the Oxford Group was a shame-based program and was mostly interested in all of the sins of the world. The creation of A.A. had the singular focus of alcoholics and was intended to eliminate the shame of alcoholism seen as a sin. It depended on others precisely because they were alcoholic and valued by others as a support to each other. It also spoke of the fact of imperfection as part of the human condition and the surrender to this fact as the way of freedom.

Bill and others spent many years traveling, promoting, and sharing the good news of the hope and success of A.A. This, of course, left many of the spouses feeling left out and lonely. The story has it that Bill W's wife, Lois, got angry with him one day several years into his recovery, and she threw her shoe at Bill. (I do not know if it hit him or not). Bill was asking her to hurry to another meeting. She was tired of only making the coffee for meetings and generally over-functioning for Bill's needs. She and other spouses attended the A.A. meetings mostly by waiting in their cars or the kitchens. It was in these kitchens that the family began to support each other. Lois realized she and other wives also needed help with their own resentments and anger. Various family groups had developed independently. Bill had attended another meeting in 1950 and met with the family groups. He returned home and encouraged Lois to try to organize them. Thus, she and her neighbor, Anne B., began the laborious and rewarding process of starting Al-Anon. Today there are over 26,000 groups worldwide. So, these Sisters of

Perpetual Vengeance (as one joke goes) benefited from this remarkable and inexpensive program for mental health, which offers a restoration of sanity and support to get you back on track. In today's meetings, there are many other relationships besides wives. Parents are sadly in abundance. In 1957, a 17-year-old boy named Bob started Alateen and there are 2300 in the world today. Smart teenager. Bill W. also assisted in the formation of Narcotics Anonymous for anyone using drugs other than alcohol. Nar-Anon is the family group.

It is normal for most family and friends to feel that they do not need any help. After all, 'the addicted one is "the problem". Sometimes a family member may still be stuck in the past while the person with an addiction is zooming along into recovery and gaining new outlooks because he/she is attending the meetings. The family believes that if the person with an addiction gets better, so will they. My experience tells me that when the family is still angry and resentful after a year into the end of the drinking/drug use, it is a clue that maybe they might have some healing to do. It is also my experience that the person with an addiction begins to laugh again and the family members are still in a frown and keep bringing up the past. I like to think of the family who has been in a car accident. The person with an addiction is the driver and gets the most attention and help in healing. The family and friends are also injured, and no one pays much attention to them. Just because the driver has help mending their broken leg does not mean the passengers' broken arms and concussions are being addressed. It is even worse—the passengers are expected to give smiling understanding support to the driver while still being bruised, limping, and broken.

In its wisdom, Al-Anon gently guides the passengers to a focus on themselves. New attendees usually hope for a focus on the person with an addiction and are surprised that the mission of Al-Anon is a path to recovery for those who have been in a relationship with the addicted person. Everyone affected needs attention and support to heal from the carnage of addiction. It is of note that most inpatient and outpatient treatment centers do not get insurance coverage for a family program.

1. Family and friends need to learn necessary things which help their recovery:

2. We are powerless to change anyone else—we are licked.

3. We need to admit this and find something more significant than self to lean on.

4. We need to learn about this disease and adapt our thinking to the fact and change our attitudes.

5. We share with others what we have learned.

6. Know that because we need to change what we do, does not mean the situation is our fault.

7. Getting back to your authentic life is a good thing. Or, maybe, finding your own authentic life.

All of the meetings are carefully structured and confidential. It is a program that carefully guards against personality conflict. It is about principles. It is not about religion—it is about spirituality. It is also interesting to know that the universal truths and wisdom in the 12-Steps are also found in all the great writing of the world:

- ➤ The Talmud
- ➤ I Ching
- ➤ Ancient Egyptian works
- ➤ The Bible
- ➤ The Quran,
- ➤ Spanish Jesuits writing from 500 AD

> Atheistic Philosophy

It is a smart choice for a person with an addiction or significant other who truly wants to make a change, to immerse him or herself in 90 meetings in 90 days. It takes many sandbags to turn a river. It takes many voices and new ideas to change thinking. For the person with an addiction, getting off the drug is the easiest part—the golden key to success is what you do to maintain and grow…12-Step meetings have been that path for thousands. Father Martin, who was a pioneer in this field and lectured around the world, loved to tell jokes. His advice to the audience (in treatment facilities and other locations) was to compare a parachute jump with the road to recovery. He said it is always good to follow the instructions.

Now for some fun. I used to give a lecture to the clients in treatment for their addiction. I stood at a large chalkboard and asked a question: why do you not like those meetings? I also asked that question to the group of family and friends. Soon, a long list appeared and finally I could hear some laughter.

A sample from people with an addiction: (and sometimes, the family)
- I hear the same old drunk-a-logs.
- I am too tired, too busy, too bored, live too far away. (even though I would drive miles for a drink/drug).
- I hate the smell of smoke—I am allergic to it.
- I have to work—too expensive for me to go to meetings ($1.00 a night)
- I have more important things to do.
- There is more to life than those meetings.
- The meetings depress me. (alcohol is a depressant)
- It's all too weird.

- It feels like a cult.
- I am not a talker, especially to strangers.
- It does not help me to hear other people's problems.
- I might see someone who knows me—especially from work. (and you might see them, too).
- The meetings last too long (1 hour).
- I need to get things done and make up for lost time (like I need to starch the flag!).
- Everyone else is so much worse off. My problem seems so small.
- I'm not into the God thing.

From Families:
- I hate to hear wives complain.
- All they talk about is the person with an addiction.
- They never talk about the person with an addiction.
- It is not MY problem. I have given this enough of my time.
- I will be fine if he/she just shapes up.
- I cannot relate to those people—they are different from me. (We need to learn to focus on the connections and not the exceptions).
- Fill in your reason.

These may have some truth, but there are deeper reasons people resist and stay in denial about their need to change and recover.

The Reasons We Resist Attending Are Usually The Very Reason We Need to be There

1. We are limited. It is hard to internalize the reality that we do not have control of much. We are not omnipotent. Al-Anon speaks of the 3 C's. We cannot Control, Cure or Cause addiction in others. We do, however, unknowingly Contribute to an environment where addiction loves to flourish. It is a truth that high-achieving/responsible people are often the most resistant to feeling powerless.

2. We might feel shame or guilt, and we do not relish the thought of spending an evening revisiting pain.

3. It seems unnatural to ask for help. It is suggested that we get a sponsor. That is not a friend. It is someone who will keep you thinking right and confront when needed. Friends will always love and agree with you. A sponsor will suggest growth.

4. We are often deluded about how we are. This is called Denial. Families can list many painful and negative feelings about how they have felt but will usually say, "I'm fine" when asked. The person with an addiction, of course, is numbed and anesthetized and is far from the reality of how they are.

Think of this experience for all of us. It is like a root canal. The difference is that the person with an addiction has the Novocain and the others do not.

5. Attendance at meetings is an implied admission that I am a person with an addiction or family member, and it might be my fault.

6. I might still want to use chemicals still. Family and friends may fear that they must also stop drinking.

7. I am afraid of change. I might have to change patterns of my life and learn new behaviors.

8. I have a fear of the unknown.

9. I have a fear of being blamed. I much prefer to blame others.

I have to share at this point. I was so sure that my mother-in-law was the cause of my husband's drinking. She was a problem. And she, of course, said that he did not drink until he was married. Well, I was glad to inform her that he drank all through high school. It is sad that we never got to sit together at some family program to learn the truth about addiction. No one was to blame. Addiction has a life of its own. It is its own entity. I am glad to report that we eventually got on the same page.

We have a fear of the truth. We take it all so personally. The truth may hurt, but it can be dealt with. I repeat that we do not take personally that which is so personally happening.

    10. I am afraid of what people might tell me to do. Or what they will think.

These reasons for resistance are natural and normal. Do not let them stop you. Mrs. Delaney, who ran a recovery home long ago, once told family members, "You should scare yourself a little every day." It cannot be any more frightful than to do nothing.

A few more thoughts on attending "those meetings." For both the person with an addiction and others, it may feel like Stark Raving Sobriety. As much as I hated to admit it, there were similarities in persons with an addiction and family recovery: Everyone needed to:

> ➤ Change attitudes, feelings, and actions.
> ➤ Understand that if nothing changes, nothing will change.
> ➤ Address our emotional needs.
> ➤ Discover the relief in sharing and communicating with others.
> ➤ Get help with our tangled thinking (A.A. calls this 'stinking thinking').
> ➤ Find a place that celebrates us, not just tolerates us.
> ➤ Know that my intrinsic thinking needs to be monitored.

> Not forget the past. It is hard to relate to an old toothache and all too easy to forget. There is a need to remember the past and avoid a euphoric recall.

> Bond again to the human race. Come out of isolation and trust interdependence with others.

> Get honest with stories and facts and feelings. One heals best with the courage to share.

> Ask two questions:
> - What am I doing that I need to stop doing?
> - What am I not doing that I need to start doing?

It becomes a process in attendance. I went from clams and resistance to viewing self and life as a whole study in exciting pieces of information.

So, I encourage you to attend several different meetings and do not judge. Keep an open mind. It is like finding the right partner, or restaurant or shoe. You will know when it pleases you.

The Change Process

In 1977 the processes of change were identified by Prochaska and DiClemente in what is known as the transtheoretical model of behavior.[8] We often talk of a need to change. This is difficult to do. Because we need to change what we do does NOT mean that the situation is our fault!! Change is a process, not an event. It requires awareness, patience, and time. Change is the process of See-Say-Do. First, we must become aware of desirable change (either to something or away from something). Then we must talk about it and finally, we must do it.

---

[8] *Prochaska, James O.; DiClemente, Carlo C. (2005). "The transtheoretical approach". In Norcross, John C.; Goldfried, Marvin R. Handbook of psychotherapy integration. Oxford series in clinical psychology (2nd ed.). Oxford; New York: Oxford University Press. pp. 147–171. ISBN 0195165799. OCLC 54803644.*

There is familiar and lengthy information on the STAGES OF CHANGE, but I like to keep it simple. For instance, an example—the process of re-painting the living room which is now a worn-out color.

Pre-contemplation Stage

One is unaware of the need or resists the idea of painting the wall blue. Maybe you never even thought about it. We begin to move to the next stage with some consciousness raising. Perhaps someone comments on it, or you are about to put your home up for sale and notice the need for decoration.

Contemplation Stage

You become more aware of the scuffs and faded areas and the things that maybe the house would sell better if you painted the room. You have not committed to the task. You consider the pros and cons. You move toward the next step once you decide the labor might make the sale more attractive.

Preparation Stage

You intend to take action soon but have decided to paint. Soon—any day now. Off to the hardware store to purchase needed supplies.

Action Stage

You vow not to procrastinate any longer. You turn down better offers for weekend fun. You paint.

Maintenance Stage

You wipe off all fingerprints and keep walls clean and free of damage. So, it is with the problem of becoming aware of a need to change when we are discussing addiction. This can be true for the person with an addiction or any significant others.

The phrase "hitting bottom" is often used to describe what needs to happen for the person with an addiction to become more open to the idea of getting help and changing their life. This is also true for the family member. The idea of change is often a by-product of something painful. The "bottom" varies. One grandmother came to treatment after her small granddaughter told her she "smelled funny all the time." Another might NOT be motivated after a severe car crash.

Some family members have a high tolerance for drama and stress and others may confront the problem after seemingly small issues. It is true that many families, unknowingly, keep rewarding the addiction with the enabling behaviors. They prevent the pain and "bottom" from happening. They usually have no help in really understanding the situation and the need for deep change. What we see as 'helpful' is often just prolonging the time to a desire for change. Enabling becomes disabling.

It is so typical for humans to resist change. We like what is familiar, even if uncomfortable. As a family member, if you ever attend an Open A.A. meeting and hear a speaker, you will often listen how their process of change occurred. From complete denial and delusion of the fact he/she had a problem, to an event that started the awakening, to some thought of seeking help, to some attempts at control and toying with the notion of quitting, to getting some guidance and a direction for treatment and showing up there.

Recovering people with an addiction often say that recovery is easy—you just have to change everything. That means "wet faces and places". I like to think of a pie chart of Change that has been divided into eighteen pieces. Half of the pie is about Why People

Change and half is Why People Do Not Change. (or Why They Relapse or Fail to Maintain). Think of an 18-slice pie:

Why People Change:

1. To avoid pain

2. To gain increased self-confidence and mastery

3. Are reinforced with good feelings (have a supportive community)

4. Can see and want something better for themselves- Hope.

5. Grow and Experience spirituality

6. Learn from experience and mistakes

7. Become less self-centered—have children

8. Grow in maturity and understand One Day at a Time

9. Gain new awareness/education about self/disease

William White wrote in a blog, "nature will find a way; so will recovery." Mr. White has been studying multiple pathways of recovery. The diversity of recovery stories shares a central theme that forms the connecting tissue across secular, spiritual, and religious frameworks of recovery. This thread is a "sustained and irrevocable commitment for personal change." White states that change can come quickly or slowly, and many factors interact to set the "detonation point" of recovery initiation. Envision this as a push/pull dynamic. The 'push' is whatever one wishes to get away from or avoid and the 'pull' factors are attractive possible outcomes for recovery. Both the push and the pull can motivate one to seek or maintain recovery. They can be seen as PAIN and HOPE. Away from more pain and toward hope.

Is this change process also not true in many life situations? Leave my job and hope for better. Leave my spouse and hope for better. Leave this car and seek better. Leave my self-defeating behaviors and hope for better? Leave my potato chips and hope for celery? (maybe not). This is a massive simplification: For complete article see blog@williamwhitepapers.com

Why People Do Not Change (or Relapse)

1. Do not deal with the grief of loss (of old lifestyle or self-image)

2. Failure to grow into uncomfortable new feelings of success (It is OK to be OK.)

3. Failure to develop support systems

4. Failure to maintain supports

5. Failure to learn new coping skills

6. Continue to isolate from others (even in a crowd)

7. Failure to grow spiritually

8. Want immediate results (Time and patience are needed.)

9. Failure to replace old attitudes, activities, and connections with new choices

Another sharing that demonstrates how small changes bring big rewards. When my son returned home after treatment for his marijuana use, he walked into the kitchen and casually announced that he needed some new shoes. My old self would have jumped at this opportunity to have a fun time shopping with him, to reward his newly found sobriety, to help. He was in college and about 6 feet 2 inches tall. I loved his humor and company. I had my mouth open to offer the money or a trip for shoes. Then, I remembered. Instead, I cheerfully said, "When I need new shoes, I will let you know." We both laughed and we both got the point. He eventually purchased some himself with his earned money. This was a small step toward independence and self-esteem. For me, it was a small step in knowing that he would still love me even if he bought his own clothes. Probably he would love me even more for thinking him to be a man. There is a quote about this: "How do you make a man? You thinketh him so[9]." It is a respectful thing to do.

A Man Named Ernie

I never met Ernie Kurtz. He died in 2015. I had met his wife while working in a treatment center in Michigan. She was creating a curriculum for social workers at her university and had arranged to have some students at our facility. Ernie had written a book in 1979 called, *NOT GOD: A History of Alcoholics Anonymous* (Published by Hazelden). While contemplating the content of this book, I tried to leave an e-mail with Ernie to ask his permission to include thoughts from the book. Much to my surprise, he responded. It was November 2013. I shared that I had tried hard to give a lecture to the patients about the content of his book— probably the most challenging task ever given or heard. Feeling that it was wise to try to explain what happens in 'those meetings' to increase respect and reduce the mystery and, hopefully, encourage attendance, I plunged ahead into paraphrasing his brilliant work. Keeping It Simple was not simple. His email response was so warm. He gave me his ready permission to include any material.

---

[9] James Allen; As a Man Thinketh; Digireads: Overland Park, KS, 2016

Ernie had written *NOT GOD* as his doctoral dissertation at Harvard. He was a priest and entered a 3-month treatment for alcoholic priests and, due to his A.A. attendance; Ernie became intensely interested in the history of that group. He left the priesthood and began to teach at the University of Georgia. Ernie met and married Linda, and their long marriage followed. He co-authored books with Katherine Ketchum (The Spirituality of Imperfection) and befriended and mentored Bill White (Slaying the Dragon). Both of these books contain a wealth of information on the history of addiction and recovery. Ernie mentored and collaborated with them for the rest of his life. Great friendships developed. Bill White shares that in Ernie's final contributions he wanted us to celebrate the growing varieties of A.A. experience and add legitimacy to secular styles of recovery within and beyond the fellowship of A.A.

At his funeral, Ernie was referred to as "the Shepherd of A.A. The one who looks after the one sheep who is lost. The shepherd cares for the whole flock." Ernie Kurtz exhibited a profound influence on the field of addiction and recovery.

What follows is a very simplified paraphrasing of the *NOT GOD* book. It is about what happens in the 12-Step meetings that makes A.A. a therapeutic success. It explores the connections between A.A. and other philosophies of existence. Ernie alerts us to the old advice that these programs are "to be utilized, not analyzed."

Statements from the Book

1. We yearn, yet we are limited, which is a contradiction. There is a core insistence that we are limited and need to

surrender to our human finitude and essential limitations of being.

THE ALCOHOLIC DOES NOT HAVE A LIMIT—HE IS LIMITED. He/she can make progress, never perfection. You cannot will what cannot be willed. We can only move in directions. Some examples of this include:

> ➢ I CAN will knowledge—not wisdom
> ➢ I CAN will submission—not humility
> ➢ I CAN will self-assertion—not courage
> ➢ I CAN will congratulations—not admiration
> ➢ I CAN will physical nearness—not emotional intimacy
> ➢ I CAN will dryness—not sobriety

He also speaks of the laughter one hears in meetings. "The laughter one hears in A.A. meetings is not laughter at the speaker. It is laughter at self. This is why it is so healing. Any good meeting will have laughter, the humor that comes from the embrace of this image of imperfection."

I am here reminded of one speaker who elicited roars of laughter from his audience at an open A.A. meeting. He had stolen a train. Really? And where did he plan to take it to avoid being arrested? The laughter means acceptance of our contradictions of self as we attempt to transcend our limits.

I also like to think of all the family examples of this. There are a myriad of stories which reveal our attempts to keep the person with an addict from using their drug. We cannot control the outcome of another. But we do laugh together when we can relate when someone else reveals what they unsuccessfully did that we also tried. Laughter is healing and a good sign of recovery. Brené Brown, Ph.D. who wrote *The Gifts of Imperfection* calls this the Knowing Laughter.

2. A.A. prescribes LIMITED CONTROL and LIMITED DEPENDENCE

The person with an addiction seeks control over feelings and their environment and loses control. The person with an addiction drinks to deny dependence and depends on alcohol. SO…One day at a time. Maybe one minute at a time is do-able. Do not say, "I will never drink again." Instead say, "Not today." They do not say "avoid all alcohol." They recommend "do not take the first drink."

The famous Serenity Prayer: Advises to accept what you cannot change (like a brain wired for addiction), change what you can, and have the wisdom to know the difference. You do not surrender your freedom to drink–you gain your freedom not to drink. Wow! I cannot drink becomes I **CAN NOT** drink. WOW again.

To be human is to be mostly dependent. We need others. A.A. embraces a new relationship with others who are also essentially limited, and they find a positive identity in their limitation. One goes beyond one's limited self, transcends self, and enters this new relationship with like-others. The problem is not dependency on alcohol. The problem is depending on alcohol. How about depending on others who 'get it.

3. THE THERAPY OF MUTUALITY

A.A. teaches three mutualities:

➢ Make a difference *
➢ Honesty *
➢ Dependence*

A.   Making a Difference

The founders of A.A. knew of this basic human need of dependence on others. The story of the Man in the Hospital Bed is well known. Bill and Bob were struggling to find people with addictions to help and had heard of a very ill alcoholic now hospitalized. They visited him. What was remarkable was that they told this man they needed HIM to help them. Thus, the man in bed felt needed and not burdened with a sense of failure. He was needed to help Bill and Bob stay sober. It is said that we search for that for which we are needed. Giving is good for you. Other people with an addiction need your presence precisely because you are a person with an addiction.

B.   **Being Honest**:

You need to learn to avoid self-deceit—of self and others! The pain of addiction is the corruption between seeming and truly being. "To thine own self, be true"[10] is imperative. One must learn to avoid self-deceit.

Another personal story: My oldest son (now 33 years sober) once had a sponsor, Al, who would sit in the front row while my son was giving what they call an open talk. (His story). Today, my son looks back fondly at the number of times Al would merely sit there and flick his lighter if he knew he did not hear the truth. Words were never spoken, but the power of it remains today.

C.   DEPENDENCE

Both dependence and independence are factors. Ernie states that each enables and fulfills the other. We are neither totally. We all have a periodic need for dependence intertwined with an equally essential need for independence. He states the basic neurotic

---

[10] Shakespeare, William; "King Richard the III"

conflict is Dependency vs. Independence. They are complementary issues, and we are neither totally.

Because we are mostly limited, the 1st Step asks that we accept we are powerless over alcohol (drugs). By surrender to this fact of dependence on alcohol, one gains power over it and achieves independence from it. Funny how that works!

Shame

A.A. is a therapy to deal with shame. The guilt-therapies do not work. A.A. normalizes the human condition and the stories at the meetings drive home our ordinariness. We are Not God. There is the shame of infraction when I have done something. There is the shame of shortcoming where I am something. We use denial and chemicals to hide shame from ourselves and as a defense against "weaknesses." Shame may be disproportionate to the event or fact. Shame does not respond well to being yelled at or told to shape up. In fact, that may escalate the shame. Exposure to oneself lies at the bottom of shame (it feels like being exposed). A.A. has a focus on the deficiencies of self and the need to accept our deficiencies.

Guilt is internal, has a sense of "I am not good," and arises from some infraction or wrongdoing. Shame has a sense of "I am no good" and arises from obvious disapproval, which is seen and may be appraised by others. I had a high school friend who had a frequent problem with blushing. She was always ashamed about this—and quite powerless over it. She was even ashamed of her shame. A.A. treats both shames. The shame of their infractions and wrongdoings and failures and the shame of feeling blamed for their limitations and shortcoming of not being able to "shape up." Guilt implies that one has a choice. The core of the pain in shame arises from the failure of choice.

I once asked the man in my life just how he knew he was an alcoholic. His simple answer: "Because, after the first drink, I could not guarantee how much I would drink." A social drinker always can tell you—even if they want to get drunk! The person with an addiction must accept the fact that one is too many and 100 is not enough. A true alcoholic loses choice. That is why one beer is too many. A person with an addiction must stop taking this limitation personally. Brain chemistry. Guilt motivates compliance. Surrender is the acceptance of shame.

Denial is the preferred defense system to conceal weaknesses from one. The critical problem is the shame. A.A. breaks through the twin denials of need: I do not need alcohol! I do not need others! You are needed at meetings—you precisely and only as an alcoholic. This is an admission of your need for alcohol

So:

- I admit that I need alcohol.

- I admit that I need A.A. and others.

- I transcend myself and find wholeness in my limitations.

For the person with an addiction and those who love them:

The 12-Step programs, and other roads to recovery, are an incredible sociological movement. Not bad when you consider that just a few years ago alcoholism was treated with shock treatment and frontal lobotomies.

Chapter 7: The Boxing Ring
A Picture of What Detachment Really Means

With gratitude to Eric Moore for artistic rendering of the Boxing Ring.

The term "Detachment" or "Letting Go" is often so misunderstood. People falsely think that to be detached is the same as no longer caring, or to abandon someone. We hear that we need to "Let Go" which is also not clear. The phrase that best explains this is: I do not detach from you, but I do detach from the agony of involvement in your problem. The following pages and illustrations are said to be helpful in visualizing the steps we need to take to be more effective. Keep in mind that Al-Anon speaks of a 'Loving' detachment. How in the world do we do that when we are so affected?

In the first illustration called 'A Picture of Enabling,' you see us pitted against addiction. We are in the ring—up close and personal.

1 Enabling – ask: What will become of you if you don't STOP doing his?

ENABLING

The person with an addiction is doing what people with addictions do. Swinging about and wildly unpredictable as the chemicals determine their moods and behaviors and choices. We have joined them in the ring with well-intentioned efforts to influence them. Guess what? We will endure slugs and hits and injuries round after round. We become bloodied and bruised and injured beyond all reason. Our love is badly tested and hurt grows as does the anger.

Although none of this is our fault, we do slowly become part of the problem without realizing it. Look at the words on the ropes of the rings. These are some of the common enabling behaviors.

1.   Lecturing, Lying, Spying

Do you realize that if any of these were effective, there would not be one person with an active addiction in this country? It is what our feet do (actions) that are effective, not our mouth. I think of us as podiatrists. What could you possibly say or nag about that you have not already said five hundred times? The person with an addiction could quote you. The complaints and whining and sniveling we do only add to their guilt and need to distance themselves.

Have you ever felt that you were set-up for an argument? Then you could be blamed, and the person with an addiction would find another reason to use their chemical. Example: Have you ever been accused of being a nag and told that was the reason for their use? This is a common ploy. It all becomes the dance of addiction. As a parent of a child of any age, we always feel obliged to lecture and 'teach.' Is that not what a parent should do?

I have one parent in the group who thinks he could take his adult son in the truck to the woods for an extended camping trip. Like a captive audience to his father's advice and 'wisdom.' I can guarantee you that the moment they get home, his son will contact his friends and get high while sharing his camping with dad experience.

One realization that is helpful is to accept the fact that the person with an addiction is not capable of being rational. We are. We are forever trying to present sensible and reasonable thinking and advice to our addicted loved ones. Maybe it sinks in for a short while, but the person with the addiction soon forgets all about it. We, of course, stay in the ring and keep on with our great ideas. Might as well talk to a tree.

Then there is the fun we have with spying. It is only a brief relief for our angst. Mostly, we spy to reassure ourselves that we are not nuts. I remember the man whose wife was in treatment. He told the story of standing in his shrubs in the rain and watching his wife thru the bedroom window to see if she was indeed drinking by herself in there! I love families. In recovery, you develop humor as you reflect on your many misguided behaviors.

2. Money

Money always affords us many ways to enable. Have you 'loaned' money, paid their bills, taken the calls and made excuses to their creditors, co-signed for cars and houses, etc.?

Addiction does not repay loans. The person with an addiction may absolutely mean to repay you. Try to be a person with an addiction on payday with a pocket of cash and see which decision you make. This is one reason the person with an addiction suffers lowering self-esteem and shame. Their honest, good intentions fall prey to the power of addiction. No wonder they become further removed from you—hard to make eye contact when you feel guilty.

3. Blame

We spend hours and maybe decades trying to determine the 'why.' I love blaming. It is so easy. It is much easier than to let myself feel that I really just do not know something.

Example: I remember, as a young thing, I blamed my mother-in-law for my husband's drinking. She, in turn, told me one day that he did not drink before he was married. Touché. (Actually, he drank heavily in high school).

We should have both been in a family program somewhere, sitting side by side learning about genetic predisposition. There is no fault to addiction. Unless you want to go back and blame your great-great-great-grandpa.

I also remember two fathers in a family group. One dad shared that he felt his son was in treatment because he had also been an alcoholic in the past and was not an attentive dad. The other man spoke up and said that he had overindulged his son in every way and that had caused his son to drink. I rest the case.

Blaming is such a waste of time. It keeps us busy, but it also drains our energy and is ineffective.

4.   Making Excuses and Cover-Ups

There is only one reason that people with addictions use drugs (and alcohol is our most common drug). The reason is that they are addicted.

Do any of these sound familiar?

> *My husband is just tired at the end of the day.*
> *My daughter has never liked herself.*
> *He misses his children.*
> *My wife has friends who like to drink.*
> *Her mom was a drinker.*
> *His dad died when he was young.*

> *She got divorced.*

And—on it could go.

We must not confuse what is casual and what might be contributing. It is true that life is full of pot-holes struggles and pain and loss and some harsh realities. It is true that we all have grief and issues. The fact is that many people push through life without the use of mind and mood altering chemical use.

The man takes a drink—the drink takes a drink—the drink takes the man.

The trick in life is to learn how to deal with the vicissitudes of living in an emotionally honest way. While intended to be temporary pain relief, the use of chemicals as a solution often becomes the problem. While the psychological and environmental factors are essential, it is the biological factor that is the most influential genetic predisposition. So, if you are on a drinking college campus and your girlfriend dumps you, and you had alcoholics in your family tree–a word to the wise.

The other enabling behavior to examine is how much we cover-up what is going on. Sometimes we really do not see the problem for what it is. We call this denial. That denial is when we do not see what we see and do not know what we know. Sometimes, there is the form of denial when we fully know there is something wrong and we keep the secret. Addiction just loves it when we do not talk about it–when we isolate even in a crowd. Do we think that to deny a fact will make it untrue? We mostly make cover-ups to ourselves.

5.   We Take it Personally

Will you all please find a Q-tip and keep it in a place where you see it frequently. It is a reminder that none of this has anything to do with you. Al-Anon will tell you that you did not cause it, you

125

cannot control it and you cannot cure it. Why do we not believe that? The Q-tip is a reminder to

Q-UIT   T-AKING   I-T   P-ERSONALLY

It is not your fault, never was, never will be. Period. We simply are not omnipotent enough to give addiction to anyone. (Read that again).

It is true that we can hurt each other, fail each other, not love each other—but that only causes pain and not addiction. It is also one of the glories and gifts of a recovery program that we can make amends and forgive and heal the relationships.

6.   Infantilize and Custodial Care

'How do you help make a man? You thinketh him so.'[11] Here is another good line: You want to be supportive but not custodial.

2 Quit Taking It Personally

The peace corps did not give food to people, and they taught people to plant corn. This is an example of not being custodial.

People ask me when is it enabling and when is it helpful? Great question. When does healthy enabling become toxic disabling? Do you 'baby' and infantilize the person with an addiction? Do you do for them what they should do for themselves? Do you know that over conscientious people are the worst at over functioning?

Example: A woman whose husband was in treatment shared that she learned to dry-wall to keep her husband's business afloat.

---

[11] James Allen; As a Man Thinketh; Digireads: Overland Park, KS, 2016

Mothers have a tough time with this—I have talked with many of them who continue to over function for their 40-year-old sons. Sometimes, things should be allowed to collapse so that something far better might emerge. The person with an addiction, as the disease progresses, often can become more and more dependent. This often eclipses us, and we get pulled slowly into functioning for them. It then becomes the norm. I remember how shocked I was when a therapist said that over functioning was as much a dysfunction as under-functioning. Wow!

Even if the person with an addiction is behaving in infantile ways, it is effective to continue to maintain an attitude in your tone and voice that reaches for their maturity and possibility.

7.   Being a Drinking Buddy or Drug Runner

It is not unusual for a family member to either acquire the substance or to join the person with an addiction in the drinking/usage. We do this to share time, or to avoid abandonment, or to seek approval. I once did an aftercare group for 12 wives whose husbands had been in treatment. We met for two years and then disbanded. Four years later, they wanted a reunion. We met. Six of the wives said they were now also in A.A. They had discovered that alcohol was also very important to them, even though two years earlier they had not realized this.

There is nothing wrong with social drinking—it is the alcoholism that is like cancer of the family. I always suggest to family members that they not drink at all for 12 months. You do not know how important something is to you until you stop doing it.

As for the rum-runner, it is often an attempt to not have the person with an addiction in the car or on the highway. You have become a well-meaning accomplice. Some of our dilemmas are not easy.

8.   Chronic Anger

This is so awful for us. It kills us. Our anger does not harm the person with an addiction. It is a cover for our deep hurt. I always prefer anger to hurt. Anger empowers. Hurt seems like standing in bubble-gum with a broken heart. In our anger, we often do great harm. I remember the old parable about the man who was trying to teach his young son about the destruction of words spoken in anger. The father asked his son to go to the fence outside and drive 100 big nails into it. The boy did. The father then asked his son to remove the nails. The boy did. The father then shared that the removal of the nails was like an apology—but the holes remained.

There is one great truth, the more you allow yourself to be used, the more anger you will feel. Well, guess what? You are the only one who can decide what your boundaries are. How many times have you let yourself be used? Addiction is all too eager to use you. Money, housing, food, bail, car, medical help. You have to decide what you can willingly do without resentment. It is the only way to stop stock-piling anger. That anger will give ulcers and problems to every part of your body. The list is endless. Ground teeth, poor sleep, strokes, blood pressure. The truth is that all the anger in the world from us will not motivate anyone to get sober/clean. Another good line for you: expectations are pre-arranged resentments.

I suppose that you think you are protecting your heart by staying angry. We do not die from grief, but we do die from not grieving enough.

I also have to share a sexist thought. Imagine. I think that we socialize men to be the 'fixers.' We give them tool belts for Christmas. We count on them to fix the garage door, the broken toilet, etc. Then, along comes a problem that involves the most important people in their lives—addiction in a spouse, child, parent. Men need to understand that they cannot 'fix' a person with an addiction. They try hard and harder. Anger is the usual feeling that is the result when all efforts fail. This anger will harm them. Men more than women, suffer the barbs of their anger. They often solve the problem with a sharp cut-off. A closed heart.

I never buy this. Their heart aches. It is just that they feel powerless and inadequate. The reality is that there are some things you cannot fix in life. It is no measure of your worth if you cannot "fix" someone else! Some women will be angry that I do not see them as capable of tool belt skills. If you are gifted, I admire you. I have trouble with light bulbs.

9.   Refusing Help

It took me 5 years to really understand that I needed to go to Al-Anon. After all, I was a nurse! Nowhere in this universe is there any education about how to live with a person with an addiction. With luck, you might land in some family program in a facility. Or you might hear about some 12 Step program, or you might have a friend who is aware of, or you might stumble into a helpful book. Mostly, however, we are flying blind. It is absolutely OK to be a beginner in this journey. I have watched family and friends come and go into education for the past 30 years. Some attend one meeting, some walk out of that meeting, some stay for years. There is much to learn.

It is an enabling factor to remain innocently ignorant. You will benefit greatly to read, listen to others, share, make mistakes, laugh and join others who understand all of your questions and situations.

10.   Overreaction

Once you learn the facts of addiction, you can adopt an attitude that goes with those facts.

Example: The grandmother of a heroin-using granddaughter who was living in a tent has been crying for years over how much this girl lies to her. The grandmother was consumed with her grief. Once she heard the group talk about the commonality of lying with addiction, she began to feel less reactive. She learned some responses to give. We often give too much drama to too little event. Once we overreact, the focus goes on us. This is what addiction wants.

She learned that the defense of lying and distortion was self-preservation for the person with an addiction. Not intentional. It is how the toxic brain protects the person from realizing the mess they are in. The grandmother was able to feel more loving, less reactive and more effective. She had control of herself for a change.

11.   We Have No Rules, Only Wishes

It seems we keep drawing lines in the sand, and then we step back and draw another. Soon our back is against the wall. How many times do we take a stand and then melt away on our resolve by the next day? We lose credibility every time we do that. So, most of us are beyond that point. You need to start a new day. Do not say what you do not mean. This means you must give careful thought to your words.

A sign: 'I said maybe, and that's final." Recognize it? Parents of adolescents are particularly vulnerable to this enabling factor. We mostly have wished. "I want you home by 10" (maybe). Spouses cannot have 'rules' with each other, but you can certainly draw a line on what is acceptable behavior for you to live with and what is not. Then you need to take action.

Example: A father of an adult son was in a go-home session after the son had completed treatment. The son promised all sorts of good things about his plans for recovery and future. The dad listened to it all and then just said, "Son, I am going to watch your feet and not your mouth." Good advice for all of us.

12.   Ignoring and Adapting

There is a problem when we have our head in the sand. It is hard to breathe. You can ignore addiction, but it is truly progressive and chronic. Sometimes we need a break from the stress of it, and we ignore it, but it is not going away. It is also bad news for us when we keep adapting and adapting to the progressive nature of this disease. You begin to feel like you are losing pieces of yourself. Your health, your values, your dreams. Just how far are you willing to get out of shape in your own authentic life to adapt to addiction?

Example: I remember one wife who agreed to group sex at her husband's request. She wanted to please him and thought his drinking was because she was not interesting enough. She had a dreadful time in her family recovery with her resolution of what she had done.

The main question to be answered by you is at the bottom of the boxing ring page on enabling. What will become of me if I do not stop doing this?

Look now at the boxing ring called LOVING DETACHMENT. Notice that we are now just outside of the rope. We have not left the arena. We have not gone away. We have not abandoned the person with an addiction. The rope has, however, made all the difference. We are now with a more unobstructed view of the situation, and we are out of reach of the fighting. We can see more when we are not suffering black eyes and blinded by anger and resentment. We are learning to take care of ourselves. Think of the flight attendant who advises that you place your oxygen mask on first before you can help others around you. It is the same idea here.

131

Also, note the little red heart now emerging again. It is amazing how love can resurface when we are not full of anger and exhaustion. Another feeling that surfaces with detachment is sadness which is better than anger and far less damaging to us. This is a picture of 'letting go' and how to be more effective in the

What will be become of you if you don't start doing this?

2 LOVING DETACHMENT

relationship with addiction. Please note that you are no longer in a relationship with the person as they have been beamed up into the world of addiction. A toxic substance has altered their entire way of thinking and being. Many family members, over the years, have commented that, after a few weeks of treatment, their person seems to again "be their old self." We are often amazed at how the chemicals had slowly eclipsed our loved one, and we had forgotten what they used to be like. It is like a curtain is lifted when they return to us.

Let's look at the ropes of relief in recovery. Those who make loving detachment and letting go a possibility.

1.   STOP allowing yourself to be used. This cannot be said often enough. When we keep thinking that 'this time will be different' and 'one more chance' and 'maybe' we are like volunteers to be used again. As long as the addiction is alive and well, you need to grasp that you are pitted against addiction in the body of your loved one. As long as you are giving the thinking and promises of addiction another favor, another dollar, another rescue, another chance, you will be had. If you cave in to manipulative statements such as: "You would do this to me?" "I thought you loved me," "You promised me," you are volunteering for one more resentment, more anger and hurt and the feeling of being used once more. So, stop. Only you are in charge of your decision. It is OK to be disliked by the person with an addiction, OK for you to not be popular, OK to be the target of harsh words. What you will keep is your self-esteem and the sad truth that you are not going to be part of the problem. The person with an addiction will move on to find others who will meet their needs, and nothing will change. It is an astounding fact that when you refuse to be in the boxing ring with the person with an addiction it is, indeed, the highest form of love.

2.   LEARN the facts of chemical dependency and develop an attitude that goes with those facts. (the above is from two of the ropes)

Example: People with addictions use for some reason

Fact: People with addictions use their chemicals because they are addicted. They may have reasons in life to feel bad, but who does not? They may have used their chemical initially to alter a mood, but with a genetic predisposition, the solution eventually becomes a problem. Then the chemical is its' own entity and has a life of its own.

Some then use because it is Monday or Saturday. Some use because it is raining or too hot. Some use because the Tigers won or lost. If you become addicted, you sink into a denial about your loss of choice and begin to believe the very reasons you tell yourself that you used. Their increasingly toxic brain convinces them that their reasons are valid. It is called denial. It is important that family and friends do not fall into the trap of agreeing. Again, people with addictions use because they are addicted. Period. Eventually, an addicted person must use to avoid the severe physical symptoms of withdrawal.

3. Quit Taking it Personally (The Q-Tip)

Again, keep your Q-tip handy. In spite of how blamed you are, you must remember that addiction is driving, and you are not and never were the cause of someone's choice to use chemicals. The most important gift to children of people with addictions of any age is to help them understand that they are not to blame. This is hard to grasp when you are a little person. Children always believe what the big people tell them. It is one way they can try to make sense out of their household. However, children need good information about their situation.

Example: The 3rd grade girl who waited for her mom to bring the cupcakes to school for her birthday party. No mom. When she got home, mom was drunk on the couch, woke up, told her daughter that she had left her bike in the driveway and, therefore, could not expect cupcakes. This child grew into an adult who felt responsible for everything. She did not have any help knowing that none of this was about her. She took it very personally. This is also so treatable with good information.

4. Learn to Respond Not React

I had a friend who was in recovery and lived with a man who had relapsed into his drinking. She loved him dearly. There were two of her daughters in residence. For months, he would start an argument or blame a child for something as he headed for the door and the bar. She often reacted with hurt and anger and reason. One day she just plain figured it out and said to him, "There is no need for you to start a fight before you justify leaving this house to drink. I love you and the girls love you. If you want to go to the bar, just do so. We do not need the chaos and scene before you go." He later acknowledged her wisdom, and there was no more upheaval in the house. He still would drink, but she had learned to respond, not react.

Addiction will try to push your buttons for you to be reactive. When you are, the focus goes on you. Being reactive is like handing an excuse to addiction on a silver platter. Best to stop-think-think again-do not take the bait.

Another example: When that heroin-using granddaughter called her grandmother for money for food, the grandmother very lovingly replied that she would give her directions to a food bank, but the only help she could provide was to help her into treatment. With an, 'I love you and call me when you are ready for help.' This woman had spent years lecturing, rescuing, pleading, crying, bribing and losing sleep.

It almost seems too simple to give up reaction. When we react, it feels as if we are doing something. The best response is always that you love them and will always help them get help.

5.   Get Non-Relative Help

Our families usually love us and want to support us. That is wonderful in most situations. However, when it comes to addiction, most family members are not educated about this problem and may give you well-intentioned feedback, but not effective information, which leads me to #6.

6.   Go to a 12-Step Meeting

Get a sponsor. These are support groups with the same 12-Step approach that the person with an addiction finds in their group. They are confidential and universal. It is amazing to know that you can walk into any group in any country and you do not even have to explain why you are there. Everyone is in the same boat. It does not matter who their person with an addiction is, or what drug, or what age or drama. Everyone in the room has felt the same list of dreadful feelings. Pain and powerlessness and fear are in every situation that any friend or family member can tell of. Or, you can just listen and learn. These meetings are not a religious gathering. They are not a cult. They are, however, very strange at first. Not like any you have attended. Most people go to their first meeting expecting to find out just what they can do to 'fix' the person with an addiction. This is not the purpose of the group. You do learn about how to be more effective, how to care for yourself, and how to get out of the boxing ring. Someone once said that it is good if you start these meetings in the summer, because you will stick to the chairs.

There is great wisdom in talking to someone who can relate to your situation. Try to go with an open mind and absorb what is being said. Also, notice the peace and caring on so many faces. They will suggest that you eventually find your sponsor. This is not a friend. It will be someone of your choice that you have admired during a meeting. You like what they say. You can ask them to be your sponsor. If they agree, you can put them on speed-dial to call when you are upset. They will pull you back down to earth in a caring way and help you with your thinking and attitudes.

Friends are wonderful. Sponsors are effective.

7.   Take Your Own Inventory

This is one of the steps we eventually need to eye-ball. It is when you are in a place to honestly examine your own short-comings. It is common to place all blame on the person with an addiction with little thought to our own behaviors. This is not about blaming ourselves, but it is about not letting someone else's behaviors determine ours. I remember the day I pulled into the driveway and had an ugly moment of awareness of how my husband must feel when he came in the door to me! Not pleasant. I, of course, immediately slammed the lid on the vision and had to later own that my own anger and hurt needed to be addressed and transformed. Education about his addiction helped me do this. I stopped taking it personally and began to have a far more compassionate view. Kindness returned.

8.   Set Boundaries

I did not know that I had the right not to participate in things that made me uncomfortable. I did not know that I could say 'no' to things without anger. I did not know that only I was in charge of my choices. I did not know that others were also accountable to me. I did not know what I needed to.

9.   Return to Your Authentic Life

What friends had I ignored? What activity had I postponed 100 times? What pleasure had I put on the back burner? What goal had I forgotten?

Example: A man brought his wife into treatment. At the very end of our interview, he mentioned that he had a boat and loved the water. I asked him about the last time he had been on the boat. He answered: "It has been seven years. I am always afraid that my wife will be drunk and fall overboard." It was summer, and I suggested that he skip the next three Saturdays of family programming while his wife was safely in treatment. I urged him to go fishing. He smiled, and we did not see him on Saturday.

How often do we abandon ourselves while waiting for someone else to change?

10.   Talk Trust Feel

These three mentally healthy things to do are often on the 'victim' list for us when we are involved with a person with an addiction. It truly is like a war zone. We shut down. We adapt to the impossible. We isolate. We are frightened, and the common way to survive is to go numb. It is said that numb is normal for family members. The person with an addiction does this with chemicals, and we do it with psychic numbing.

Time to defrost. Attending the 12-Step meetings is a good way to start feeling alive again. Surely you can talk, begin to trust others and recognize feelings in others and yourself.

Emotional honesty is healthy. Sharing is healthy. Crying is healthy. Laughter is encouraged.

11.   Do Your Grief Work (see chapter on grief)

It is said that to age well, there are three things that seem to be beneficial. One is to take self-responsibility (stop blaming others in life). The next is to see reality. This is most difficult and most important. You can deal with the reality, but not with delusions. It may be painful, but at least you can see truth and come to terms with it. The final factor is to do your grief work well. That means that you can say goodbye to all the lost people and situations in life in order to be able to move on and re-connect to the new. These three challenges are a lifetime task.

Can you think of an older person who seems to be stuck in some past decade? Can you think of one who is still vital and interested and invested? With addiction, there a myriad of losses. Learn to cut them loose and move on. It takes time but is well worth it.

12.   Over Conscientious People

If you are reading this book, you may be one of those highly responsible and highly functioning people. Thank heaven for you. However, learning to detach lovingly is "highly hard" for you to do if you have had successes in life. Because of this trait, it will be a hard swallow for you to surrender to your powerlessness. The fact that we cannot control the outcome for others seems so simple to read and so tough to believe and tougher to internalize. You will come to see that you can use your great talents except with people who are making their own choices. We can learn to be supportive and not custodial. (My favorite line to remember).

Chapter 8: The Wall of Denial

The definition: Denial is a mechanism or process people use to protect themselves from the pain of realization. It blocks awareness and is a wall against unacceptable reality. It is not the same as simply denying what you are aware of. Example: "I did not break that dish," or "I did not say that." When one is fully aware of the truth, this sort of denial is simply lying, and you know it.

The denial most dangerous is the kind that is unconscious. It is self-delusional. It is when you do not see what you see and do not know what you know. Can you remember the time you heard a distant bell? It is somewhat like that. You heard it, but you did not hear it. If someone asks you about it, you might then recall the sound.

Do you remember the days of those graphic art pictures? At first glance, they look like just a pattern of lines and squiggles. But, if you train your eye to see it differently, you can see a picture emerge; like bridges, people, or dinosaurs. Once you see thru the surface picture into the deeper picture, you can never again not be aware of the latter.

Another experience comes to mind. Remember when you were a kid and some pictures hid things? You were asked to find the ten figures in hiding. Like the tea cup and the rabbit, I would try to un-see them and failed every time. There they were! That is a lot how denial feels in hindsight.

Someone once said that there are three signs of maturity in life. We must learn to take self-responsibility (stop blaming others for our choices), learn to do our grief work well (life is all about hello and goodbye), and see reality. And, of these three challenges, the most difficult is to see reality.

For the person with an addiction and everyone else, denial is a huge wall against recovery. You must see the truth if you are to deal with it successfully. Denial denies reality and, therefore, is dangerous. It is only my mind giving me a false sense of protection, and I did not know that until I did.

An example: One man said that while his wife was Lost in the Sauce, he was Lost in the Land of Denial. He said, "I was so lost I did not know I was lost." He was referring to his complete lack of understanding of the situation he was in.

In hindsight, he realized that he had built the wall of denial all by

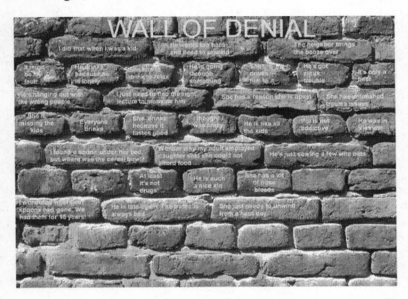

3 Wall of Denial

himself. Every time his wife was drunk, he made excuses for her need to drink and found it to be "understandable" considering the stress or conflict she verbalized. He decided that alcohol was an acceptable outlet—like chocolate or smoking.

As the months passed, he felt that the cement holding the bricks of the wall was beginning to crumble under the weight of truth.

141

He stated that he progressed from the innocent ignorance to "something is not right," to the reality that his wife needed help. (He still was not sure that he did!) He recognized that his Wall of Denial was in the interest of unconscious self-preservation.

Being in the state of denial is, of course, a very enabling condition. No one sees what the problem is—not the person with an addiction or family members. Why is it that we see people and situations as we need them to be and not as they are?

Some other examples of denial:

> The mother who found the spoon under her daughter's bed and wondered where the cereal bowl was.
> The wife who was a nurse and thought her husband had a sinus problem and would call his office and make excuses. (More like a pint of Vodka)
> The parents who always think it is a "phase" and know that their child would never lie or get involved with drugs.
> The wife who had a late-night call from her husband who said he had to work late and that the music in the background was what the night janitors always played.
> The sibling who knows a lot about her brother's drug use but blames his friends and makes excuses for him to the parents.
> The wife who puts the kids in the car and drives around to see if she can find her husband's car and, when she does, tries to "understand."

As a final thought, I recoil when I hear someone being "accused" of being in denial. It is something you cannot help until you force yourself to look deeper and to consider painful options to what you are so sure is true. And, as the joke goes: Denial is not a river in Egypt.

Chapter 9: Projection

The definition: When you attach your unconscious and negative feelings onto another person. The thing to think of: When you used to play Hot Potato as a child, did you ever do this? While a timer is set, or music is played, you and several others are in a circle and keep tossing a potato quickly from one to another until the time is up. Of course, you did not want to be the one left holding the 'potato.' Loser.

3 Hot Potato

Projection is an unconscious defense system that is rather common. Many people with addictions rely on it heavily. It is a shield against the reality of what is going on. There are many other defense systems: denial, lying, minimizing, deflecting. Projection is why addiction is often partially called a family disease—it is one of the ways that family and friends become automatically emotionally involved.

For the person with an addiction, it is a false solution and just a trick of the mind to protect you from pain. It is a way to reduce the internal nightmare of their feelings and helps lighten the load of desperately negative feelings.

Remember this: The person with an addiction is progressing in their disease and their internal collection of negative feelings is growing. At the same time, however, they are medicating, anesthetizing, and numbing themselves. "Feeling no pain" as the saying goes. Those true feeling sink further and further into the abyss of denial, and yet, they do find a way out. Rather like measles. Eventually, they surface as attitudes, feelings, and behaviors that bring relief to the true and unrecognized desperate emotions. As the disease progresses, so does the guilt, remorse, and self-hatred. Life is becoming more uncontrollable and unpredictable. The value system is slipping away. They feel powerless against what is happening. In this way, perhaps, the relief of projection could be seen as an alternative to suicide.

FOR EXAMPLE: Let's look at the alcoholic mother again. She was heavily drunk and asleep on the couch when her 7-year-old daughter arrives home from school. The mother had promised to bring cupcakes to school for her daughter's birthday. The guilt she feels as she remembers and sees her daughter's sad face is overwhelming. That guilt is then projected onto her child and she lashes out with something like, "I told you to clean your room. You cannot expect me to do nice things for you if you are so irresponsible." Her daughter swallows her own feelings of hurt and catches the Guilt Potato. She then internalizes the thought that she was responsible for her mother's mood and decides that she should try harder to be people pleasing or more perfect or some other impossible attempt to seek approval and self-esteem. She is doomed to a life of trying to stay ahead of guilt and inadequacy. Little children do not know the alternative. They usually take on the problem to maintain an idolized view of their parent. Is it not so sad? She, as an adult, may seek out people to "fix" and take care of. It is such a misplaced sense of self. Wise counsel for children of people with addictions: Do not marry a "fixer-upper" and do not be a "fixer-upper" yourself. This is not the same as a healthy relationship where caring for and about is reciprocal.

The best advice I ever got was not to marry someone who needed a fix-up. Better to find someone who occasionally wanted to stop on the way home from work for "one beer" and did! Please do remember that projection is an unconscious and automatic act. Do not approach the person with an addiction and say, "Aha, I found out what you do to me!" A person with an addiction does not do anything TO us but in spite of us. We just happened to be in the way. It is hard to ask you not to take it personally if you are personally and emotionally harmed, but it is the truth. It is not about you—it is a projection of their self-loathing, and you are the target and chosen one to carry their internal load.

Another way to visualize how this works is to think of a large bucket of lead. It is beyond heavy. You need someone else to grab the handle and help you carry the load. Projection works. I can get someone else to carry my heavy feeling. But it does not end here. Amazingly, the enabler and alcoholic begin to focus on the catcher of the potato. The recipient of the bad feeling usually becomes reactive to it because we have quickly and unknowingly become infected by some negative emotion. We now feel the guilt or hurt, or shame, or pain, or anger, or fear, or blame, or loneliness, or powerlessness, or helplessness, or low self-esteem that just came our way. The attention often then goes on us as we become reactive. The unconscious result is that the person with an addiction senses some relief. Remember, once more, that this transaction is swift and unconscious. Therefore, we often share the same feeling life of the person with an addiction. Have you not had the experience of feeling good then having some conversation with the person with an addiction and suddenly you feel defensive and are trying to explain yourself? You once more have the Guilt Potato in your lap.

I remember that on Family Program Day at the hospital, which began at 9 a.m., it was not unusual for families to arrive a bit late. The weather was nasty at times, and the distance was long. Patients would often stand at the lobby window eagerly awaiting the arrival of a loved one. It was not unusual to hear, "You're late," as the greeting, and the family would break out in a long list of the morning's obstacles. They had gotten up early, packed up the kids and lunch for all, gotten gas, getting lost, etc. Can you see that the patient was feeling guilty for being in treatment? Guilty for asking anyone to give up another day in their interest? Guilty for asking for cigarettes or money or clothes, etc.? That guilt immediately landed on the visitor and the day started poorly. In the later family group, we helped families simply respond to this by saying, "Yes. I guess I am." Nothing more. No guilt, no explanation, no potato. They loved it. Remember: YOU DON'T HAVE TO GO TO EVERY ARGUMENT YOU ARE INVITED TO.

If we fail to break the cycle of reacting to projection, our time together with the person with an addiction is often a dance of the two outer circles interacting over and over. (See following circles). This is not an emotionally honest relationship and surely not intimacy. This is more like case management, retaliation, and war. True intimacy is a connection and exchange between the two inner circles. Emotional honesty with each other.

You can learn, with awareness and practice, to let the hot potatoes hit the floor. It becomes easier with practice. It happens so swiftly that you might not realize it until the next day when you reflect on the argument. Examine the times you were feeling peaceful and then suddenly felt defensive, hurt, diminished, or controlled. Clue!

You do not need to be the scapegoat for some else's toxic feelings. Let that spud hit the floor and let go of the bucket.

In our dreams:
Would it not be wonderful if family and friends could find some sort of help and education about all this at least two years before the person with an addiction finally gets some help? We might then be in far better shape to lend effective and anger-free support and a clearer view of what recovery is needed for all. Alas and all too often, we are wounded and contaminated by the trauma and too fresh from the "War Zone" to be very objective. Therefore, a heavy AL-Anon or Nar-Anon meeting schedule is so recommended for the family to start their healing. Too bad there is no inoculation for Hot Potato Disease.
Let's refer to the two circle chart of projection.

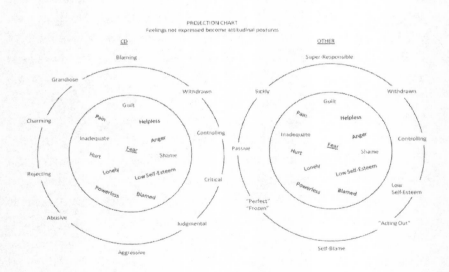

4 Protection Chart

As you can see in the behaviors seen in the outer circle of the 'OTHER' (US), the behaviors we develop (or copy from a parent) lead to problems of our own. I remember one lady who had an alcoholic husband and supported the family with her high-powered job. She eventually lost that job, got speeding tickets, developed illnesses, and engaged in behaviors out of our value system. All of this sober and drug-free. What she did not have was help from acting out her inner feelings.

Some Reactive Behaviors of Family from Projection – The Outer Circle

Super Responsible

This person tries to "fix" all things. They live in high gear and are always ready to help with a myriad of good ideas. They are, by the way, the most delusional about needing their recovery, but all too happy to help others with theirs. They seem unable to distinguish to what degree their help is needed. They jump in with answers even before the questions are formed. Here is a good quote for them: (Suzanne Farham). "Even when a need exists, and we are well qualified to meet it, we are not necessarily called to respond to it. To be doing what is good can be the greatest obstacle to doing something even better."

Withdrawn

Even in a crowd of family or strangers, a person can seem to shrink and withdraw. Keeping the secret is paramount. There is a loss of self-confidence and a gain of guardedness. With or without a smile, the feeling is "everything is fine, and I cannot talk about it." You may be feeling shame or guilt or blame and surely, loneliness.

Controlling

A cover for helplessness or powerlessness might be efforts to control. The behavior is seen as bossy, hovering and attempts to control what you can. It is like having a perfectly lined-up silverware drawer, or an immaculate lawn. You are trying to counter-balance what is so terribly out of control—your life. And looking good is often a cover for low self-esteem, and for being controlled by forces, you cannot control. Perfectionism is common.

Low Self Esteem

Even a person with initial high self-esteem can be worn down by living with addiction in a loved one. Like a slow drip of water on stone.

Is there someone else trying to climb up their ladder of self-esteem by stepping on your rungs? Are you in a relationship where you constantly need to pick up your self-esteem and confidence from the floor? It can be subtle. Is someone else being critical of you— or judging, or blaming, or rejecting or abusive? Sometimes it can be the intellectual ascendancy of the person with an addiction, who is trying desperately to put their foot on your next rung to climb their way back up. I once more advise you to keep that Q-tip handy and to stop taking any of this personally.

When you think about it, feeling good about yourself is simply a decision to feel good about yourself. It is, of course, aided greatly by doing "esteem-able" things. In my nursing career, the para and quadriplegics often had good self-esteem simply due to the remarkable person they were in everyday exchanges.

Self-Blame

Do you find comfort in the delusion that anything others do is your fault? This comfort derives its power from the belief that 'if this is my fault, then I can fix it!' Just because someone is blaming you does not make it so. Just because someone says something, does not make it true. That might include messages from your parents. I know one lady whose childhood was filled with people telling her that she was not very smart—today she has her Ph.D. and was a beloved school principal.

Parents are particularly full of apology and guilt. How enabling this is. There is a risk of overindulging and weak boundaries as some apology for real or imagined past harm. I am not saying that we do not need to forgive each other and move into today. Of

149

course, we do – and some of the harm is far more grievous than others. The 12-Step program is valuable in this effort to become better together. But it is not useful to remain stuck in self-blame and guilt.

A story: A woman shared that her son, about 5 years clean and sober, was finally talking to her about his memory and impressions from his childhood. He was escalating in anger and hurt, and she was trying to share with him that she had an entirely different memory of the situation. This, of course, made him even more upset. He finally set her straight with what he needed. He said, "I do not want you to explain or defend or argue with me. I just need you to listen to me." She got it! When he had finished, she asked if she could respond. He agreed. She then said this very healing and sincere thing to him. "I am so sorry that this happened to you. It is surely not what I ever would have had in mind for you. You were so wanted and so loved. Is there anything I can do now and today that might make it better for you?" He eventually replied, "No." She then added, "If you can ever think of anything I might do to help, let me know." She also added that she would appreciate it if he could no longer keep blaming her and bringing it up.

She honestly did not remember what he was so hurt about. It did not matter. It only mattered to him, and the perspectives would never agree. It only mattered that she expressed her sadness and regret over his memory and offered a present-day hand of love. She also felt that this conversation helped reduce her sense of blame.

Perfect or Frozen

It is like trying to stay ahead of the broom. If you are always ahead of anyone's needs, requests, expectations, wishes, or thoughts, you might be safe. Being perfect or frozen (hidden and totally not heard from) means you can survive or avoid any further assault from an angry parent or spouse or child. Living like this is a shutdown of the free spontaneous self. You have caught the hot potato of someone with abusive, controlling, and critical behavior as his or her defense system. Perhaps all the feeling in the inner circle of the person with an addiction leads to this behavior. Regardless, no child can figure this out and they just try harder to achieve the impossible. Can you imagine a life trying to be perfect always? It is quite a price to pay for another person's attitudes. In groups for children of people with addictions, they learn that it is not their fault, they cannot change or cure anyone, and they are encouraged to express their true feelings. And, they surely learn that it is OK to not be perfect. Mistakes are the fertile ground to grow wisdom.

Passive

This survival reaction and behavior is also a reaction to a feared onslaught and seems like a safe harbor. If I have no opinion, do nothing and create no waves, maybe the storm will pass by me. The problem with this is that I might get stuck in my shelter and my survival decision.

A word about being a People-Pleaser. If you always say YES to everything, how can anyone believe you if you never say NO? When you always agree (not to rock the boat) and then begin to build walls of resentment because you did not want to say 'yes,' you then begin to distance yourself from others. In a healthy relationship, both can say Yes and No, and the honesty of that is refreshing and respected.

Sickly

Sharon Wegscheider, a pioneer in family treatment, once researched records in a manufacturing plant to investigate the number of medical files of any employee who had been identified as an alcoholic. To her surprise, there were far thicker files for their family members! As a family member, you are stressed (and not medicated to numb their pain) and their bodies felt it all. On the charts of family members was cancer, headaches, dental problems (grinding teeth), hypertension, gastrointestinal issues, etc. Not to mention accidents on the job, highway, and emotional conditions.

A Final Story

An exhausted husband brought his wife into treatment for her pill and alcohol abuse. The nurse was watching him and assured him that the doctor would be there soon for admission. He looked like a wreck. His wife was smiling. Upon further exam, the wife was admitted. The facility had thought that he was the patient. Sometimes, you cannot tell the players.

Some common examples of Hot Potato projection from addicted child to parents:

Table 1 Hot Potato Chart

THE INNER FEELING	CHEMICALLY DEPENDENT SAYS	PARENT FEELS
GUILT	YOU DON'T LOVE ME WELL—YOU HAD ME!	GUILT GUILT
FEAR	ANY FORM OF VERBAL OR PHYSICAL AGGRESSION- THREATS/ABUSE	FEAR
BLAMED	YOU ARE A ROTTEN PARENT I AM NOT YOUR FAVORITE	BLAMED BLAMED
HURT	I HATE YOU! I WISH YOU WOULD DROP DEAD	HURT
LONELY REJECTED	NO LONGER TALKS WITH YOU SHARES NOTHING/AVOIDS	LONELY REJECTED

LOW SELF-ESTEEM INADEQUATE	BOB HAS A NICER DAD SUE'S MOM IS REALLY COOL YOU GUYS ARE SO LAME	INADEQUATE LOW SELF-ESTEEM
HELPLESS	OUT OF CONTROL BEHAVIOR I AM GOING TO KILL MYSELF	HELPLESS

So many times, the question arises: Just how do I not catch the hot potato?? It is true that you need to practice being responsive and not reactive. It is so automatic to want to answer without much thought. You will get better in time and with trial and error. Try to be aware of what was just said that puts you on the defensive and needing to explain. That is the Potato clue. Take your time to think. Think of the circles and how you are feeling. Do NOT react, explain, and excuse yourself. Why not just let it all pass? Think about what feeling just got tossed your way. That is how the other person is feeling. Respond to that as you wish. Keep your cool. Refuse to be on the defense to their offense. It only puts the focus on you and off the real issue. People with addictions are great at distraction. Your reactive response is like handling relief to them on a silver platter, as they are now free not to see their reality.

Also, look at the outside words of the two circles. That is like a figure 8 that describes the relationship in addiction. Around and around. Your defenses and mine, over and over. Hardly healthy. What recovery can hope for is a connection between the two inner circles of feelings. That is true intimacy and genuine relationship with emotional honesty.

A final quote from Ann Beattie

"Do everything right all the time and the child will prosper. It is as simple as that, except for: fate, luck heredity, chance, the astrological sign he was born under, his order of birth, his first encounter with evil, the girl who jilts him in spite of his excellent qualities, the war being fought when he was a young man, the drugs he may try one too many times, the friends he makes, how he scores on tests, how well he endures kidding about his shortcomings, how ambitious he becomes, how far he falls behind, circumstantial evidence, danger when it is least expected, difficulty in triumphing over circumstances, people with hidden agendas, and animals with rabies."[12]

Chapter 10: Intervention

There are two kinds of interventions: formal and informal. An intervention is when an event comes between two other things such as between a person with an addiction and their denial that they need to seek help. An informal intervention is when some unplanned happening occurs. I remember one grandmother who sought treatment after her young granddaughter told her that she "smelled funny all the time and I do not like being near you."

It is a common belief that a person with an addiction has "to hit bottom" before they want help. This could be a loss of job, family, health, and home. It can also be of a lesser magnitude. All too often, the 'bottom' is never reached. It is also a sad truth that the family and friends may unknowingly get in the way of the bottom as they 'help' the person with an addiction one more time. Little do they know that they are rewarding the addiction by alleviating the pain and inconvenience of the many inevitable consequences of addictive use. In the talks heard in an Open A.A. meeting, family and friends can hear the stories of how the pain of

---

[12] Sunbeams - Issue 287, November 1999 - The Sun Magazine.
https://thesunmagazine.org/issues/287/sunbeams

remaining addicted was greater than the pain of facing what a recovery would require. Pain can be a tipping point. Some people with addictions tell of how they had to tell their families to stop enabling them. Imagine.

Formal interventions are not a new idea, but they are still not utilized often enough. Those of us in the treatment field assumed that the world knew about them until a Gallup poll revealed that we were talking to ourselves and the public remained unaware of the possibility. A recent TV show has made the process more familiar. I must add, however, that it is not common to have any yelling or blame in effective intervention. Snoopy said, "A kiss on the nose does much to turn away wrath."

A formal intervention is prepared for, rehearsed, and can be orchestrated by a professional. The participants consist of some people who care for the person with an addiction and can join forces to confront the person with an addiction lovingly with their memories, feelings, recalled incidents, hope for help, and their intent not to support the problem any longer. All anger and blame are put on the shelf for this occasion. The goal is to relentlessly chip away at the denial and delusion of the person with an addiction. The power of the group is far more effective than to try to confront the problem by yourself. It is then a one versus two situation. It is you against the person with an addiction and the disease. You will lose.

Imagine being the person with an addiction who unknowingly walks into a room full of people who love and care about you. You are asked to sit and listen and are informed that you can respond later. Facing you are your spouse, children, friends, minister, neighbors, relatives, and employers. Anyone who knows you well enough and has first-hand experience with your behaviors. They want to save your life. It is hard not to crumble in the face of the reality and love and hope that reaches out to you. Eighty-five percent of interventions are successful in convincing the person with an addiction to seek help. It is important to find an Interventionist who has had training and experience.

A guaranteed and unexpected benefit from the process is the family relief and cohesion. The education itself changes family thinking. The sharing and coming together is a major force in family healing. Not all family members have the same experience or opinions. It is healing to listen and learn from each other. This coming together will dis-empower the addiction in the family. It lets in some sunshine and reduces or destroys the power, control, and isolation that addiction demands. Families will often improve even if the person with an addiction does not agree to treatment (sometimes it has to marinate until they agree to seek help). I call it 'success' if the power of addiction is lessened and the family members can begin a new path for themselves.

Doing an Intervention has yet another reward for participants. It reduces the sense of guilt to intercede. The ball is in the other court. The seed is planted. They have said it all. They have crossed the finish line. They have come to the end of being part of the problem. The hard thing at this point for family and friends is to stop doing what they need to stop doing!

I refer you to this website: lovefirst.net. And to the book by Jeff and Debra Jay called *Love First*, published by Hazelden. 1-800-328-9000. This highly professional couple has spent years in the field of addiction. The website had an abundance of information about interventions.

Chapter 11: Barriers to Recovery

Many years ago, Dr. John Grimmett gave a speech at a North American Association of Alcoholism Programs in Utah. He stated that it was commonly seen, but not always present, that men with alcoholism needed to break out of their rigid and stereotyped pattern of self-destructive behavior to benefit from help. He called these the barriers to recovery. These are ways of thinking and behaving that interfere with the process of learning a new path to living. All of them render the person to feel lonely, frustrated, bitter, angry, untrusting, helpless, trapped, or anxious. They find relief in alcohol. The true relief is through changing attitudes, beliefs, and biases.

The HELP BARRIER is responsible for the denial and resistance to seeking help. The problem is the ego that feels it is in control. This does not feel comfortable when the 1st Step of A.A. speaks of powerlessness. And the first word in the 12-Steps is 'We.' It feels like inferiority to others to reach out for help. Humility and surrender to others are the desired path, but that Ego keeps demanding 'I can do this myself.'

You are more likely to get your way when you have more than one way. The task of remaining humble is part of the reason to continue to attend the meetings—a weekly reminder of the nasty consequences of picking up the first drink again. The fact that we need others in life is healthy. It is wise to know when to surrender and to know your limitations. It is wise to be interdependent with others who can share their experience and hear yours.

The third man in A.A. was in the hospital when Bill W. and Dr. Bob went to visit him. They did not present themselves as his rescuers. They asked him to join them at a meeting to deal with their mutual alcoholism. They said that they needed him. And, needed him precisely because he was also alcoholic. We are mirrors of each other. I see you in me and vice versa.

Better to depend on others than on alcohol. You can surely need others and not lose yourself. There is an A.A. joke that if you are only talking to yourself, you are in a bad neighborhood.

The Perfectionist-Failure Bind

There is no such thing as a perfect way to recover. Many paths exist. I once asked an audience of people with addictions in treatment if they had experienced a parent who was a perfectionist. Over half of them raised their hands. They had often felt like a failure as a child when the parent was not pleased with their effort. It followed that they then felt a strong need to be perfect in adulthood to feel adequate. The only problem is the impossibility of that. We are not Super-Man/Woman. Often, in recovery and to make-up for past unacceptable behavior, they set goals that are too high and unrealistic. The predictable failure then circles back to the sense of inadequacy. It is OK not to have all the answers.

This expectation of perfectionism is often projected onto others (the children or spouse) and, if they fail, elicits anger from the person with an addiction. This internal tension is compared to walking on a tightrope through life. I once heard of a group of college students who were so anxious about doing well on a test that they were unable to pick up a pencil. The college then had them take a class on how to be mediocre and how to feel fine about yourself when you made a mistake. They all passed the test.

It is also not unusual for a sober spouse hiding the household pain, to become very perfectionist. The spices are always alphabetized.

The Tunnel Vision Dilemma

This is described as seeing life and people through a long, dark tunnel with a small hole at the end. Like having blinders on. One does not want to be confused with all aspects of a problem. Decisions are made in a short-sighted manner and an incomplete recognition of reality. They only want to perceive what they want to. Poor judgment follows and so does added frustration and failure. The world is seen through rose-colored glasses when a drink seems to relieve all the fears and feelings of helplessness and failure.

It is like a right or wrong straitjacket. The rigid thinking leaves no room for process nor options, and there is a super-sensitivity to criticism. What follows is rejection by others and a deep sense of loneliness (even if seen as 'the life of the party').

Life and all of its decisions require consideration of gray areas. Black or white is just too simple at times. An example of this from an A.A. meeting where one man was complaining about his wife. Another responded quickly with, "Well, just divorce her!" I leave you to think about that. One of the great benefits of attending meetings is the exposure to other ways of thinking. There is a relief when you realize that there is an option to impulsive thinking or feeling frozen. Again, you are more likely to get your way when you have more than one way. And, you may get your say but not your way.

Paralysis of Loneliness

Look into any bar. See depression, hopelessness, boredom, and apathy. A common feature of the solitary drinker alcoholic is really a deep feeling of loneliness. Even if they seem to be happy, a closer look will reveal that their relationships to people are mostly superficial. They have not learned the art of give-and-take. Achieving a balance between these two is characteristic of a mature adult. Two-way relationships may be quite lacking, even

160

though there are social skills. Once more, the use of alcohol makes it all feel better. "Poor me, poor me, pour me another" is an A.A. joke. (not really a joke).

Double Bind

This is when two contradictory forces are at work on a person.

Like:

> ➢ Go away, close.
> ➢ Help is wanted, but advice is rejected.
> ➢ Structure is needed but fought against.

The tensions and anxiety from all the above can be reduced or alleviated only through changing attitudes, beliefs or biases. It takes time and attendance. Some people say they were born while sitting around a table at a meeting. And the price is right.

I included this discussion in *I LOVE YOU—BUT NOT YOUR ADDICTION* because it is important for others to develop a compassion for and deeper understanding of this disease and those who struggle with it. Actually, I do not think these barriers to recovery are exclusive to the person with addiction. Does it not ring any bells for some others in this recovery process?

Chapter 12: Staying with an Addicted Spouse

Many people ask about this and wonder if it is OK. My immediate response is to ask if there is any violence in the home. Nothing violent is OK. And, of course, this is totally a personal decision with many variables and factors at play. As complicated as it may be, and as dangerous at times, it is never wise to remain in a physically abusive situation. There is also a prevalence of emotional abuse—both silent and verbal—in many homes that are under this duress.

Children, of course, are totally dependent and not aware of their choices or options. Adult spouses have more choice. If one was a survivor of an abusive childhood, it might be strangely familiar in the marriage. Or, it might be a place from which to flee as soon as possible. So many stories and so many paths.

It is surely OK to love a person with an addiction. That may be a strong influence to stay. It is also OK to leave someone you love if that person is no longer part of a healthy relationship. Huxley said, "The choice is always ours."

A man in group once described his Three Stages of Staying. The first stage was that of victim. He was unaware and in full denial of his wife's drinking and had many excuses for her usage. He ignored his own feelings and was highly driven by his sense of responsibility and delusion about the true nature of the problem. The second stage was the growing sense of resentment and anger. He still did not have clarity about the alcoholism or his own enabling behaviors. He volunteered himself to be used at every opportunity and felt like a hostage in his life and home and marriage. He felt trapped by some unseen and relentlessly unhappy situation. Finally, months and years later, they both got into a treatment facility and he gained a new view of the problem.

He attended multiple Al-Anon meetings, sought counseling, and began to internalize the knowledge, which transformed into new attitudes. The wife did relapse and had a series of treatments. His education and growth continued and, at the end of it all, he still chose to remain in the marriage. But this time he was in the third stage and considered himself a volunteer. It gave him a sense of freedom. He was making the choice to remain—no longer a victim and no longer trapped. He chose to stay for his own reasons. These included his vows of so many years ago, their financial situation, his concern for her and the fact that his wife's choices were separate from him. He stopped feeling and displaying the anger with her—she was, after all, simply being an alcoholic. He began to take better emotional care of himself. He shared his feelings with the family and got support. At the time of her death, there were some long-absent moments of tenderness shared.

What his detachment accomplished was a sense of freedom for himself and an open the door to more kindness. He has accepted his powerlessness as he gave up his delusional sense of control. Sadness followed, but not many regrets or guilt. When just one member grows and changes attitudes through education and support, the entire tone of a household can improve.

Chapter 13: Recovery of Relationships

In recovery, the central operating principle of the family members needs to swing from the drinking or other drug use to the development of 'self.' Someone once said the goal would be to have relationships with both men and women that do not operate at the expense of self and to have a self that does not operate at the expense of the other.

The 12-Step program is a wise "holding environment" for the relationships while things improve. Jokingly, a treatment center had said that we should all put duct tape over our mouths for about a year and only remove the tape if we had something kind and positive to say to each other. During this time, of course, one needed to keep focused on self-support, education, and 12-Step attendance. This is because the "we" of any healthy relationship is based on individual identity. This self-identity, even if once in good shape, can become very trampled in the fog of addiction for the person with an addiction and anyone who loves them. Self-identity needs to be recovered or discovered.

Can you pat your head and rub your stomach at the same time? The great opportunity and challenge of recovery is the need to attend two paths and focuses. The first begins the healing from all the wounding and trauma of the experience. The second path takes us forward into something new, rewarding, and healthy. Once the person with an addiction has entered some beginning recovery program, many people feel the initial plan is enough merely to move on with nothing ever shared or discussed. Family and friends think of the person with an addiction as "the problem" because the person with an addiction is easily identifiable. Thinking this way is major denial and not easily broken. It was once quoted that the hardest person to live with was not the person with an addiction but was an un-recovered family member.

One cannot argue with the immense value of time and more time in the healing process, but it is not enough. It is akin to stitching up a deep wound that has not been treated for infection. Eventually, the debris finds its way to the surface either in ourselves or the relationship. We cannot hope to take our dormant wounds into forward healing and wish they would remain inactive forever. Early and committed attendance in Al-Anon, or another path to healing, is recommended. It does not matter whether you "like it" or not – think of it as a necessary treatment for your heart and the hurt.

This chapter is relevant regardless of the relationship you are thinking about such as with a spouse, significant other, sibling, friend, child, relatives, and parent. Basically, any two people who are willing to work on the repair will do (one hand cannot clap by itself).

There is an abundance of literature and therapies, which address the need for relationship improvement. Also, there is an abundance of trauma and stress besides addiction, which can create havoc in any relationship. Examples are chronic illnesses, chronic mental disorders, unresolved trauma, death in a family, gambling, excessive anger, food, sex, shopping, busyness, poverty, bankruptcy, workaholics. These can all become the family central organizing principle and stress-producers. The granddaddy of all is an addiction because of the toxic brain component, which prevents any rational approach and seems to be so rigidly locked into the system.

The relationship that troubles you today may have been very healthy before the addiction altered things. On the other hand, it may not ever have been. What is certain, is that when drugs are added, it becomes a three-way (the drug is the added partner) and a chemically altered way for people to communicate and relate.

All relationships will bend toward the unhealthy state regardless of how well they 'used to be.'

Many books, articles, and professionals can be helpful. When you add the complication of addiction to the scene, there are additional suggestions to follow on the "how do we get better together" path. If you were seeking professional help, you would be wise to select a counselor or therapist who is deeply familiar with addiction and relationship issues.

I cannot possibly cover it all, but I would like to mention a few of my favorite things. What is a Healthy Relationship? What is an Unhealthy Relationship? We all seek connections. We can do this by our family roles, our feelings, our rules, and our behaviors. These connections help us feel safe and secure.

> **Unhealthy Connections**
  When the central organizing principle is the chemical, the connections are often caretaking. We slip into case management as things change. Think back. How much more are you functioning for someone else than you were a year ago? There is nothing inherently faulty about being kind and helping others. But, when that 'help' is harming them or you, there is a problem. Also, we often 'harm,' 'infantilize,' and 'disable' the person with an addiction with our good intentions.
> **Give and Take**
  Does it feel like a relatively, equal behavior? It all becomes a one-way street eventually.
> **Resentment**
  (Expectations are prearranged resentments). It is described as 'brown bagging' by stuffing all the disappointments in a bag for later explosion and fuel. Keeping score is hard.
> **Guilt**
  This is a killer of any honest intimacy. It is a cancer.

➤ **Mutual Rejection**

As the anger and guilt grow, so does the behavior of distancing oneself. It seems to be a contest of Hurt vs. Hurt.

➤ **Worry**

This is a useless use of our energy and time, but very common. There are several mothers of adult children in my group. They do not hear from their sons or daughters, so they keep the connection alive by worrying about the addicted person. We worry as a sense of connection. We spend energy on trying to find any information at all about the addicted loved one. If we finally do succeed at this, there is a sense of momentary relief. Soon, however, the anxiety of not knowing begins to build and we are trapped in the repetitive cycle. Does this not sound a bit like the addict seeking their drug? Al-Anon is very effective in addressing this behavior. It is OK to laugh, go to a movie, and enjoy your life even if the person with an addiction remains involved in their drug. If worrying were effective, there would be not a single person with an addiction in the country.

➤ **Manipulation**

Very little remains a direct and honest conversation. We try to manipulate each other into the answer, behavior, and outcome we want. Most people know the manipulations when the phone rings and the request is for money. How many family members also recognize their attempts to control the outcome of someone else's life? The cancer spreads. Have you ever lied or omitted a truth in the hopes that the person with an addiction would make a better choice? Ex: Many times, a spouse has not "passed on a message" that seems connected to a dangerous situation for the person with an addiction such as a phone message from the people with addictions 'using buddy'.

- ➢ **Win-Lose**

  Along with manipulation, we keep some mental score, such as trying to feel superior and not inferior. It is our anger and the feeling of 'getting back' for some hurt. So, did you have the last word? So what! It is an empty victory.

- ➢ **Mutual Pain and Loss**

  "We are in this together." Both can become MUTUALLY DEPENDENT, and the RULE OF SILENCE and SHAME keeps us BLAMING and increasingly caught in the whirlpool together. WE CLING TO EACH OTHER AS A WAY TO FEEL SAFE WHICH IS, OF COURSE, A DELUSION.

There are infinite variations and degrees of the above, but it does seem that the relationship becomes slowly eclipsed into an unhappy mess. Whatever became of the hope for love and closeness and honesty? Well, Chucky entered the scene. Let us think about what a HEALTHY relationship feels like. It is possible to enjoy, love, depend on each other, and not be kidnapped into anything else. You can indeed focus on your own authentic life and move into relationships where you maintain your freedom of choice. When the central organizing principle is closeness, love, and intimacy, you can have personal safety and comfort. "Freedom without intimacy is empty. Intimacy without freedom is unacceptable."[13]

Henry Ford was known to quote Everett Hale's words on the importance of working together.

Coming together is the beginning

Staying together is progress

---

[13] Unknown

Working together is success.

I have always liked the image of a relationship as two people together on a mountain climb. The base camp is where they join daily to share, enjoy, and nourish. The rest of the day is spent individually following their trail and life around and up the mountain of life and looking forward to the end of the day to descend again to their safe place to greet a trusted friend. Soup, a warm fire, and someone who is so glad to see you. What is so "healthy" with these two mountain climbers? Just what connections do they share?

"They support the differences and individuality of the other.

They allow and encourage growth in the other.

They know how to have fun together and separately.

They respect each other's spirituality and may share it.

They have mutual concern for each other and are inter-dependent.

They know how to disagree well.

They have a pride in the feeling of "us."

They take self-responsibility and own their own 'inventory.'

They communicate their feelings and respect the others' opinions.

They each have a healthy sense of self.

They can share interests and tasks.

They are friends." (Anonymous)

WOW! Who would not want to have this in their life?

Next, I would like to share just a few more of the many thoughts from a variety of authors, therapists, and recovering people. It is only the very tip of the iceberg of information and directions you may utilize to begin your journey of healing. Some are simplistic, some are fun, some are thought provoking, some are a challenge, some may seem silly to you, some may appeal to you, and some may not.

Know that problems give us opportunities. M Scott Peck (The Road Less Traveled) believes that it is only because of problems that we grow mentally and spiritually. The people in my group for family and friends (and in Al-Anon) are eventually able to state that loving an addicted person has been a surprising wakeup call to some needed new ideas and feelings and behaviors for themselves. They have found peace, some humor, and unleashed regard for the person with an addiction and themselves. They have found a supportive community and a place to 'be real' in the world with those who share their unwelcome dilemmas. They have shed their shame, innocent ignorance, and guilt and feel the enormous lifting of the weight of believing they could change the person with an addiction. A lady on the elevator to an Al-Anon meeting said, "All I know is that I feel much better when I go to this meeting and not good if I stay home."

What follows are abbreviated thoughts from a variety of authors. Some are useful in the return to self and some address the growth of healthier relationship with others.

Thoughts that Help me Focus on Myself, My Recovery, and My Growth

"Make Peace with Your Past"[14]

---

[14] Bloomfield, Harold, MD; Making Peace with Your Past; Harper Collins; 2000; NY, NY.

Dr. Bloomfield believes in the remarkable resilience in humans. He suggests the following to help heal old wounds and reverse the damage.

Reframe the Past

We cannot change the past, but we can re-frame and control how we experience it. (Eventually, we must give up all hope of a better yesterday!). Ask yourself how the experience has made you stronger or what valuable life lessons did it teach me?

Break the Shame Shackles

He states that shame is the cancer of the spirit. Shame makes us feel worthless and unlovable. Ex: I will always be nice, so no one will ever hurt me (from an abusive childhood attempt to alleviate the pain).

He encourages that we break those early decisions and know that shame is a lie and that you are worthy of love and respect. Really? Are we doomed to keep operating on a decision we made when we were young?

Release the Pain

It is suggested that you write letters to everyone who ever hurt you. You do not ever have to let anyone see them, so do not hold back on what you have to say. Let out all the rages that have been festering in you. Do not censor the letter. Research shows that those who write about past traumas heal faster from illnesses and have stronger immune systems.

Stop the Slow Acid Drip of Regret

Your health and peace of mind are affected by repetition of the "if only..." and "I should haves." Our past mistakes or omissions need to be forgiven by ourselves. What we need to do is resolve to act differently from now on. After all, what did you know at the time? What did you not know at the time? Think of who you were at the time and you may discover that you did okay under the circumstances.

I often shudder at my choices of the past and would not make the same one today. But I have great compassion for that woman 'back then' and know she did her best with what she knew 'back then.'

Move from Grief to Gain

(See the chapter on Grief). No matter how long ago the loss occurred, it is crucial to allow yourself to feel the emotions you may have suppressed. In the loss of a loved one, try letter writing again-a farewell letter. Express whatever comes up-the love and sadness and the rage, terror or other emotions you may feel wrong for having. Get it out.

Practice Acceptance

Like the movie 'Groundhog Day". Old hurts that keep being rehashed in your mind gain power. Do we hope the ending will change? Dr. Bloomfield shares that peace comes from accepting what was for what it was and moving on.

Cultivating Gratitude

This is so vital. No matter what happened in the past, remind yourself that you have so many gifts to be thankful for. You may even find that you become grateful for your troubles because of all you have learned from them. I always start and end my day with a long list of "gratitudes." It has been said that this may be the highest form of prayer. I know for certain that it is a mood changer and always for the best.

Break the Habit of Blame

"Blame is not something you heal–it is something you choose to stop doing." It is self-destructive behavior. Blaming others may bring you the cozy sympathy of others, but it also leads to chronic resentment, which damages you. Ending the bitterness of blame does not mean that you let those who hurt you off the hook. It does not mean you ever want to have lunch with them (my thought). It just means you are taking charge of your well-being.

Find Inner Peace

No matter how traumatic the past has been, Dr. Bloomfield believes you can tap into a source for your peaceful place. This will allow your mind to clear. He suggests these to help create calm: yoga, meditation, a walk-in nature, a hot bath, a good massage, soothing music, prayer, deep breathing, and pleasant memories. Whatever will distract you to find the inner peace.

Create a Satisfying Future

It is said that living well is the best revenge[15]. A great way to make peace with your past is to become the person you always wanted to be (or begin to think about that!). He states that we are the author of our own story and a new chapter can start anytime we choose.

He suggests that you visualize it, write it out, read it over time, decide what you need to do to achieve it, what steps are needed. His reward is that creating a life that is fulfilling to you will remove the sting of the past. [16]

---

[15] George Herbert; Welsh Poet 1593-1633
[16] https://www.prevention.com/mind-body/emotional-health/recover-unhappy-childhood)

From Robert Burney

Codependence: The Dance of Wounded Souls

How do you set boundaries for yourself?

The purpose of having boundaries is to protect and take care of ourselves. We need to be able to tell other people when they are acting in ways that are not acceptable to us. A first step is starting to know that we have a right to protect and defend ourselves. That we have not only the right but the duty to take responsibility for how we allow others to treat us."

Setting boundaries is not a more sophisticated way of manipulation, although some people will say that they are setting boundaries, when in fact they are attempting to manipulate. The difference between healthily setting a boundary and manipulating is when we set a boundary, we let go of the outcome. It is impossible to have a healthy relationship with someone who has no boundaries, with someone who cannot communicate directly, and honestly. Learning how to set boundaries is a necessary step in learning to be a friend to ourselves. It is our responsibility to take care of ourselves, to protect ourselves when it is necessary. It is impossible to learn to be loving to ourselves without, owning our self—and owning our rights and responsibilities as co-creators of our lives."[17]

Just What is "Detaching with Love?"

When I feel responsible FOR others:

---

[17] (http://www.joy2meu.com/Personal_Boundaries.htm)

- ➢ I fix I rescue I protect I control
- ➢ I carry their feelings
- ➢ I do not listen
- ➢ I feel tired. Anxious, fearful, liable
- ➢ I am concerned with answers circumstances being right details performance.
- ➢ I manipulate feelings people outcomes.
- ➢ I expect others to live up to my expectations.
- ➢ When I feel responsible FOR others, I am caretaking.

When I feel responsible TO others:

- ✓ I am sensitive
- ✓ I show empathy
- ✓ I encourage, share, I confront
- ✓ I level, I listen
- ✓ I feel relaxed, free, aware, high self-worth
- ✓ I am concerned with–relating person to person, feelings with the person.
- ✓ I can feel my feelings, express my feelings, let go of my feelings, trust, let go.
- ✓ I expect others to be responsible for themselves and their actions. When I feel responsible TO others, I am practicing self-care.

Some thoughts on communication. The Dirty Dozen

FROM: Thomas Gordon

Parent Effectiveness Training

These are communication blockers. We need to stop doing these things if we desire a more informative and satisfying conversation.

1. **Criticizing**
   Making a negative evaluation of the other person, their actions or attitudes.

"You have no one to blame but yourself"

Name Calling

Putting down or stereotyping the other person

"You are nothing but a male chauvinist!"

2. **Diagnosing**

Analyzing why a person is behaving as they are by playing amateur psychiatrist

"Just because you were rejected as a child---"

3. **Praising Manipulatively**

Making an exaggerated judgment of another person

"I know what a good friend you are and that I can count on you to--"

4. **Ordering**

Commanding the other person to do what you want to be done. "I want it finished right now!" "Because I say so!"

5. **Threatening**

Controlling the other person by warning of negative consequences. "You'll do it, or else!"

6. **Moralizing/Preaching**

Telling the other person by warning of negative consequences. "You shouldn't think of divorce. Think of it as breaking up the family".

7. **Excessive Inappropriate Questioning**

Close-ended questions that can only be answered 'yes' or 'no.' "Aren't you sorry you did that?"

8. **Advising**

Giving the other person a solution to their problems. "If I were you…" (I call this Alanonandonandon)

9. Diverting
Pushing the other person's problems aside.

"Don't dwell on it" "Get some sleep" "You think you've got it bad-"

10. Logical Argument
Appealing to the facts, and logic without considering the emotional factors.

"Look at the facts. He/she does not even call you…"

11. Reassuring
Trying to convince the other person not to feel the negative emotions.

"Don't worry—it's the darkest before dawn."

Another anonymous quote to think about:

"The art and skill of being a good listener is the noble half of any conversation. It is also a skill that can be learned from or improved upon."

Ask: Do I listen to learn or to argue?

Scott Peck also felt that, "you cannot truly listen to anyone and do anything else at the same time."[18]

(I wonder what he would have said about the technology today and how often we multi-task while conversing with someone!).

---

[18] Peck, M. Scott; The Road Less Traveled; 2003; Touchstone; NY, NY.

Listen

When I ask you to listen to me and you start giving advice, you have not done what I asked.

When I ask you to listen to me and you begin to tell me why I shouldn't feel that way, you are trampling on my feelings.

When I ask you to listen to you and I feel you must do something to solve my problem, you have failed me, strange as that may seem.

Listen! All I asked, was that you listen. Not talk or do—just hear me.

Advice is cheap. Ten cents used to get you both Dear Abby and Billy Graham in the same newspaper. And, I can do for myself. I'm not helpless. Maybe discouraged and faltering, but not helpless. When you do something for me that I can and need to do for myself, you contribute to my fear and weakness. But, when you accept as a simple fact that I do feel what I feel, no matter how irrational, then I can quit trying to convince you. I can get about the business of understanding what's behind this irrational feeling. And when that's clear, the answers are obvious, and I don't need advice. Irrational feelings make sense when we understand what's behind them.

Perhaps that's why prayer works, sometimes, for some people because God is mute. He doesn't give advice or try to fix things. "They" listen and let it work it out for yourself.   So,   please listen and hear me. If you want to talk, wait a minute for your turn, and I'll listen to you.[19]

NOW

---

[19] (http://www.sapphyr.net/largegems/pleaselisten.htm)

Thoughts that help me think about recovery with another person.

Five Spiritual Strengths of a Relationship – Ernie Larson[20]

He states that the opposite of these is death of the relationship.

- ➤ Straight Talk - No mind reading, be direct
- ➤ An emotional commitment
- ➤ Personal responsibility - Like the 4th step in Alanon which advises owning our behaviors.
- ➤ Fighting fair
- ➤ Daily nurturing – Some advice that partners share at least 5 positive validations daily.

Recovery of Relationships

From: David Treadway (and author comments) Before It's Too Late[21]

Addiction and its devastation often leads to relationships that are reactive and enmeshed. To 'detach' is often misunderstood. It does not mean abandonment or loss of caring for someone. My favorite quote: "I Do not detach from you, but I do detach from the agony of involvement in your problem."

Before we explore Mr. Treadway's ideas, let me try to help you understand the concept of enmeshment. It is when I have a cold and you sneeze. It is when someone asks me, "How are you?" and I respond with, "He's fine, thank you." It is when a couple is under a dual controlled electric blanket and he keeps dialing down because he feels too warm and she complains of feeling cold as she keeps dialing up on the control dial crossed wires. It is like

---

[20] Stage 11 Recovery: Life Beyond Addiction; Harper Colins; Ny, Ny; 2013

[21] Treadway, David; Before It's Too Late; W.W. Norton & Company; NY, NY. 1989.

trying to see how close you can manipulate two drops of mercury before they meld into each other.

The picture of two hands with fingers intertwined is the feeling of enmeshment. It can feel cozy and safe. But what happens if one hand has a problem and takes the second hand captive and sinks in that problem? Down they both go.

4 Enmeshment

Detachment on the other hand is to b

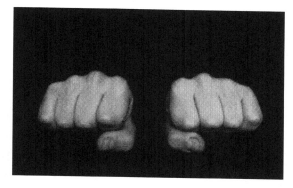

5 Detachment

for themselves.

The picture of two whole hands sitting side by side is the feeling of detachment Those two hands choose to be close, can support each other, but remain separate and independent at the same time. They are each a whole self which allows remaining in the relationship without losing pieces of myself to the problem of the other. What healthy support can I give you if I am also drowning?

M. Scott Peck Wrote that love is the free exercise of choice. Two people love each other only when they are quite capable of living without each other but choose to live with each other.

The enmeshed fingers must be reactive. The detached fingers are free to respond.

I first saw David Treadway when he was giving a lecture about couples recovering from addiction in their lives. He has had a successful career in family systems and couples therapy and has lectured and written widely. What impressed me so many years ago was how, during the break in the long program, he sat on the edge of the stage and simply answered the many questions. So real. So unassuming. So easy to approach. That is also the flavor of his book *Before It's Too Late* that remains useful today.

Upon contacting him to see if I could paraphrase his work and include it for sharing, he wished me luck and asked only for a footnote mention. Gladly. In his practice of recovering couples (and very applicable for any two people!), he was using a year-long plan. The rules were simple: both people had to agree to participate willingly and truly want to find their way back to each other. Remaining drug-free was also required for both.

There were six stages: Each stage needed to be fairly well mastered before moving onto the next. In cases when a once mastered stage was needing more time, it was necessary to backtrack to that step and reinforce it until the time came to move forward again. Sessions with a therapist were as needed along the path.

Stage One - Disengagement

Think of those clasped fingers. Imagine how hard it is to pull apart two water glasses that are stuck together. We need to address the enmeshment and pull apart psychologically. Pulling apart can feel so foreign and unfamiliar, but it is of major importance if one is to grow. Disengagement ends reactions to each other and gives us space to respond and expand.

This stage is the most difficult and may take several weeks. Attendance nourishes it as 12-Step meetings encourage a focus on 'self and discourage focus on the 'other.' Al-Anon is a natural program to promote becoming aware that you are a distinct self. (I know one lady who remarried her husband after years of their recovery and insisted on keeping her maiden name as a reminder that she was separate).

There is a vast difference between selfish and self. There is a vast difference between self-centered and SELF-centered. Many family and friends do not yet understand that the idea that putting your oxygen mask on first before you can help others is not selfish or self-centered.

Other self-developing paths might include employment, school, or any activity that helps one become more aware of their own authentic life, needs, feelings, strengths, gifts. Remember that it takes two healthier people to create a healthier relationship. And it takes a whole sense of self to be healthier.

"The tragedy of her life is not that he left her, it is that she never showed up."[22]

When we separate, it is in the interest of autonomy and connection. Sounds strange, but it is true. Think of the two separate hands still capable of closeness but not hostages to each other. This first stage is to separate but acknowledge the pain and the hurt and hold onto your anger. Stop beating each other with it. You can take it to your Al-Anon meetings, therapy, or your pillow. Just not each other. What this does is stop the predictability of the system. The tit for tat.

Stage Two - Differentiation

---

[22] Unknown

Do you remember those two stuck glasses that you tried so hard to pull apart? What usually happens when the suction is released? Your two hands fly apart much farther than needed. Now that you have pulled apart, there is a need for healthy distance but not miles and miles. Also, if you try to get too close too fast with the work of healing not yet accomplished, there will be disappointment and frustration. So, what might help this state of the relationship possible to be differentiated? Two things:

> Agree NEVER again to bring up the past if you mean to use it as a weapon. There is a contact for both to sign. It does not mean that you will never be able to discuss the past, but NOT NOW. You need to be more stable and less reactive. The agreement is at the end of this chapter. Copy it, agree with your partner, sign it. You can even sign it in the book if that would work better for you.

Think of what bringing up grievances will accomplish. Pardon my medical background, but I always think of our hearts like an open wound that needs to be tenderly cared for. When you get a scab on a wound, you do not keep picking at it or tearing it off. You leave it alone and protect it. I sometimes think that a heart bandage would help. If your long-term goal is to heal and grow closer, then you might be able to sign the contract never again to clobber each other with past harm. Become an expert tongue-biter. It is common for a person, especially if you are losing an argument, to dredge up the past as a means of victory. You will lose the war and create even more distance.

> His next great idea to aid in differentiation is to learn to listen! This will also promote more closeness as I will see you more clearly and stop taking you for granted if I keep my ear flaps open and receptive and resist the urge to comment, argue, criticize, find fault, react, and defend

myself. Just absorb what you hear without comment or reaction. Be a sponge.

What is it We Fear About Listening

If you always need the last word, you will die with a bag of last words and not much closeness to others.

What Dr. Treadway asks at this point is a daily exercise. Set aside time without distraction. Start small–maybe three minutes. Take turns just listening to whatever the other wants to share. You do not need to fix anything or even like what you hear. Just Listen! As you get braver and more comfortable, increase the time. Do not discuss it at all later–walk away and do whatever but marinate in what you heard. Listening is the better part of communication. If you already think you are a good listener–ask the people you live with if they feel heard by you. What these two suggestions accomplish is a way to pull apart, but not too far. One can begin to become aware of the other as separate by really hearing them. Not dredging up the past will also prevent further distancing. At this stage of the process, many people may experience some depression. Usually, they wish that they had known this years ago. You may have to go back to Stage 1 for a while. It is always OK to refresh.

Stage Three: Negotiation

This is a skill that successful relationships know about. It is similar to a business deal and useful when there is a stuck place. It is not about feelings and not about winning or losing and not a contest. It is now possible to do this rather adult negotiation with a focus on an agreement to the deal. Positive solutions to small problems are now possible.

The rule is that there is not past talk. Stick to solutions. Success is measured when you can 'keep a deal. 'The deal needs to feel "equal" in value. For instance, I used to ask couples to share some small and frequent conflict. Not unusual for a wife to complain about the elevated toilet seat and not unusual for the husband to agree to pay attention to this issue if she would only stop hanging her washed delicates in that same bathroom. With a lot of laughter, they would shake hands on 'the deal.'

It became more of a challenge to find something of equal value when one sister wanted her brother to stop smoking. She finally agreed to do his laundry for a year. Once again, successful negotiations may seem so foreign after months of never resolving any conflict or succeeding at anything. Success is a stranger and feelings of it may make the losses of the past seem worse. Talk about this with someone– like a sponsor. IT IS OK TO BE OK.

It is important that, after the handshake on the exchange, both parties feel like winners and the 'deal' seems fair. It is also important to have a few laughs together. That brother and sister had been alienated for months.

Stage Four: Conflict Resolution

The goal is to learn to be in conflict and not necessarily resolve, agree or 'act out.'

Contrary to the days of addiction living, it is healthy to be able to stay angry and remain in control. People refer to the Dance of Anger during the crazy days of the chemical being the main event (even though unacknowledged). It is such a game.

Harriet Lerner wrote a book by that title as she explored the patterns of anger in relationships. Anger is such a presence in the relationship during addiction and can remain so in recovery. It is a cover for hurt. Anger guarantees distance and destruction.

185

Fighting well is a skill and can be cathartic. It is good to clear the air—just not good to make things worse. Ask yourself what your role model was? Did you see adults fighting when you were a kid? What did you learn to do or not to do? Some people never saw fighting between their parents. Does that mean that someone was lying or just people pleasing? It may have kept the peace, but it was not honest if there were pseudo-agreements. Some people witnessed violence from yelling to homicide. Some people witnessed a role-model practice the fine art of being passive/aggressive—when you 'get back' at someone by what you do NOT do!

I remember one wife who always asked her husband to stop and pick up bread and milk (he had offered) and who never once remembered the request. Do you think she got angry after a few years of this? I will bet he smiled to himself.

You were fortunate if you saw your role models fight well. Even in a healthy disagreement, it may take one or both some time to 'cool off.' Seldom do both arrive at this at the same time. Be patient. Learning to 'fight healthy' takes practice. There is a list of Dirty Fighting that is not in Treadway's book. Author unknown: 10 NO-NO'S to think about:

> SPY: Look for shortcomings of the other. Keep track of them. Throw up all unpleasant incidents.
> TIME YOUR ATTACK: Fight to win-especially when the other is tired.
  - When they come home from work
  - When they are on the way out the door
  - When they are absorbed in something else (ex: football)
> SHOTGUN ATTACK: Do not stay on topic. Hit from all directions. Bring in all old issues. Bring in money, parents, girlfriends, and boyfriends

- ➤ TEASE Puts other at a disadvantage. "Where is your sense of humor–I was just kidding."
- ➤ OVER-KILL, BOTTLE-UP- GUNNY-SACKING:
  For the quiet type. Hold in all your feelings so you 'don't hurt your partner.' (or yourself). But one day you explode and hit partner with it all.

- ➤ MARTYR: Give in to others wants but look sad. Make them appreciate your sacrifice. Rub it in until they feel guilty.
- ➤ SPOUSE ANALYZER AND LABELER:
  Be an amateur psychiatrist. Learn such words as inadequate, dependent, neurotic, paranoid, insecure human being, over-sexed, animal, frigid.

- ➤ DO NOT LISTEN:
  Know you are right. So why waste time listening? While the other is talking, you use the time to plan your attack.

- ➤ USE SILENT WARFARE:
  "What's wrong?" "Nothing." Do not give a clear message when you have a bone to pick, Let him/her figure it out.

- ➤ INSIST ON MAKING UP AT ONCE:
  Something must be wrong with the other if they do not recover as fast as you do.

- ➤ BACK TO 'BEFORE IT'S TOO LATE"

Going back to Treadway's Conflict Resolution, he suggests practice fighting at home. The two people are tasked with setting time aside to 'fight.' He suggests that they only allow one-half hour, followed by **immediate** attendance at 12-Step meeting that is nearby. The following are the argument guidelines:

- ➤ No bringing up of the past
- ➤ Stay on the subject
- ➤ Set a timer, and stop all talk after 30 minutes

When the 30 minutes are up, go to the car, go to the meeting and do not discuss the practice fight on the way to the meeting. There is a reason for this. During the 'fight,' it is easy to break the rules, escalate, lose yourself in the argument. It is so easy to slide off the topic and become enmeshed again. When you attend a meeting, it helps you gather yourself and feel whole. When you feel whole, you become a healthier self and can be in conflict and maintain your boundaries.

It is OK to be angry and be in control. What is not OK is to lose control and lose your point and your boundaries. Dirty fighting is a hollow battle. Far better to be clear, direct, and respectful, even if loud. Any two people can practice this enough to succeed eventually. Just as a side comment, in any disagreement in your life, it is a great advantage not to allow yourself to be pulled or manipulated off the topic. You can always say, "Right now, we are talking about this. We can talk about what you want to at another time." Get back on track. Very powerful stuff.

Another common challenge is to be certain you are addressing what is bothering you. It is not unusual to present a hurt or concern under the guise of another topic. Ex: Asking about a checkbook entry rather than what is really on your mind.

STAGE 5: Resolution of the Past

Please note that this is not Stage 1. By this time, the two people have had some success, are feeling more stable. Now is the only time that sharing about the past might be successful. Ashleigh Brilliant wrote, "Sooner or later, we must give up all hope of a better yesterday."[23] We need to face the tragedies of our history together. There are so many lost dreams and wishes and so much emptiness.

I think it is helpful to finally have a sense of "we" as you look back and recognize that Chucky was in the relationship. He is the enemy–not each other. "We" can have a strong sense of survival– 'we' share responsibility. The blaming must stop as 'we move into surrender and resignation and forgiveness. The shields need to drop.

A sense of separation from the past is possible. We are now in the present. I think of the movie 'Princess Bride" where the two people are running through' the Fire Swamp (which is full of danger and beasts and boiling holes). They finally emerge and can look back at the Swamp and know they survived it all.

There is a sense of relief and pride in selves. If indeed, we do not resolve the past and create this image of separation, the past will always be happening. Know that the perceptions of the past will seldom agree. Learn to listen and accept the others' perception. Why argue? Better to learn from each other and put it to rest. I can remember several situations where numerous siblings were in a family session and their parent was in treatment. It was amazing how differently they each saw the history of their family and perception of the addicted parent. Almost like four separate households and each certain that they were right!

One primary thought from this stage is that there may be one or several "UNFORGIVABLES" on your heart. They need not end the relationship. Hopefully, forgiveness can come your way, and many roads can lead to this. However, there may be few things that seem just stuck in your heart. One of the most common I heard

---

[23] Brilliant, Ashley; I Feel Much Better now that I've given up hope; Brilliant Enterprises; 1984

189

was from wives who were so deeply hurt when their mate did not make an appearance at the hospital when some child was born. Too drunk.

Well, Treadway had a common-sense trick for this. He said that if you struggle with these lumps of hard resentments in your mind of heart, you can wrap them in some imaginary container (I used duct tape wrapped around a shoe box), wrote MY "UNFORGIVABLES" on it with big black letters, and then threw them away as far as you could into some deep imaginary dark cave or hole—never to be seen or heard from again. In other words, it is OK to have some things you never need to forgive, but you can still get rid of them. This works. What eventually happens, in recovery, is that the day will dawn when you both can revisit the past in a rational tone and tell the story, but this is soon followed by "Yes...but..." and they move on to tell of the balance in their lives today. Again, and I repeat, this Resolution of the Past is possible after several months in the preceding stages.

STAGE SIX: Sex and/or Intimacy

Working on Stage 1-5 is itself intimacy. There are many roads to 'intimacy' with another. It is when you feel a special closeness to another. Do you know someone with whom you communicate well? Is there a person you work well with, have a sense of humor with, share values with, share an intellect with, can be social with, have fun with, share spirituality with, or have a common sense of being 'my sort'? Lucky are you if you have a variety of people in your life where you feel one or more of these easy connections. They all bring a sense of closeness and living well together. Many couples confuse sex with intimacy. Although fun, this is not the answer. In the work of recovery, the answer is in the necessary healing which can lead to genuine closeness.

We cannot think our way out of a problem we behaved our way into.[24] Just know that we cannot simply return to where we got off track in our history with someone. It takes some effort and the realization that we are now farther down the track than when we derailed.

It Takes a Family: A cooperative Approach to Lasting Sobriety

By: Debra jay

Structured Family Recovery®

This amazing new book is the first to approach the recovery process while seeing the entire family as the client. There has been much to address family and friend education and healing, but this is an amazing path for all follow in a well-organized and common-sense approach for all in the circle of a need for recovery. The

---

[24] Covey, Stephen; The 7 Habits of Highly Effective Families; Golden Books, NY, NY; 1997

person with an addiction is but one part of the whole. Everyone involved is of equal concern.

The book is inclusive of so much that I think of the saying about How Do You Eat an Elephant? Answer: One bite at a time.

Structured Family Recovery® (SFR) is a new and comprehensive approach to long-term support for all concerned. It is inspired by the highly effective Physicians Health Program that has been utilized for years and claims an 85% success rate for sobriety. This PHP has several components that define their path to success. Debra Jay has beautifully adapted these into possibilities for a family to practice and incorporate into their lives.

The SFR® journey is not about airing past hurts (which she calls Dropping Bombs). It is focused on the weekly family sharing of everyone's progress in their recovery. What is so brilliant is the fact that the sharing of this, along with other weekly discussions and topics will automatically begin and enhance the healing of all. There is a clear guideline for actions in the case of a person with an addiction or family relapse.

The entire idea is designed to create a feeling of connection and mutual regard and support. There are several ways to utilize this book. There are now therapists trained in the utilization of SFR®. You can access them by phone for a one-time conference call and guidance, you can access them as needed, you can hire them for a few sessions, and you can utilize them as needed. There are clear steps described as to how a family can start the process. Jay recognizes that not all families are intact enough to enter the SFR® process, but it is also a fact that any close friend who is willing to be part of the healing is welcome. She reports families that have successfully created a "do it ourselves" system.

I have recommended the reading of this comprehensive book even if you do not think it is possible to implement the SFR®. There is a plethora of information on every page and tons of resources. The fact is, that treatment itself is not recovery. Because the active addiction is not in play is the beginning and now makes it possible for the recovery to begin. The trauma must be addressed. Somewhat like a fire that has been extinguished but recovery now looms. SFR® is not therapy. Its sole goal is "to get the family to a better place." The attitude is one of kindness and gentleness (even if you must fake it to make it!). The SFR® system is a weekly family phone connection with a plan for each hour. This book tells you how to arrange this. The year is divided into four quarters with a wide array of topics and readings and assignments and sharing. There is a chairperson or "leader" There are tools and checklist. There are clear (very doable) assignments. There is an explanation of the 12-Steps There are topics we need to know. There are things we need to do. There are weekly reports, discussions, and plans. There is always phone help from the SFR® counselor if needed. There are clear guidelines for actions in the face of anyone's relapse.

Jay explores the fact that motivation, itself, is not enough. It might be powerful for a short time, but it fades. (Think of a New Years' resolution). What has a more positive effect for all of us is a connection and caring and hope. She has given a hand-held, clear, intelligent, loving, process for anyone to follow in the interest of sustained recovery. This model has a focus on the changing of self and a clear direction for the family team for long-term success. It may seem overwhelming to think that SFR® is possible for you. Start with baby steps. It is true that our behaviors change our attitudes. Jay recommends that you read the first 34 pages. Here is a quote from page 34.

> *"When families get involved in recover, they find a new and vital integrity. People learn to say what they mean and do what they say. Each person strives to admit when they were wrong, forgive others for their shortcomings, and honor the progress everyone is making as a group. Truth is not used as*

a weapon and love is not used as an excuse for inaction. With everyone in recover, the family—which now includes the person with an addiction on this shared journey—begins to feel safe."

The website is love: www.first.net/structuredfamilyrecovery/

So, after reading all the above, you are asking, "What is the point of this chapter?" It is simple. It is normal for families and friends to keep the focus on the person with an addiction and their "recovery progress" and not to believe there is a need for their own involvement in anything. Pretend that two years have passed, and you are still non-trusting, hurt, angry, and resentful. The person with an addiction can do nothing to make it heal. You must. You were also in this war zone, and only you can tend to your wounds. This may seem unfair, or you can try to see this as a great opportunity for you to grow and mend. Many relationships do not survive the recovery if only one person participates. My hope for you is that all of you can someday feel peace with each other, even if you decide to separate amicably. It is massively worth the effort.

WE, THE UNDERSIGNED, DO AGREE NEVER AGAIN TO BRING UP THE PAST WITH EACH OTHER IF THE INTENT IS TO HARM OR WIN. WE UNDERSTAND THAT THIS WOULD BE DESTRUCTIVE TO OUR HOPE AND GOAL OF HEALING OUR RELATIONSHIP.

WE SIGN THIS AGREEMENT ON_____

NAME: _____

NAME: _____

WE ALSO UNDERSTAND THAT THERE WILL BE A DAY WHEN WE ARE MORE STABLE AND RESOLVED, AND WE SHALL BE MUTUALLY ABLE TO DISCUSS THE PAST WITHOUT REACTION.

Chapter 14: Children of Alcoholics

I like to call this chapter "The View from The Floor, as author Alice Miller often referred to small children of alcoholics. There are COA's (children of alcoholics), ACOA's (adult children of alcoholics), and a state of being referred to as CO-DEPENDENCY (whose behaviors, attitudes and feelings often spring from the breeding ground of the above). There are support groups for all.

It is nothing new to mental health professionals to be welcoming those have been impacted by a childhood laced with stressors and challenges. It was in the 1960's that so many of the presenting problems were seen in children of alcoholics, and it all began to make sense. So much in common. So much to share. So. much to heal. So much to figure out and leave in the past. What was so powerful was the movement that began to identify living with an addicted parent as the commonality. Pioneers in the field of addiction gathered and wrote and started a national movement to help the healing of these children (of all ages). In 1969, R. Margaret Cork wrote *The Forgotten Children.* This social worker studied 115 children who lived with one or two addicted parents. Sis Wenger read the book while she was on vacation and this was the inspiration for her creation of National Association for Children of Alcoholics (NaCoA). The work of this organization and others has relentlessly reached out to identify, support, and educate those who could not help themselves.

Maya Angelou said, "Children's talent to endure stems from their ignorance of alternatives." I keep thinking of all the little people who manage to survive the most difficult of situations. We could say that they developed choices or automatic reactions or modeled behaviors to get through the day. I prefer to think that they developed survival skills. Hats off to them. When you do not have the power to change the threat to your sense of wellbeing, you find ways to survive.

I think of a man in-group who had two fighting and violent, addicted parents. He said he lived in fear. His father would shoot at rats in the house and had been abusive to all. His mother once hit him with a bat. He was manipulated at age seven by an adult male into a hotel room who, under the guise of 'going on an adventure,' tried to molest him. He ran. He could not find anyone to come and pick him up. He learned to trust no one and to keep everything to himself. Years later, he was dealing with his deep anger and learning the joy of sharing with others and trusting some and finding his way home to himself. Is he not a miracle?

Of course, there are less dramatic and intense situations, but many have felt the need to develop the four main survival skills so common to children of alcoholics.

> **Denial**
> **Rigidity**
> **Silence**
> **Isolation**

These four skills guaranteed your survival. There is just one problem–they are not great coping skills for life! We can continue to use these survival skills in the workplace and our relationships. Life has many situations that require skills beyond survival. Do we not need to take a look at those decisions we made when we were small? How are they working today?

It has been said that the COA household for a child is both a blessing and a curse. As a blessing, one can feel proud that they learned to be competent, responsible, strong, productive and in control. Or proud of your sense of humor, charm or ability to be helpful and invisible. It is a curse to be ignored, abused, hurt, and helpless. Feeling alone and angry and fearful or guilty and confused is not unusual. The family may seem like most others except it is a breeding ground of despair behind the face of denial.

Do we not need skills that allow us to reach out for help, consider alternatives, deal with reality, and know that you are more likely to get your way if you have more than one way? These are coping skills.

If you are fortunate enough to find your way to some 12-Step program or other growth means, the development of effective and healthy coping skills sneaks up on you. It is in these recovery situations that a person may experience the relief of sharing, the amazement of seeing the reality of their situation, the wonder of hearing new ways of thinking and feeling and the joy of feeling safe and understood. All of this and, in the 12-Step program, the price is right.

One can learn to respond and stop the reactions which keeps your power intact. One can learn not to take the situation personally (even though it feels very personal). One can learn it is not about your worth as a person and that you are lovable despite another's inability to love. One can learn to focus on your own authentic life and to either return to it or develop it. One can learn to stop letting yourself be used. One can learn that is OK to seek help and OK to be OK. One can learn to grow to the point of forgiveness, and, finally, truly understand the meaning of loving detachment. This is coping at its finest.

COA's also may be left with what some call a perpetuating attitude because of a past event. This keeps you from living in the present. For example, if you felt shut out as a child, you may always filter your life through this pain. You may continue to feel shut out even if the present-day situation is not one of exclusion. Or, if you felt blamed as a child, or responsible for someone else's poor choices, you may continue to feel responsible for others. Or, if you felt unimportant as a child, you may continue to discount yourself. Uncovering these 'buttons' that get pushed is one goal of therapy or merely discovering them as others share the story of their growth. A quote: "We have issues in our tissues."[25] Our survival skills are surely not effective when pitted against addiction.

➢ **Denial**

Denial may keep our hopes alive, but when the truth is not faced, nothing will resolve. Truth often is painful, but at least you are clear on the situation.

If the truth was not spoken in your household, like seeing your parent on the bathroom floor and there is some blood, and someone tries to explain that "dad is just napping." Or is the message being "do not talk about this at school because everything is "fine."

I again smile when remembering the mother who found a spoon under the bed of her daughter and wondered where the cereal bowl was.

➢ **Silence**

The household rule is often Do Not Talk, Trust or Feel. One children's book is called 'Elephant in the Living Room.' Everyone steps around the pachyderm, ignoring it. Crazy-making! What elephant? Many have stated that the entire family 'walked on eggshells.'

➢ **Rigidity**

A child learns about good/bad, black/white, and life with no gray areas. A COA never knows what is behind the door when coming home from school. Is the coast clear? Is mom drunk? Is dad in a bad mood? Is there fighting? I

---

[25] https://www.yogispirit.com.au/blogs/chronicles/issues-in-our-tissues

anyone sitting around naked? This child does not learn the concept of processing things. He/she cannot plan to have a birthday party, or talk about it, or invite anyone to their house. They have to wait to see how things are at the moment. Friends are seldom invited in. This leads to rigid thinking in life. Life is full of gray areas and the need to be flexible.

"You are more likely to get your way if you have more than one way." It is also true that trusting a good moment or a pleasant time is often difficult due to the history of so many of them having been quickly turned into disappointment after the alcoholic had consumed more than 'a couple of beers. 'Sometimes, the COA will sabotage their happiness to alleviate the anxiety of expecting it to crash.

> **Isolation**
COAs have secrets. They feel alone, even in a crowd. The feelings of shame or guilt are overwhelming to some. There is little trust in seeking help and no experience working as a team with others. Often there is never a 'best friend,' although sometimes COAs find each other.

Children of People with addictions, young or old, need to hear that they are not their story. They need help finding their way back to their authentic self.

An artichoke is a good visual. The heart and core of this vegetable are the most desired. The leaves represent all the layers and layers of defenses, attitudes, and feelings that can protect the precious heart. Recovery is the process of peeling away the leaves.

I no longer am silent. I no longer feel responsible for others (although I remain responsible TO them). I no longer feel like things are my fault. I no longer use anger to push others away. I no longer am emotionally dishonest. I no longer ignore my feelings. I no longer measure myself by my circumstances. I no longer have to be a 'people pleaser.' I no longer have a high tolerance for inappropriate behavior. Leaf by leaf.

In the 1980's and 1990's, therapists researched and wrote about the concept of children growing up in the alcoholic home. The view of resiliency was introduced. Dr. Steven Wolin and Dr. Sybil Wolin created "The Challenge Model"[26] and listed seven factors that might limit the amount of damage and promote well-being and self-esteem. They viewed this as an interplay of Damage and Challenge. They felt that exposure was not the whole story. Vulnerability and mastery also play an essential role in determining response to stress.

So, is resiliency a quality in the child or their environment? Robert Ackerman (1987) also explored some variables.

- ➢ The degree of addiction is present. The child's resiliency to stress
- ➢ The gender of the alcoholic and the child
- ➢ The age of exposure to the alcoholism
- ➢ Positive off-setting factors
- ➢ Cultural considerations and family values
- ➢ The child's perception of the family and self-esteem

The hope is that the predicament of being born to a family with addiction will not be cause for stigma, but instead seen as a growth opportunity and a challenge where the survival stances are to be applauded. Werner (1985) felt that negative outcomes from a toxic environment are not inevitable and may be buffered by

---

[26] Wolin, Steven MD; Wolin Sybil Ph.D.; The Resilient Self: How Survivors of Troubled Families Rise above Adversity; Villard, NY, NY; 1993

constitutional characteristics of the child and by qualities of the early caregiving environment.

Let us look at the seven resiliencies identified by Wolin.

> **Insight**
This begins if a child senses something is wrong, and then expands it to knowing and seeing family dynamics and roles. They see that the problem is not them and begin to understand about people and themselves. Children with insight later do well.

> **Independence**
Kids begin to disengage from parents emotionally. Adults may separate eventually. This independence from toxic parent's accounts for successful adaptation as emotional independence is crucial for adjustment. The degree of independence by resilient children will parallel the extent of intrusion of their boundaries.

> **Relationships**
This is the interdependence-to derive love, acceptance, and emotional gratification from others. Resilient children go from interaction to connecting with other adults in their world, bonding with friends, siblings, and spouses to form the attachments they need. COA's need for alternative anchors. Sometimes, they actually can feel closer to the person with addiction than to the sober parent.

> **Initiative**
This is the buoyancy, the capacity for problem-solving, and belief in personal control found in resilient children who do not buckle or accept the view of themselves as helpless. They branch out and explore their options. Perseverance with determination. Practical skills develop.

They become productive and refuse to acknowledge obstacles. Like a Queen, they discard all nuisances.

➤ Morality

This is the quality of ethical conduct in which resilient children give themselves the necessities of purpose in life, self-respect, and dignity. It begins with questioning parental behavior and by wondering when their parents are good or bad. Later, moral reasoning becomes incentive to action and they judge. "Resilient children do independent moral arithmetic"(Wolin).

They separate from family values and form their own.

➤ Creativity

They find a way to express their conflicts in some creative form. In childhood, creative play with imagination is protective. Later, they compose their work with thought and art and self-expression.

➤ Humor

Humor is a natural restorative. It helps discharge tension and changes perspective. Adversity morphs into laughter and a playful state of mind. Humor seems to protect us from the wounds of trouble. It also elicits positive attention from others.

So-when COA's possess strong resiliencies and have only a modest number of vulnerabilities, and they can be successful survivors. If they are simply overwhelmed by the past, with few resiliencies, they may be casualties. Many are a checkerboard of strengths and weaknesses.

It is also of note that some of the resiliencies may be over-developed and one can become 'stuck' in them. For example, it helped a child to survive by developing strong independence.

However, as an adult, that person needs to understand the necessity and wisdom of asking for help when needed.

As this peek into the family that struggles with addiction, I am left with one main truth. So much more is subject to generational transmission than the actual predisposition to addiction. It is said that for every person with an addiction, at least seven family members are impacted.

Chapter 15: Home Contracts

Eight Samples

Before we look at some Home Contracts, I want to state that it is never the fault of the addicted child if the parents seem to be "split" on their approach and at odds with each other. It is easy to see the addicted child as the cause for all the drama and trauma, but the truth is that it is the full responsibility of the parents to stop blaming each other or any "reason" that their child is addicted. It is time for parents to get help, form an aligned position and be consistent in their unified approach. It is well known that when two parents are of different responses to the situation, the person with an addiction knows how to manipulate one against the other and then leave the parents arguing with each other as they leave the scene. This is highly enabling and disabling.

What follows are samples of Home Contracts to be used within residence adolescents or adult children still in residence. These show a variety of various contracts that have been used. It is only to show examples and a wide variety of parental thoughts for a contract. Of course, when a child is of adult age, you have more options for consequences. But consequences are important no matter the age.

I often think that parents have more Home Wishes than Home Rules. We are vague and inconsistent in our expectations, if, indeed, we have any at all. This is unfair. It is fair to let someone know your expectations and fair to know the consequences if the rules are broken. Parents need to create their contract according to your rules and wishes. It is, indeed, your home (unless, of course, your child is making the mortgage payment).

It is suggested that you read over these examples and create your contract. Do not make it too complicated. One set of parents had a 10-page contract and asked that the shower tiles be wiped clean daily. Stick to what matters. Most contracts have a major rule that the child must remain completely drug-free, attend a recovery program and contribute to the household maintenance and contribute some financially if they are employed (adult). The contract can also include comments from the child regarding what they need from their parent(s). A meeting is then held, and the contract reviewed and revised as agreed upon. All parties then sign and date the contract. It is somewhat like a business deal, and it is important to have signatures. The contract may be revisited and negotiated over time as needed.

The bottom line of this contract idea is that it ends the confusion. If the child does not honor what they have agreed to, then it is their decision to no longer reside there. (ADULTS). This is preferable to having parents feel that they must 'kick my kid out'. With adult children, it is their choice to remain or not and NOT the decision of the parent. It might be a new feeling for the child to have to take responsibility for their decision to break the contract. If the child is under 18, the consequences will most likely not be a loss of residence but must be impactful enough to matter.

Remember that you want to be supportive but not custodial. While following through on your contract, there is no need for anger or threats. This can be done lovingly, and it does not mean that the relationship ends. It simply means that you are refusing to let the disease of addiction reside at your address. Do not be concerned with being popular or liked at this time. You are pitted against their addiction, and this requires consistency and clarity and resolve.

Remember that you love them but not their addiction. In the long run, if your child recovers and grows, you will be thanked. You can attend an Open AA meeting and hear any number of people with addictions who will share how their family finally stopped enabling them to continue their disease.

There is one more piece of interesting information for you to read before looking at the examples of Home Contracts. Someone once asked a large group of adolescents who were high-risk kids (already involved in drug use) to advise their parents. They then rated their parents on how well they did.

I found it amazing and helpful to peek into their minds and realities. Read and learn.

ADVICE TO PARENTS FROM HIGH-RISK KIDS (Source Unknown)

	QUOTES	Always	Sometimes	Never
1	Make the rules clearer.			
2	Parents should present a united front.			

3	Don't give us everything we want.			
4	Don't do everything for us.			
5	Don't live up to discipline.			
6	Don't allow us to control the boundary line, because we'll keep changing it.			
7	Make reasonable consequences, ones that you can keep, then hold to them no matter what.			
8	If you are divorced or not getting along with each other, don't use us as a tennis ball.			
9	Don't discuss the rules with us or ask of if we agree with them or like them - we don't, but we need them.			

10	Don't lecture for hours -we're not listening anyway.			
11	Don't let us wear you down.			
12	Practice what you teach- if you get drunk or high, we'll use it as an excuse to get high ourselves.			
13	Don't make empty threats.			
14	Don't compromise.			
15	Don't blame our friends, our school, or society for our trouble.			
16	Don't give up on us.			
17	Don't say we're going through a "stage."			
18	Start discipline early on.			

19	Don't fight our battles, smother or overprotect us.			
20	Don't look the other way.			
21	Don't be intimidated by us, don't back off, don't walk on eggshells with us.			
22	Don't be afraid to confront us in public if we are too outrageous.			
23	You don't have to prove that we did something wrong. It's not a court of law. If you suspect us of something, you are allowed to accuse or challenge us even if you may be wrong.			
24	Don't clean our room for us - that's our job.			
25	Don't let us talk you into leaving us at home when you go			

		Always	Sometimes	Never
	away- we're probably planning a party.			
26	Realize that there is no such thing as a 5-person party -"parties" are usually 50 people or one _____).			
	Quotes Page 2	Always	Sometimes	Never
27	You're not obligated to supply us with money when we go out, especially when we've been acting out.			
28	Don' t "baby" us. You 're asking us to grow up, but you sometimes talk to us like we are children.			
29	Don't keep threatening rehab -just do it.			
30	Don' t send us to our room as a punishment- we will protest to trick you, but we love it there.			
31	Don't let us bargain with you.			

32	Take time with us to just talk.			
33	Don't leave money out - we'll probably take it.			
34	Don't trust your friends - we may be getting high with them.			
35	Don't say, "It's up to your father (mother). Don't refer responsibility. Don't send us to" double check."			
36	Ask for telephone numbers of friends we say we're going to stay with- then call the number to make sure we're really there.			
37	If we've ignored your curfew, don't ball us out when we call you in the middle of the night.			
38	Don't fall for half-truths.			
39	Don't fall for our friends "ass- kissing" act. Sometimes we make pacts to impress each other's			

	parents. Then you'll trust us and let us go out together. If our friends offer to help with the groceries or take out the garbage, be suspicious			
40	It's not a good idea to put our bedroom on the first floor.			
41	Don't fix special meals for us, let us eat at separates times or in other rooms.			
42	Don't let us have our telephone or TVs.			
43	LEARN ABOUT OUR ADDICTIONS! Learn what drugs look like, smell like, what we look like, and how we behave when we're using them.			
44	Always check that we are attending intramural sports, getting extra help. are attending that "chess club meeting" when we tell			

		Always	Sometimes	Never
	you that we have to stay after school.			
45	Check the windowsills for butts.			
4	Don't give us random money- it's too easy to use it for drugs.			
47	Check the position of the fan in our room- be suspicious if it faces out toward the window.			

	Quotes page 3	Always	Sometimes	Never
48	If you're looking for drugs, be sure to check the light fixtures, under mattresses. (especially your mattress). socks, deodorant containers, heels of shoes, etc. - we pride ourselves in clever hiding places.			
49	Don't let us have locks on our bedroom doors.			
50	Don't be afraid to invade our privacy. If we're in trouble,			

	You should read our letters, check our closets, and check our friends.			
51	Be suspicious if we sleep a lot, have red eyes or runny noses.			
52	Be suspicious when we: wear cologne, use mouthwash, chew gum, wear hats, or dark glasses.			
53	Don't fall for the line- But all the other parents let them.			
54	Stick to the rules.			
55	Don't give an inch!			
56	Believe it or not, we want you to catch us, stop us, and outsmart us.			

AREAS FOR HOME CONTRACT

1. Alcohol/ Drug-Free Home
2. Curfew
3. Phone Calls
4. Privacy
5. Friends-Safe and Unsafe
6. Household Chores
7. Smoking
8. What Feels Disrespectful
9. How Will Respect be Demonstrated

10. How to Have Peaceful Resolution of Conflicts:
    a) I Will
11. Things I will do for Myself
12. When I Get Angry, Upset or Depressed, I Will:
13. When I Go Out with Permission, I Will Inform Parents:
    a) Where
    b) Who
    c) When Returning
    d) Call With Any Change
14. Will Attend AA/NA
15. Places I Will Not Go
16. People I Will Not See
17. Friends I Will See
18. School:
    a) Regular Attendance-
    b) At Least Cs
    c) Homework
19. Car Driving
20. Family Relationships
21. Music/TV

Contract to be dated and signed by all involved.

Might list consequences under each area.

RULES OF THE INN

THREE CARDINAL RULES IN OUR HOME:

1.

2.

3.

FIVE MAJOR RULES IN OUR HOME:

1.

2.

3.

4.

5.

THESE ARE LISTED to MAKE CERTAIN THAT WE ARE CLEAR. THEY ARE DESIGNED TO HELP OUR FAMILY BE A SAFER PLACE AND IN SUPPORT OF YOUR GROWTH AND MATURITY.

To Our Sons:

There was a time when we were the only adults in our home. As children, you depended on us to run the house for you. We cooked, we bathed you, we cleaned your clothes; we cleaned the house, we maintained the yard, and we provided your clothes and entertainment. We did all of this willingly and lovingly. We wanted to do it, and we loved doing it.

As time went on you grew up, but we stayed the same. We continued to cook, clean your clothes (mostly), clean the house, maintain the yard, and provide you with some if not most of your clothes and entertainment. We did this out of love, but with an increasing sense of it being inappropriate and unfair to both you and us. Sometimes we may have resented doing so much of the work while you did little to help. We realized that we were allowing resentment stand in the way of loving you. We realized that we made you feel useless in your home.

Today we are four adults. We know you need and appreciate our home, our love, and our support as you finish your education and become independent. We also need and appreciate your love and your contributions to running this home. To end that, we are establishing the following rules.

You will...

1. Make time to do your share of the work around the house. You don't need to have a schedule of jobs. Look around and see what needs to be done. Ask
    a. Some of the jobs that need to be done regularly (or $1/4^{th}$) of work around the house include:
        i. Doing the wash, and sorting and folding clean clothes.
        ii. Doing the dishes and emptying the dishwasher.
        iii. Taking care of Sylvester, his food, his water, and cleaning his litter.
        iv. Putting things (telephone, cups, and glasses, etc.) back where they belong.
        v. Doing yard work (raking leaves, cutting the grass, shoveling snow).

2. Make time to communicate your feelings and plans and be together for meals regularly.

3. Keep your bedroom and bathroom as clean as the rest of the house. This means a good cleaning every other week.

4. Be home by 1:00 a.m. at the latest. If you cannot be home by that time call us, preferably before we go to sleep.

5. Allow yourself 6 to 8 hours of sleep before school and work, and get yourself, to school and work on time, without anyone waking you up.

6. Stay clean of alcohol and drugs and attend weekly group meetings for support as long as it is necessary.

Signed,

SAMPLE HOME CONTRACT

1. Curfew
   a. 10:00 p.m. - school nights
   b. 11:30 p.m. - school nights with special permission for a job or particular event
   c. 12:30 a.m. - Friday, Saturday or Holiday evenings
   d. Parents to be notified at least one hour in advance of curfew for any anticipated
   e. deviation.
   f. <u>Violation Consequences</u>
      i. First violation - curfew ½ hour earlier for one-week
      ii. Second violation -: grounded, no outside activities other than to and from school or job for one week.
      iii. Next violation - loss of privileges (to be specifically defined) for two weeks up to one month.

2. School
   a. Regular attendance at all classes
   b. Adherence to all school rules
   c. No school absences unless sick or excused by parents
   d. Maintain at least a "C" average
   e. Participate in some extracurricular activities such as music, drama, and sports, as
   f. approved by parents.
   g. At least an hour of home study for homework completion daily on school days
   h. Adherence to homework requirements as established by teachers; completion of
   i. assignments.
   j. <u>Violation Consequences</u>

       i. Loss of privileges as benefits violation.

      ii. Loss of car or driving privileges for one-semester

    iii. Curfew 9:00 p.m. school nights, 11:00 p.m. other nights

    iv. No outside activities until improvement is seen.

3. Job

   a. Obtain a part-time job that will not interfere with school within thirty days.

   b. Employment should be where employees are not known drug users.

   c. Employment income to be used to purchase personal items - cosmetics, clothes, CD' s.

   d. Parents are not to be expected to continue to finance such purchases.

4. 4. Chores

   a. Make bed, pick up clothes daily, clean room at least weekly.

   b. Do home chores when asked without arguing or procrastinating.

   c. Take or show initiative to do things around the house, garage, and yard without being

   d. asked or told.

   e. <u>Violation Consequences</u>

       i. First refusal - loss of outside activity privileges for one week.

      ii. Second refusal - loss of additional privileges such as a car or special event attendance for two weeks to one month.

5. Car/Driving

a. Ensure that the car is always in good repair and safe condition.
b. Maintain proper insurance and licensure.
c. No moving violations.
d. No one who has been using drugs or who is in possession of drugs to be in the car at any time.
e. No more than four people to be in the car at any time.
f. <u>Violation Consequences</u>
    i. Loss of driving privileges as befits violation (time period to be specific).

6. Dating/Friends
    a. Not to be in the company of known drug users.
    b. Attempt to seek out non-drug users as friends.
    c. No visiting of known drug user hangouts.
    d. Bring friends home to be introduced to parents.
    e. When going out with friends or to be at a friend's home, leave name and telephone
    f. number.
    g. <u>Violation Consequences</u>
        i. Loss of privileges as befits violation (time period to be specific).

7. 7.Family Relations
    a. No rude or hostile behavior.
    b. Participation in family activities, special occasions, holiday festivities, without
    c. argument.
    d. A show of respect, and patience with family members of all ages.
    e. No outbursts of violent (verbal or physical) behavior or threats of violence toward
    f. family members.
    g. <u>Violation Consequences</u>

    i. Loss of privileges.
8. Music/TV
    a. Volume of stereo not to exceed three at any time.
    b. T.V. program selection to be approved by parents.
    c. Music no to be of the type that glamorizes drugs or violence.
    d. <u>Violation Consequences</u>
        i. Loss of music or T.V. privileges.
9. Drugs/Alcohol
    a. No drugs or alcohol to be brought into your room, or your home, at any time.

Signed and Agreed By:

_____

Dated: _____

Signed and Agreed By:

_____

Dated: _____

HOUSE RULES (1)

Developed on:

_____

By: _____

Dated: _____

By: _____

Dated: _____

By: _____

Dated: _____

We have agreed to live by the following guidelines while we share
a parental/adolescent relationship:

No Alcohol/Drugs in the home:

_____

Curfew:

_____

Telephone calls:

_____

Visitation with non-custodial parent:

_____

Phone calls to non-custodial parent:

_____

Privacy:

_____

Visitors:

_____

Who Visits?

_____

Where Entertained: _____ How late will visitors
be welcomed? _____

Music:

_____

Household Chores:

_____

Smoking:

_____

Respect:

How will respect be demonstrated?

_____

_____

_____

What things feel disrespectful?

_____

Five guidelines for peaceful resolution of conflict between parents/adolescents:

1. Agree to a time-out and remain calm.
2. Treat each parent and adolescent with respect. No name-calling, put-downs, or threats. Attack the problem, not the person.
3. Listen to understand.

4. Expect Success. When you express feelings of warmth and optimism, you help the other side feel less defensive and more receptive to your point of view.
5. Seek outside support.

BEHAVIORAL CONTRACT/SUBSTANCE ABUSE

Teenager: _____

A. These are the goals/issues I will work on at home and/or in school:
   1.

   2.

   3.

   4.

   5.

B. These are the positive things I will do for myself:
   1.

   2.

   3.

   4.

   5.

C. When. I get angry, upset or depressed I will:
   1.

2.

3.

4.

5.

D. These are the time commitments I will follow:
1. I will be in the house at_____ on weekdays, Sunday through Thursday.

2. I Will be in the house at_____ on weekends.

E. When I go out, I will obtain permission from my parents and inform them:
1. Where am I going?

2: Who are you going to be with?

3. Who is providing the transportation?

4. When I plan to return?

5. I will call them if I change locations.

F. I make the following promise about not using drugs/alcohol:

_____

_____

_____

_____

G. I agree to attend at least_____ Alcoholics Anonymous/Narcotics Anonymous meeting(s) every week, and will attend the following support group(s):
1.

2.

H. I agree not to go to the following places (where I am sure drugs/alcohol are sure to be):

1.

2.

3.

4.

5.

I. These are the people I will not call or see:

1.

2.

3.

4.

5.

J. These are my friends or acquaintances with whom I will spend time:

1.

2.

3.

4.

5.

K. The following family member(s) agree to participate in counseling:

family member   family member

family member   family member

agency/counselor   frequency

HOUSE RULES (2)

1. School
   a. Regular attendance at all classes
   b. Adherence to all school rules
   c. No school absences, tardiness, missing individual classes or leaving school grounds unless sick or excused by parents
   d. Maintain at least a 2.5 average no "D's" or "F's"
   e. Participate in some school extracurricular activity of your choosing
   f. Adherence to homework requirements as established by teachers - complete and tum in all assignments
2. Drugs and Alcohol
   a. •Zero use of Drugs or Alcohol
   b. •Zero possession of Drugs or Alcohol
   c. •Continue with drug counseling program as recommended
   d. •Random drug testing
3. Curfew
   a. •Discouraged on school nights but no later than 9:00 p.m. unless special occasion with
   b. permission
   c. •Weekend nights - 12:30 p.m. unless special occasion with permission
   d. •Parents to be notified at least ½ hour in advance of any anticipated problem/deviation
4. Chores
   a. •Make bed, pick up clothes daily
   b. •Clean room at least once a week

    c. •Do home chores when asked without arguing or procrastinating

5. E. <u>Car/Driving</u>
   a. •No tickets
   b. •No one who has been using drugs or who is in possession of drugs to be in the car at any
   c. time
   d. •Keep the car clean - inside and outside
   e. •Advise parents of maintenance issues

6. <u>Dating/Friends</u>
   a. Attempt to seek out non-drug users as friends
   b. No visiting of known drug user hangouts
   c. When going out with friends:
   d. Check in regularly via phone
   e. Leave name and number where you can be reached

7. <u>Family Relationship</u>
   a. •Greet and acknowledge those who come into the home or a room
   b. •No rude or hostile behavior·
   c. •A show of respect and patience with all family members

8. <u>Lying</u>
   a. Absolutely no lying about anything - no exceptions

9. <u>Violation Consequences</u>
   a. Loss of privileges as befits violation, e.g.
   b. Loss of car or driving privileges
   c. Curfew hours shortened
   d. Grounding - loss of outside activities

HOME RULES

A. Drugs and Alcohol
   1. Zero use of drugs or alcohol

2. Zero possession of drugs or alcohol
3. Random drug screens
4. Successfully complete the OPTIONS program
B. School
   1. Follow all school rules
   2. No unexcused absences or tardiness from any classes
   3. Complete all homework assignments on time
   4. Be prepared for tests and quizzes
   5. Obtain C's or better in every class
   6. Be subordinate to all school staff members
C. Family relationships
   1. Be respectful to all family members
   2. No rude or hostile behavior
   3. No hitting the family pets
   4. Be considerate of other's feelings and needs
   5. Always be truthful Dating and Friends
   6. Have drug free friends and boy/girlfriends
   7. No friends over to the house without permission
   8. No visiting boy/girlfriends house when parents are absent
   9. Check in every 2-3 hours when out
   10. Get permission before going anywhere
D. Chores
   1. Keep room clean and tidy on a weekly basis
   2. Do household chores when asked without arguing or procrastinating
   3. Clean up after yourself (don't leave stuff lying around the house)
E. Violation Consequences
   1. Loss of privileges (phone use, grounding, no friends over, computer use)

_____'s CONTRACT

HOUSE RULES (3)

As parents who want to support you and who care for your welfare, we are happy to welcome you back home to continue your recovery and help you rebuild your future. It is important, however, that we all understand and agree on House rules. These rules were developed to make sure everyone's basic needs are respected so that we may be positive forces in each other's lives during this arrangement, which will not exceed six months.

1. **<u>Mom/Dad Rules:</u>**
   a. Zero use/possession of drugs or alcohol. Drug testing will be done as needed.
   b. Actively continue 12 steps to maintain your recovery.
   c. Attend recovery-related meetings at least 4 times a week.
   d. Be home on weeknights (Mondays-Thursdays and Sunday) by 11:30 and 1 AM on Fridays and Saturdays.
   e. Make time to do your share of work around the house. No schedule is necessary, look around and see what needs to be done. Some of the jobs that need to be done regularly include:
   f. Loading/Running dishwasher, taking out the trash or rolling out trash cans every Wed night,
   g. Vacuuming/cleaning common areas etc.

2. **<u>Breaking the Rules:</u>**
   a. If you break any of the rules, you are telling us you no longer want to live in our home and receive our support. You will have 5 days to find another place to live. You will not receive our financial support.

    b. If you relapse into drug/alcohol use, you must go to detox immediately. If you don't, you will

    c. have 5 days to move out. If that is your choice, we will not support you financially.

3. <u>Your Rules:</u>

    a. Do not interrupt me or disregard what I have to say. Listen to me.

    b. Respect my wish to not confront or talk with me when I tell you that I'm too angry to talk.

4. I will discuss any issue with you once I get myself under control.

    a. Treat me with the respect that you would give to an adult.

    b. Do not nag me; one reminder is fine.

5. <u>Financial Support:</u>

Until you finish your IOP, we will provide the following financial support to you as long as you follow the House rules:

    a. Lodging, utilities and use of the house

    b. Groceries and necessary personal hygiene items

    c. Paying for your Health Plan premiums

    d. Paying for medical/dental expenses/prescriptions not covered by your medical plan

    e. Pay for personal needs (clothing/shoes)

    f. Pay for your cell phone plan

    g. Transportation and other expense necessary for you to maintain your recovery

A. After you complete IOP, we expect you to do the following within 30 days:

    1. Find a job.

    2. Pay at least $200/month in rent

3. Pay for your share of your cell phone expenses ($50 /month) d. Pay your own living and recovery-related expenses
4. Get your own regular transportation to NA/Al-Anon meetings and events or contribute to the gas ($10/week) when we take you.
5. Pay your bills/obligations on time.

B. Family Values
1. As a courtesy, tell us when you leave the house, who you will be with, and approximately when to expect you back. This is NOT for approval
2. Attend Church with the family.
3. Have dinner with family regularly.
4. Mind your manners/Be respectful.
5. Nurture your health and well-being.

OXFORD/SOBER HOUSE OPTION

A. If, after completing your IOP, you want to move to an Oxford House, the following conditions apply:
1. Tell us at least a month before you expect to move.
2. You pay for the move-in and deposit expense at the Oxford House.
3. For as long as you continue to actively work your recovery, we will pay rent, medical/dental expenses, food and personal needs for no more than 6 months. However, we will withdraw all financial support if you get evicted and don't come home.

Signatures:

We Agree to follow the <u>Rules</u> specified in this Contract, Understand what happens if they are broken, are Aware of the

Family Values and Understand the Oxford House Option. This Contract is valid until a new Contract is signed.

Name

Date

Name

Date

Name

Date

When Your Child is an Addict

Sometimes the hardest things we have to do as parents of adolescents who are using chemicals are the things we need to stop doing. When you are in a relationship with someone who is operating from an addiction, there are many opportunities to be "helpful." These opportunities are all the behaviors, attitudes, and feelings that we have been taught by our families and by religious ethics to bestow upon someone we love who is having a problem. When we try to alleviate the pain and discomfort of our children, it is deemed to be kind and loving. This is normal, natural, automatic and not all effective if the problem is a chemical dependency.

When up against the power of addiction, a logic reverse of what we have been taught must be used. It holds that doing less is doing more. This logic states that the most loving, kind, and helpful response to addiction is to allow pain to happen and to allow the addicted persons to feel the discomfort of the consequences of their behavior. Most of us only wake up and take a different course of action when the discomfort increases. Think of a toothache and how to postpone the trip to the dentist. Think of a bad relationship or an uncomfortable workplace situation; we take action when it is more painful to stay than to change.

The conflict that evolves when we step aside and allow others to have their pain is that it puts us outside of our value system. This seems very unloving, unhelpful, and uncaring. And, so "un-parental." Parents are supposed to teach, protect, rescue, shield, and sooth against all adversity. Anything else can feel like a failure. We do not know, or we lose sight of the fact, that really effective parenting promotes independence.

We need to recognize addiction is powerful. Many of our well-intentioned, benevolent and responsible efforts are really like putting out an oil well fire with a squirt gun. Pain can be our most powerful ally. Pain can be a friend. Allowing the pain by allowing the consequences is truly the most loving and helpful response to addiction. When you are pitted against someone's addiction (and it is so important to remember, that it is not the person you are pitted against, but the addiction), you are really in a battle with the person's denial, delusion, and compulsion. If lecturing and yelling and rescuing were effective, we would not have a person with addiction in the country!

Pain is their alarm clock, their call to action. Pain is what we have the most trouble allowing, yet it carries the greatest hope for change. Pain is not the worst thing that can happen; it can be a motivator.

The hardest behavior change for a parent is to stop taking the situation personally and to see clearly that the most effective and loving behavior is to let the child take full responsibility for bad behavior. The logic switch is truly loving, helpful, and respectful. "I do not detach from you, but I do detach from the agony of involvement in your problem." Our children need us to stop reacting. They need us to stop taking it personally when they are acting out of chemical use. They need us to be clear, constant, and consistent. They need us to be on the job, vigilant and educated about what's going on. They need us to stop worrying about being popular, and they need us to present a unified front, as parents, with the "Rules of the Inn." They need us. Period.

(http://www.nacoa.net/pdf2/julaug03p4.pdf)

Chapter 16: Some Non-Physical Do-it-Yourself and Group Exercises

In most family programs there are a variety of exercises and hand-outs. Some of these are for fun, some for self-awareness, some for an outline of the topics you just addressed, some to be taken home as homework and some to be stuck to the refrigerator for frequent viewing. I have picked a few of the many.

One of the hopes behind these exercises is to help the family member begin to put the focus on themselves. During the active addiction, our attention and energy have been focused on the addicted person. (Like the squeaky wheel that gets the attention). The healing of ourselves really begins with self-care and self-awareness. Most of the exercises may be done by yourself. They are surprising. What is an extraordinary benefit of the group exercises is the unexpected fun of common understanding and surprising humor that surfaces?

It is very soothing to realize that we are not alone and not unique and that so many others understand. The laughter arises from how often we thought we really could control the person with an addiction. This is called a Knowing Laughter. We are as delusional about our ability to control someone else as the person with an addiction is about thinking they can control their disease. We are so endlessly creative and exhaustive in our efforts to control the outcome for someone else, and it is such a relief to let go of that delusion. It has been said that addiction has three lynchpins:

> ➢ Delusion
> ➢ Control
> ➢ Denial

Five Breath Vacation   (Martha Belknap: stress relief for kids)

Purpose: quiet relaxation between activities

- Sit comfortably and close your eyes. Be aware of your breathing.

- Listen to the sound of your breath.

- Feel the air flowing gently in and out.

- On your next breath, imagine a beautiful place you'd like to visit. As you breathe out, feel yourself traveling there.

- On your second breath in, notice the colors of your favorite place. As you breathe out, enjoy this scene in every possible way.

- On your third breath in, listen to the natural sounds of this place.

- As you breathe out, be aware of the quietness you feel inside yourself.

- On your fourth breath in, notice all the beauty surrounding you.

- As you breathe out, relax into full enjoyment of this time and place. On your fifth breath in, feel yourself traveling home again.

- As you breathe out, stretch your arms and open your eyes.

- Tell some about your wonderful five breath vacation.

The Teen Years---Then and Now

A good exercise for parents of child in treatment. Always amazing and fun to realize that we were what we were then. What is it like to be a teen? How has the teen experience changed over the last several decades? How has it remained the same? The best way to find out is for those who are teens and those who were once teens to share their experiences with each other.

1. Quickly jot down the first words that come to your mind when you read the following questions. Teens, think about your present experience. Adults, reflect on your experiences as a teen,

   a. How do/did you spend most of your time?

   _____
   _____

   _____
   _____

   _____
   _____

   b. With whom do/did you spend most of your time?

   _____
   _____

   _____
   _____

   _____
   _____

   c. What are/were your goals and dreams?

_____

_____

_____

_____

_____

d. What are/were your greatest fears?

_____

_____

_____

_____

e. What kind of future for yourself, your country and the world do/did you envision as a teenager, looking 20 years into the future?

_____

_____

_____

_____

f. Who are/were your heroes and role models?

_____

_____

_____

_____

g. If you have/had a problem or something you are/were excited about, with whom do/did you share it?

_____

_____

_____

_____

h. What family responsibilities do/did you have?

_____

_____

_____

_____

_____

_____

i.) On the average, how much time each day do/did you spend with your family?
What do/did you do together?

_____

_____

_____

_____

_____

_____

j.) What are/were the greatest pressures on your generation?

_____

_____

_____

_____

_____

_____

2. Discuss as a group if possible.

    a.) How are the experiences of being a teen "then" different from being a teen "now?"

        _____

        _____

        _____

        _____

        _____

        _____

    b.) How are they similar?

        _____

        _____

FINISH THE SENTENCES: A concept of sentence completion from Nathaniel Brandon

Choose Parent

What I resented the most about you was:

_____

_____

What I wanted you to change the most was:

_____

_____

_____

_____

What I loved the most about you was

_____

_____

_____

(Answer both questions whether you are male or female)

Being male in my house meant

_____

_____

_____

_____

Being female in my house meant

_____

This exercise may increase your own awareness of your experience as a child. As we age, we may begin to see their good intentions behind parental negative behaviors. Sometimes, it is possible to re-frame a resentment into an appreciation.

CHANGING DEMANDS TO PREFERENCES

1. What pushes my buttons? (Makes me really angry)?

I really get angry when someone

_____

_____

_____

_____

_____

2. What am I emotionally demanding from them? He/She must:

_____

_____

_____

If they do not do this, I feel I am

_____

_____

_____

_____

RESTATE:

I prefer that he/she

_____

_____

_____

But, if they do not do this, I am still

_____

_____

Examples of Demands and Preferences

1. I really get angry when someone assumes what I feel
2. I am demanding that they listen and hear and understand me
3. If they do not do this, I feel ignored and misunderstood and unimportant.

Restate

➢ I prefer that you hear me and understand
➢ But, if you do not or cannot, I am still important

THE 'I QUIT ' LETTER

This is a popular handout. Most people laugh when asked if there is some annoying person in their life that they have tried to change.

Obviously, this is a stretch far wider than about the person with an addiction.

An Example: Dear

_____

For years, I have wanted you to stop smoking pot.

I HAVE

_____

Hidden it, flushed it, yelled at you, not spoken to you, controlled your finances, not given you messages from your friends, (searched your belongings/room), called you names, ignored what you want;' thrown out your smoking pipe, refused to let you in the house, been rude to your friends, kicked you out, nagged you and lectured and threatened.

I want you to know that I am no longer trying to get you to change. This is not done in anger, but in acceptance.

Love, _____

THE I-QUIT FORM:

Dear_____

For Years I have wanted you to

_____

_____

_____

_____

_____

I have

_____

_____

_____

_____

_____

_____

_____

_____

_____

_____

I want you to know that I am no longer going to try to get you to change.

This is not done in anger, but in acceptance.

Love_____

_____

This letter is not sent as an attempt to manipulate. You must really be ready to quit all the efforts to change the person. It is useless to be angry any longer. They will change the behavior, or not. What might occur, however, is a shift in the usual dance.

Some people with addictions have said that it was very frightening when the yelling and anger turned into detached responses. There was a sense that something was changing in the system. The predictable back and forth was no more. The dance we do with addiction becomes the routine eventually. They do this, and we do that repeat and repeat. It creates some discomfort when we change the dance step we are doing. One man said that he had never been so afraid as the night he came home drunk, and his wife was cheerful, and there was not one angry word from her lips—she simply kissed his cheek and went to bed. She had come from an Al-anon meeting. He soon went to treatment. He could sense the seismic shift.

What is the benefit, however, is that you can live your day with more focus on your plans with less anger in your system? If anger were effective, there would be not one single addict in this country. Think about that.

Another Exercise About Control and Powerlessness (Step One)

This is more fun in small group discussion and sharing, but also worth thinking about on your own.

Ask:

What does it mean to you to be personally powerless? When have you felt that way?

Where do you feel this in your body? How does it affect your self-image?

I ask you to stand in front of a wall. Place your palms flat on the wall and then move it back at least 8 inches.

OR

Ask one person to lie flat on the floor. You lie next to them or you can stand. Your task is to get the

flat out person to stand up. As the effort and volume of attempts increases, there is clarity that the person flat on the floor will simply not budge UNLESS THEY WANT TO. What is interesting to see, however, is how exhausted the motivator has become.

The point is to feel your powerlessness. Learning just what we can do that is effective and what we cannot becomes a valuable lesson.

Ask:

➢ What messages did you get from your family about being in control? What messages did you get from church, school, the culture and what does it mean to you?

> How have your attempts to 'help' or control the addicted person affected areas of your life? (health, relationships, work, feelings about yourself).

GUILT VS. RESENTMENTS???

There is not a form for this question, but I ask you to think about which you prefer.

Here is the dilemma: If I do something unclear to me about whether to proceed or not–ask this:

Do I say YES and then feel RESENTMENT OR do I say NO and then feel GUILT? WHICH IS PREFERABLE??

The choice is limited-resentments or guilt.

My own truth is that resentments tend to linger and hang on for years, and guilt is much easier to banish from my mind. Guilt seems more available for resolution. Resentments have such a long shelf-life. So-do I bail you out or not? Do I let you use me or not? Do I agree to lie for you or not? Etc. Etc. Etc.

It becomes easier and easier to not participate in whatever problem the addicted person needs to deal with. Remember, there are two kinds of business: Mine and Not Mine. It is also possible to say NO with kindness and firmness. If you do not know what to do, ask if your effort is toward recovery or not. Do nothing that is not in the interest or direction and possibility of recover.

One mother in group has learned to say No to her daughter's request for money but offers her a ride to the local food bank. She has stated that it feels so free to remain loving and not part of the problem.

"I MESSAGES"

This is a simple guide to help restate our feelings without using harsh and angry and blaming tones and language.

"I" MESSAGES

I FEEL

_____

WHEN

_____
_____

BECAUSE

_____

I NEED YOU TO

_____

Be specific   EXAMPLE

➢ Describe behavior or situation·., not person
➢ Describe how you feel

"I feel safe and worried when you come in late because I wonder if you are safe."

A LIST OF WORDS ABOUT OURSELVES

Fourth Step of the 12-Steps refers to our inventory. I also call them: **I**nteresting **P**ieces of **I**nformation **A**bout **M**yself.

Self-Pitying		Unselfish, thoughtful of Others	
Resentful	_____	Not holding grudges	_____
Critical	_____	Charitable	_____
Suspicious	_____	Trusting	_____
Angry	_____	Patient	_____
Tense, Apprehensive	_____	Relaxed	_____
Emotionally Uncontrolled	_____	Calm	_____
Withdrawn	_____	Outgoing	_____
Jealous	_____	Living in Attitude	_____
Fearful	_____	Confident	_____
Selfish. Self-Indulgent	_____	Generous and Loving	_____
Domineering	_____	Yielding	_____
Self-Righteous	_____	Uncritical	_____
Stubborn	_____	Agreeable	_____
Intolerant	_____	Forgiving	_____

259

Dishonest with self		Truthful
Depressed, gloomy	_____	Optimistic, Cheerful	_____
Smug, Narrow-Minded	_____	Open-Minded, Generous	_____
Feeling Superior	_____	Humble	_____
Expecting Too Much Too Soon	_____	Realistic	_____
Hypersensitive	_____	Willing to Admit Faults	_____
Despondent	_____	Hopeful	_____
Sullen (Silent Treatment)	_____	Having Sense of Humor	_____
Apprehensive of The Future	_____	Living 24 Hours A Day	_____
Procrastinating	_____	Being Prompt	_____
Aimless and Indifferent	_____	Finding a Purpose	_____
Worrisome, Over-Anxious	_____	Serene	_____
Ungrateful	_____	Thankful for All Blessings	_____
Prone to Gossip	_____	Practicing Confidence of Others	_____
Obsessed with Own Problems	_____	Helpful to Others	_____

260

The list of 30 negative and positive traits has been used in AA and Al-Anon groups for a long time.

THE BOOGEYMEN EXERCISE

This concept was a part of the work that Sondra Smalley pursued in her lifetime exploration of co-dependency and intimacy. She looked at how we tend to distance ourselves from others with the defenses we use. It is true that we first need to see something if we are to change it, followed by talking about it, followed by doing it. Not always easy. There is a saying that, "If you want to keep your eye on the devil, you invite him to the pow-wow." This exercise is one that helps us walk around the Boogey Men and keep an eye on them and know them better.

(It is so easy to know and keep an eye on the faults of others and not so easy to see our own). I do prefer to call all of our traits INTERESTING PIECES OF INFORMATION about myself, rather than BAD or GOOD things.

> ➢ All of us have plenty of both. We need a realistic view of ourselves that we are not all sinner or all-saint.

> ➢ We can get stuck and know that we need to change something but have no clue as to how. It takes some courage to change some things and may also be painful.

> ➢ These Boogey Men may be how I act, feel or reside in some belief I hold.

> ➢ What we need to invite to the pow-wow are those pieces of information about myself that stand in the way of emotional honesty and closer relationships with others.

Take a moment to work with the list of 60 traits. Notice that they are seen as Interesting Pieces of Information about yourself. The positive traits probably enhance your relationships, so we do not do anything to change them-except pat yourself on the back. It is the harmful pieces that we need to address.

It is a Step One exercise because of the feeling we have of powerlessness over them. They seem automatic and even unconscious. Nonetheless- all prevent closeness.

As a personal note, I remember the very day that I pulled the car into the driveway and had a fleeting moment of perception about what my husband probably found greeting his arrival. Anger.
It had become chronic. I did the usual thing and quickly ignored that piece of information about myself. Nothing changed. In time, however, my anger became seen as a defense of hurt that needed to see the light of emotional honesty.

What follows is a worksheet about what blocks closeness in a relationship. Again, does your defense system destroy your support system? There are five columns. (The I FEEL column has a before and after answer.)

1. Column One: List of characteristics you have that are deterrents to closeness. (BEHAVIORS, FEELINGS, BELIEFS). List the things you DO to 'push people away and keep your distance' These are your defense systems. The Boogey Men.
2. Column Two: This is a divided column-the first half is what you are FEELING before you do what is in column one. Then add how you FELT both immediately or later on.
3. This third column is what OTHERS might FEEL when you do what you do in column one.
4. This fourth column is what others might DO in reaction to you. For example:
   a) I DO: GET ANGRY

b) I FEEL: HURT
c) THEN I FEEL: REGRETFUL SORRY GUILTY
d) OTHERS FEEL: ANGRY, CONFUSED, SHUT DOWN, FEAR
e) OTHERS DO: SHUT DOWN, AVOID ME, LIE TO ME.

Say to yourself that change is possible.

Dare to scare yourself and look a bit awkward doing the opposite of what you usually do. Try to be emotionally honest from the start. The first part of Column Two is honesty.

It gets easier!

Does your defense system destroy your support system?

Blocks to closeness in Relationships
Goal: Change
Method: See - Say - Do

Ask: How will this boogey man interfere with my recovery?

I DO	I FEEL	OTHERS FEEL	OTHERS DO

ANOTHER EXERCISE TO KNOW EACHOTHER BETTER

This is a group or solitary exercise, or for two people. Just finish the sentences.

Right now, I am feeling

_____

One of the things I wish you knew about me is

_____

It is hard for me to admit

_____

One of the ways I try to control you is

_____

One of the things I had to do to survive was

_____

One of the things I am angry about
is_____

I love it when
you_____

1 feel cared about when
you_____

If I were willing to reach out to people,
I_____

My greatest fear
is_____

What I like most about you
is_____

What I need from you
is_____

Secretly,
I_____

_____

I am beginning to
realize_____

TRAITS: YOU DECIDE WHICH YOU ARE MOST LIKE

Yet another exercise to think about. Interesting in a group and fun for self-awareness. Try to identify what lies behind your choice. Example: I am a daisy; resilient and usually cheerful.

A ROSE_____ OR A DAISY

SUMMER--------------------------------- OR WINTER

A HAMMER------------------------------ OR A NAIL

A SCREEN PORCH----------------------OR PICTURE WINDOW

BREAKFAST------------------------------OR DINNER

A TELEPHONE POLE-------------------OR A TREE

SUEDE--------------------------------------OR PATENT LEATHER.

A TRUMPET------------------------------OR VIOLIN

A CLOTHESLINE------------------------ OR CLOTHES POLE

WOOL BLANKET-------------------------OR SILK SCARF

CORVETTE -------------------------------OR MINIVAN

CIRCLES EXERCISE

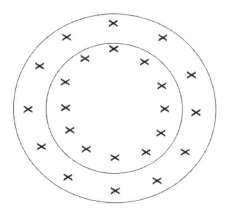

First in the center: Family and Friends

Second in the center: People with addictions

Third in the center: Anyone who had an addicted parent

A GROUP EXERCISE CALLED 'CIRCLES'

This is very powerful- to participate in or even to observe. It is a listening exercise. Ask yourself if you listen to learn or to argue? There is an inner and outer circle of chairs and participants. They take turns talking or listening. The inner circle does the talking, and the outer circle is directed to simply listen and absorb what is being shared by the inner circle. There is no cross-talk, no debating, no arguing, no correcting, no side remarks. Just listening and absorbing. The therapist asks questions and the inner circle shares whatever they want in response. They talk to each other as the outer circle remains quiet.

Communication has broken down prior to entrance to treatment and been mostly toxic and unsatisfactory. The Circles will be a new experience as the participants become increasingly open and honest. It feels like a safe place where support and caring are present. You begin to see yourself in the other. The therapist determines the questions and decides when to move on to the next sharing.

It is preferable that family members comprise the first inner circle. People with addictions comprise the second inner circle. The third inner circle is comprised of anyone in the room who was raised by addicted parents. This third circle group, of course, seats family members and people with addictions together.

Reading this book has hardly the same impact as being there in person, but I feel that seeing some of the questions asked has value. You can at least answer these questions for yourself.

Questions Asked of the Family Circle:

> ➤ How has this been for you to love someone with an addiction?
> ➤ What is your biggest resentment?
> ➤ What are you most worried about in recovery and hope will never happen? (Do not use 'fear of relapse').
> ➤ What will you do differently from now on? What do you need from the person with an addiction in your life?
> ➤ What three things do you need to change to make it easier for others to live with you?

Questions Asked of the People with Addictions:

> ➤ No one can do this, but can you try to help others understand just what it is like to be addicted?

- How do you respond when someone asks you 'why don't you just quit?'?
- What is your biggest resentment?
- What are you most worried about in recovery and hope will not happen? (Do not use Relapse).
- What do you need from your family member?
- What does your family need from you to help their recovery?

Questions asked of COAs (Children of People With Addictions)

- What was it like for you as a child?
- Is there anything true for you both then and now?
- Do you ever feel responsible in some way for the drinking? What survival skill did you learn as a child that you still use?

What strengths did you build in the midst of that adversity?

Everyone is then reminded never to discuss any part of what was said if it is not in a kind and accepting exchange. Nothing said is to be debated. This exercise is simply designed to help us know each other better.

Chapter 17: Odds 'n Ends and Unrelated Random Thoughts

Are We All Chasing the 'FIX'?

The person with the addiction is surely and eventually seen as chasing their fix. This is in reference to their drug or drugs of choice. As their enslavement to the addiction increases, so does the effort to satisfy the need. All else seems to fall away in importance. Once the 'fix' is satisfied, whether short or long term, there is a sense of relief. This is temporary but all that matters. Soon the insatiable need to once more find the 'fix' is in action and the cycle is repeated endlessly in desperate attempts to feel the relief once more. Over and over and over.

It occurred to me in the family group that this is very similar to the repetitive cycle of the need to 'fix' the addicted person or to 'fix' their dilemmas that friends and family experience. There are degrees of this, of course, but there seems to be an endless list of ideas by the family to try to control the choices and outcomes for the addicted person. The group members agreed that this cycle was true for them.

Think about this. We think of 'just one more' idea or attempt or rescue and the plan begins to consume our minds. We execute or present the plan and then we have the feeling of relief and the calming hope that 'this might work'. When it does not, the cycle restarts and our minds begin to think of the next "fix' for the problem. It builds and builds and can even eclipse our own authentic life. It is a cycle of ever-increasing entrapment we cannot control. We keep on trying and looking for that relief that comes with success. Our Home Remedies cannot succeed—learn what are the most effective attitudes and behaviors in the face of addiction.

Women or Men Who Keep Returning to the Same Abusive Relationship

We all have undesirable traits and behaviors that make us hard to live with (or at least annoying). The trick is to be able to see someone with all of their 'faults' and decide what you can accept and what is unacceptable to you.

Many women and some men keep returning to the same unhappiness hoping it will be 'better this time.' The feeling is 'I love them.' Do you know you can love someone and still leave? Think of an apple. Now think of the back side of that apple. Is it black, mushy, rotten, foul? Why is it that we only see the red part when we go for that apple? The fact is: You get the whole thing. Front and back. Eventually, one may need to forgive the person they chose to hurt them.

Speaking of Forgiveness:

When someone asks for your forgiveness, it is really what they need for themselves. Their expression of remorse is about them. It does nothing to heal the hurt of the other. The giver of the hurt never asks what you were feeling at the time or presently. What if they asked what they can do to ease your pain? When someone understands and acknowledges the feelings you had due to their behavior it can be a healing moment. This would be a good piece of knowledge for you if you were the giver of pain. Forgiveness from the other is more likely if it is not about what you need from them.

Expectations are Pre-Arranged Resentments

It is wiser if we can see others for who and what they are rather than what we need them to be. We set ourselves up for resentments every time we put an expectation on something. It is said that if we remove our expectations from someone, we are then free to receive their gifts!

A major expectation of many families is that when the person with an addiction enters recovery, they will simply return to 'how they were before addiction. Not necessarily. Try to not shackle them with what you think they should be doing or thinking. One mother wanted to know if she could now expect her daughter to keep her room neater. Maybe. Maybe not. Recovery is not an automatic growth or maturity or personality change. But, being drug-free does make those things possible.

Remember the woman who hoped her long time husband would begin to communicate. She had such expectations for his sobriety! Well, he remained silent as he had always been since their dating days. But being sober and in meetings held the hope that he might someday learn to share more. Hope is not the same as expectation.

Loving Detachment

This is what Al-anon helps us achieve. We could stop taking all of this personally, and as a reflection of ourselves, we just might be less angry. We also are in charge of how much we let others use us.

When you finally deeply understand that detachment is not abandonment or lack of caring, you are finally able to operate in the relationship with the person with addiction with much softer feelings. I can surely feel loving toward you while I learn to keep my boundaries and say NO and take care of myself.

Why must we so often resort to anger? Anger is useless to the situation and becomes part of the dance of addiction. When you detach, you can see more clearly. The person with an addiction has a disease, and it behooves you to realize that in other diseases, you would seldom fall into anger. The behaviors of addiction are what elicit anger from us, but the core disease is easy to feel compassion for. Why are we constantly surprised and angry when a person with addiction acts just like an addict?

I love you-not your addiction.

The addiction is the giver of hurt. The brain is damaged, the emotions are running amok, the coping is non-existent, and their fear abounds. The addicted person is slipping into an abyss– desperate, ill, drunk, and dialing. We, of course, being the rational beings we are, decide to take all of these slings and arrows personally. Can we not rise above our reactions to the abuse and simply see that this is a disease of destruction? Our learning to not take this personally will at least not make things worse by reacting in anger. Try sadness. Wear Teflon, not Velcro on your heart. Practice loving detachment by setting strong boundaries for yourself while holding onto a loving feeling for the person that Chucky is holding hostage.

As the parent or spouse of an adult person with an addiction at home, here is a gentler way to ask the person with an addiction to no longer live there. One wife (with small children at home) was sad that her husband relapsed after treatment. She said to him, "I am sorry that the family disease has joined us again. It is such a painful and hurtful thing for our family. Only you can manage it. I think it would be better for this household and our children if you took the disease away from our home and dealt with it. We love you and know you can do this, and I await the day you can return home." It is important to be able to separate the disease from the person and not to take it personally. It is important to protect your home environment and set your boundaries with love and clarity and certainty. This is a reality-based view of relapse.

Thoughts About Generational Transmission

We know that the genetic predisposition to become addicted is a biological fact. Becoming a person with an addiction is also influenced by social and psychological factors. What is also of interest in the study of families, is the prevalence of behaviors, feelings, and attitudes that tend to cascade down thru generations. Ask yourself what you saw your parents or grandparents do if they dealt with addiction. Were they angry? Were they caretakers? Were they over-achievers? Were they collectors of things?

There is a myriad of traits that have been noted in families with addiction present. Much is written about this. Learned and role-modeled behaviors are powerful. Ann Smith wrote 'Grandchildren of Alcoholics" and identified many similar generational behaviors. Claudia Black's recently published "UNSPOKEN LEGACY' is an exhaustive study of the generational transmission of the effects of stress and trauma that some children of addicts experience. My point is this: Not only does the person with addiction need help to stop drug use, but so does the family need some increased awareness of their roles in the situation. Some people with addictions well into recovery also attend Al-anon and begin to address 'all the other stuff.'

In many family programs there is a Sculpture performed by clients themselves. It is an impromptu play that physically demonstrates the emotional relationships and dynamics in a family with addiction. The Sculpture is a powerful tool to help people become aware of a multitude of feelings and situations and stressors from their childhood. There are family roles and 'jobs' and it is uncanny how this unrehearsed demonstration runs so true.

My most memorable sculpture was performed with members of the fire department. Six volunteered to play mom, dad, and the four kids. They were so familiar with the roles, the demonstration proceeded without much direction from me. So much has been so true for so many, a script was not necessary.

Some Frequently Asked Questions

"What do I do with all the beer cans at home?" (or any other drugs that were hidden here and there?)

I think of the movie "When a Man Loves a Woman" and remember how their little girl threw all her mother's liquor bottles in the trash can. We could all relate to her anger and hurt and the temporary relief she might have felt. It is a respectful idea to discuss this with the person in treatment before they head home (or while in an outpatient setting). It is too controlling to purge the house and other "hidey-holes" without conversation with the person with an addiction. It is infantilizing to rush ahead assuming that this task is yours. What you CAN do is present your concerns and ask if the person with the addiction if they wish for you to do this. Communicate. Ask if they would like your help or would prefer to do it themselves. It is often an impactful experience when a person with an addiction tends to the task themselves and often in the supportive company of a veteran recovering person with an addiction. Some may prefer that you take the lead, but it is time— unless asked—to stop functioning for someone else. Begin to think "we" and start inclusion again for both to participate in the many new feelings and behaviors of recovery.

It is time to stop our control and protective tendencies and time for the person with an addiction to realize they can ask for what they need on their journey to self-esteem and self-respect.

"Should I stop drinking too? I do not have a problem

It is a very supportive idea also to pledge to abstain from all mood and mind-altering chemicals. Think of eating a large piece of chocolate cake in front of a friend who is struggling to avoid sweets. There needs to be at least one safe place in this world at the end of the day for the person with an addiction. When they pull into the driveway or open the house door, the environment needs not to contain their worst enemy. Many have spoken of the relief they felt when they grazed in the refrigerator and did not bump into a can of beer. Recovery includes being on guard against the unguarded moments. Home needs to feel safe.

Very often, family members may be surprised to realize just how important their drinking was to them. One does not feel this until it stops. Maybe a person realizes that it makes no difference to them and maybe they begin to feel what a big part of the relationship it was. Family members want the person with an addiction to stop using-so why not everyone? It is quite a transition when a household or relationship enters abstinence. There are social changes, relationship changes, daily routine changes. All these changes are more easily escorted when you all use the 12-Step programs as a holding-tank for yourselves while the river turns. Others understand and will help. Two more thoughts on all of this: Sometimes, a person with an addiction will feel guilty about the idea of asking a spouse to abstain. This is a reflection of their low self-esteem. On the other hand, some people with addictions have been known to encourage their spouse NOT to abstain. This may have more than one motive, but it is also like having a drink vicariously. What is for certain is that a person with addiction must always be on guard for the unguarded moment.

What should I do when he/she comes home? And, why do I need to go to those meetings?

It is so revealing that anyone would wonder what they should DO when the person with addiction comes home. We have become so accustomed to 'doing' and not just 'being.' My answer to this: I do not know. Read a book, make soup, wash the car, take a walk, go to a movie, watch TV, call a friend, shop, go fishing, whatever.

Probably the hardest challenge will be just to be yourself. You do not need to walk on eggshells. You do not need to keep an eye on the person with an addiction. You do not need to ask a million questions.

People with addictions are equally nervous about homecoming. Some of best advice I ever heard came from a therapist who just advised everyone to put duct tape over their mouth for several weeks while they attended many 12-Step meetings. The tape could be removed only when they wanted to say something nice to each other, then it was replaced. I keep a roll of golden duct tape in my props and offer it to family members as a reminder that Silence Is Golden in those tempting moments. Some keep it by their phone.

There is so much ahead. Trust will not come home for several weeks (even if everyone becomes trustworthy!). The meetings are where we begin to heal. We all need to reach out to others in those beginning weeks. You cannot resolve so much with each other. There are too many wounds, too much still raw, too much unresolved, and too fragile. That is why I encourage you to use the meetings as a holding tank until you can begin to feel a bit better. In time, you can begin to help each other and come to terms with the past. What the person with an addiction needs is for the family to get their support, understand the language of recovery and get educated about addiction and its facts. What the family needs are for the person with an addiction to follow their recovery program, communicate with them like a responsible person. What everyone needs is to have some fun together.

How can friends help?

Friends can love us, but they can often not have the benefit of in-depth knowledge about addiction and family issues. The best and most loving action a friend can take is to attend those meetings with you so that they can have a knowing ear. Anyone can also attend what is called an OPEN MEETING. This is for AA and NA. Al-anon is always open to anyone. These open meetings often have a guest speaker, and you will learn much.

Can I learn to drink less?

My many years of employment in the field of addiction can work both for and against the credibility of my response. Am I prejudiced or convinced? Programs have appeared that promote moderate drinking for problem drinkers. Great. The difficulty is to separate heavy use from those who drink at a disease level. There are some heavy social drinkers who actually drink more than some alcoholics. The key seems to lie in the loss of choice that alcoholism creates. All very confusing and sometimes with disastrous consequences if the distinction is missed.

USA once ran a tragic item regarding the founder of Moderation Management (An alternative to AA). Sadly, she was drunk and involved in vehicular homicide. Her lawyer stated she is now in AA and faces both her guilt and prison. It is my observation that if you have to think about control of something, it is a potential problem. I never think of controlling my broccoli intake. So, imagine the energy and time and money spent in the quest to learn to control ones drinking with these management programs. That is still allowing alcohol to be of major importance in your life. This is playing with fire. Why not place that energy into the consideration and pursuit of life with a clear head and heart? What is so triumphant about a life focus of controlled sedation? I am not talking about taking a drink. I am talking about drinking to the point that you have to manage it.

Someone remarked that if you drink and feel suddenly more whole, you should probably never drink again. If you drink and it is not a big deal, you are probably good to go. And you probably will not jump up and down with the news. I should add that a responsible "management program" would refer into treatment those clients they assess as alcoholic. My beef is that this idea of controlled drinking continues to be yet another distraction from the necessity of facing the reality that people who are harmfully involved with alcohol need to cut it out. The delusion that "I am not hurting anyone" lives on. The truth is that you are.

I recall a television program a few years ago in which a living room interview was being conducted with a man in the controlled drinking program. His 8-year-old daughter was present and remains in my memory. Both father and reporter ignored her. His face reflected fear and at one point she interjected that she wanted her father to quit. No one noticed.

Over the years, I have heard a lot of creative efforts to manage the consumption of alcohol. The field of treatment has taken a beating lately with invasions from without and convulsions within. There remains, however, one constant. Members of AA sadly watch, feel grateful and know what works for them!

Chapter 18: E-mails from a Mom

She only attended the family and friends group a few times, but later said that she got what she wanted from the meetings: The permission to take actions that were more effective in the situation of her addicted son. As she later said, "You will know when it is time. I needed to learn to ask for help."

As a background to this journey for the son (I will call him Mark) and parents, his pot-smoking began in the 8th grade. Right from the beginning, Mark started stealing money to buy the pot. This drug use graduated to pills that he and his friends would steal from their parents. Parents tried different punishments and therapy. Mark would respond for 6-8 weeks and then be 'caught' again. In the 10th grade, Mark and friends were arrested for stealing from neighbors unlocked cars. Parents then sent Mark to Teen Challenge in Pennsylvania for a year. He came home in good shape and entered high school. Mark was trouble-free until his first college semester when he was arrested for possession of acid. Friends provided the bail and Mark swore it had been a one-time event. When he came home for Spring break, it was obvious that he was using something. Parents found a syringe in his room. Upon confrontation, Mark admitted to using pills (opioids, Valium) and had tried heroine "once or twice." Mother and Step-father decided to send Mark for more rehab in Maryland with the idea that he would then live with his father on discharge. Mother felt he had been sober for 5 years until current relapse, but she was told that he had continued using marijuana. The relapse back to opioids occurred when he stole a bottle of Percocet from his landlord. When he could no longer afford the Percocet, Mark began heroine. His mother states that despite residential treatments, Mark never did take any action in a recovery program and she now hopes he will center his life around staying sober.

What follows are the emails I received from the mother over a period. There are gaps of time and a few phone calls as part of the picture of this journey, but the emails tell quite a tale. It is an all-too-familiar story for many parents.

February 1

It's all so awful. I was in a hotel with him on Sunday and Monday while he detoxed because there were no beds available at places that took his insurance. My daughter took him to the ER on Saturday where they did an EKG, drew blood, gave him anti-anxiety medication and told him to go to rehab. The rehab counselor supposedly set him up for Monday said they were full now but will call you sometime this week.

His step-mom and I called multiple places and finally were able to get his insurance to give us approved providers outside of Maryland. They did not even want to speak with us because the insurance is in his name and he is 25! Step-mom called the place he is in now in PA and confirmed that they accepted his insurance and had a bed.

I drove him there yesterday, and he went willingly. He is so sick, he probably would have agreed to anything. It seems like a good place. They were very professional. Well, today I get a call that insurance is denying payment and they need a credit card for self-pay status until it can be appealed! Supposedly he does not 'meet criteria' whatever the hell that means! It all feels like a scam to me. Shouldn't they have figured out whether he met criteria before admitting him? The cost is ten thousand as self-pay. No wonder so many people die from this disease. Getting help is incredibly hard. At this point we're stuck, and I think they know that. So, my only option is to start over with finding a place, drive to PA, yank him out and bring him someplace else?!! I really do not think that is an option. Please pray that I can find the wisdom to know what to do. I know Al-Anon would say that this is his problem, but he was so sick there is no way he could think clearly and rationally enough to navigate any of this. I was sober as a stone, and it is still screwed up! If you have any suggestions, please let me know.

February 2

I did call two other treatment centers, but his dad and my husband have decided to split the cost and keep him where he is. They both feel it is best for him to be out of the Baltimore area where he was buying his drugs. I am too exhausted to deal with it anymore, so I am calling this 'God's' will and surrendering to it! Thanks for checking with me.

February 13

So, Mark walked out of rehab on Saturday. He left with no id, money, ride, etc. as I have his wallet. He somehow made it back to Maryland and got into his apartment where his stuff had been packed up by his ex-fiancé. We found out today that he had been going to his dad's house as well. They were missing the money and started checking doors and windows and sure enough found a garage window unlocked. He then stole his dad's truck today. They called the police, and they caught him in Baltimore with heroin in his possession. He was arrested but, because he has no record, it is expected that he will be released with a court date in 60 days. I feel like I am in the middle of a bad dream. What, if anything, do I do?

February 15

I ended up going to Maryland yesterday. My goal was to return his wallet (so at least he would have an ID if he ended up in a hospital or dead), and to find him a place to stay near NA. meetings for a week. I was able to say things I needed to say and whether he listened or not does not matter. I know it may well be the last day we ever spend together. More than likely he will keep using and die/go to jail. I needed to tell him I loved him, see his eyes one more time clear and blue (he seemed sober and had not used since rehab-I do not believe anything he says), hug him and then walk away.

If God graces him with the miracle of sobriety, I will forever be grateful. If he doesn't, I know I can live my life believing that I have done everything possible to help him and I will have the memory of yesterday where we had a few glimpses of the mom and son we used to be before drugs ruined him.

Thank you for being there for all of us suffering from this disease.

His mom also added later that she had stated that she could no longer be a part of his addiction in spite of her love for him. She requested that he not contact her himself, but she would speak to his sponsor for any message or update. She was setting her own boundaries with loving detachment.

March 9

I wanted some advice on the latest saga with Mark. I have stuck to my guns and have not been in contact, but both my daughter and his step-mother have reached out to him. It seems he is having psychiatric issues. Extreme paranoia—thinks people are after him, called the police at 1 am to report drones that were spying on him, blocking doors with furniture so no one can get to him. So, what now? He clearly needs intervention but what?

March 10

Mark's Dad was finally able to convince him to get an appointment with his psychiatrist. He was with her for 2 hours. She deemed him a possible threat to himself or others and had him taken by police to the hospital to be committed. I think Maryland has a three-day hold but hopefully, in that time his mind will clear, and he will agree to a longer stay. She thinks he is bipolar, and drugs have exacerbated the problem. I am so glad he is safe for a few days.

March 14

After Mark was committed Friday for 72 hours due to extreme paranoia, he signed himself out against medical advice after the hold was up. As you can see, he is no better. He thinks there is someone in the tree spying on him. I feel so completely helpless as to what to do to help him. Without a power of attorney, there is no legal recourse.

May 9

So, Mark showed up in court today. The Judge ordered him to xxxxxxxx rehab for 6 weeks as a part of his probation. When she asked him what he thought of that, he said, "I would rather look for a place out of state. That place does not have a very good reputation". My jaw dropped!! He is a homeless, jobless person with an addiction and wants to dictate where he is going to get help. She told him 'too bad' and ordered him to go there before noon. When we left the court, he asked to be taken to his car, that he would get himself to the treatment facility. His dad had the car at his place and said he could have it on the condition he went to *the DMV and take his father's name off the title. Mark had paid for the car, but his father had co-signed the loan. Mark must have had a key on him because he walked in the front door of DMV and then out the back and took the car. I checked the center console of my car where I kept $40 in emergency inside a compact, and it was gone. There is now a warrant out for his arrest. Un-flipping-believable. He is just so sick. Thank you for prayers. I am at peace with whatever happens knowing it is all in God's hands. As his earthly parents, we have done all we could.*

The parents then had him arrested, and Mark later was grateful for this, knowing his own parents had put him in jail and that he had nowhere else to go. No job, home, money, and no more rescues.

Mark went to rehab for 28 days and then moved into a sober home (halfway house), attends an out-patient program and has a sponsor. As of this writing, He is still there.

No date on the email

After completing rehab and being in the sober house for 30 days, Mark had to appear before the judge for the charge of breaking probation by fleeing that day. It was the judge's last day on the bench before retirement. She cried after how much better he looked and after hearing his apology. She told him about the countless stories she had heard over the years where the outcome was so much worse. We were all in tears by the time she finished speaking.

August 1

Good morning. I am back from the family wedding (Mark was there). Mark is 90 days sober now and looks and acts like his old self. It is amazing what the body can take. Three months ago, he looked like he was close to death. I took him to an NA meeting on Saturday morning at his request. He talks about his sponsor in the program and how he is putting sobriety first before anything else. I know to attribute his progress to God, to just take each day as it comes, but it is hard as his mom not to get my hopes up that maybe he can change enough to live recovery forever.

Email in September

We joined him at the Ocracoke Jamboree. He heard about it from his sponsor. Apparently, there is a recovery meeting every September on the island, and people come from all over for it. It was special because we took him fishing and crabbing there when he was little. He went to the meetings, we rode bikes and walked on the beach, lots of honest conversation about life, addiction, and God. We got locked out of our unit one evening, and no one was in the office. I called the emergency number, and a lady answered who had obviously been drinking. I told her our dilemma, and she said in her southern drawl, "honey, go on in the office, and you will see a wooden cabinet on the wall. It looks locked, but it's not. Just get your key and close the door back shut." When I opened it, there were keys for every room in the band but thank God we weren't thieves. (My comment—the office manager needs those meetings, too?).

October 18

Mark relapsed and now in long term treatment facility. Parents remain respectful of his continued journey.

Email in December

After we returned Mark had made his amends to my husband. He was 5 when we got married, and Mark's biological Dad had moved to Maryland. So, (step-father) was the father figure that Mark grew up with. He took him to baseball, scouts, basketball, etc. not to mention he was the one who picked him up from the police station when he got in trouble at age 15!

Anyway, I was not there for the amends, but they spoke for a long time, and I could tell there were tears. When my husband came to bed, was emotional, mostly because he thought Mark was really sincere about staying sober. Mark had apologized to him for never accepting him as his Dad, even though he was the true male role model he had in his life. He apologized for stealing from him—not most material things, but his peace. He thanked him for taking such good care of him all these years. He listened as he was told how Mark's disease had affected him personally. My husband slept like a baby that night.

Email in February

Mark was still in the sober house, and the family traveled to help recognize his ninth month of recovery. Mark continues to work his recovery program.

As an added note:

There was a time when I got a call from his mom about a dilemma she was struggling with. Mark had $7000 of his own money and was requesting that his parents release it to him. It was with fear and resignation that his parents recognized that Mark was an adult–they knew he would soon spend it on, drugs, but they decided to let go of control and release it to him. I felt it was a wise decision and perhaps money well wasted. If they had refused, Mark would have added another focus for anger and blame onto parents. Was it not wiser to kiss the money goodbye and let it be clear about who was out of control?? Who do you blame if you are the arranger of your bad outcomes? Of course, the money was soon gone, and it was shortly after that Mark entered the process of recovery.

My thanks to this Warrior Mom for sharing the emails. It gives great hope.

Chapter 19: A Word About Drugs and Some Current Trends

There are two things I want to recommend prior to this chapter. Please watch Pleasure Unwoven which is a DVD by Dr. Kevin McCauley and, online, watch the MOUSE PARTY cartoon by University of Utah.

This has been the most difficult chapter to write. One reason is that the scene is constantly evolving with new drugs and new types of treatment for addictions. The second reason for my hesitation is that family members have usually researched the drugs they are concerned about. The third hesitation of mine was the fact that family and friends much prefer to focus on the addict and what they are doing as opposed to any realization or focus on their own issues. The addict is the squeaky wheel. It is enough to know that all of the addictive drugs alter and disturb the brain circuitry.

Dr. Nora Valkow is the Director of the National Institute on Drug Abuse (NIDA). She has done brain research using PET scans for several years. In a recent blog, she states: "As a young scientist in the 1980's, I used then – new imaging technologies to look at the brains of people with drug addiction and, for comparison, people without drug problems. As we began to track and document these unique pictures of the brain, my colleagues and I realized that these images provided the first evidence in humans that there were changes in the brains of addicted individuals that could explain the compulsive nature of their drug taking. The changes were so stark that in some cases it was even possible to identify which people suffered from addiction just from looking at their brain images."

It is strongly felt today that addiction is what is referred to as a biopsychosocial disease. This means that factors such as your environment and mental state are also in play as well as the genetic predisposition. It is also highly treatable. NIDA states that 174 people a day die from overdoses. I wonder how many others die daily from the devastating effects of drugs on their bodies. Like alcohol and cirrhosis, esophageal varices, car accidents, suicide, heart attacks, etc.

What is true for all mind and mood altering illicit drugs, and some legally prescribed, is that they eventually can eclipse the person you love. The loved one and how you knew them to be slowly fades away with an altered mind, confusing behavior, and into a world unknown. We become sucked into the situation with little information or support or guidance. Ironically, an informed circle of family and friends is the most loving and effective environment for an active or recovering person.

There have been several cycles of drug epidemics over the decades. Due to the current and dreadful opiate crisis I feel it necessary to make a few comments for families. The most important fact is that if you are in a relationship with a Heroin user, it is imperative that you keep NARCAN (Naloxone) nearby. This is an antagonist which blocks the effects of opiate use and is easily administered. You can find a brief and clear demonstration of its use on training videos on the internet. This emergency drug is used by first responders and has saved many lives. If you find someone in an overdose condition, this Narcan is to be given nasally and immediately. An overdose can be detected if you find a non-responsive person with labored or shallow breathing or pinpoint pupils. Give the Narcan before you call 911. Some states have programs that provide training and free Narcan. Call your pharmacy or fire or police department to find locations to acquire some. The current trend is to not require a prescription.

A Few Facts
- ➢ Opiates can very quickly lead to addiction.
- ➢ The Dept. of Health and Human Services stated, "Over 76,000 died in 2018 from Opioid overdose.
- ➢ Not all overdoses are fatal.
  - o Many users have experienced several overdoses. The sad thing is that, following their rescue and revival, not many are linked to an aftercare support system.
- ➢ 56% of overdoses occur at home.
- ➢ As necessary as it is, there is some thought that Narcan may encourage some addicted people to increase their amount of opiate use to 'get a better high' now that they feel the security of a Narcan rescue.
- ➢ After the revival from Narcan use, withdrawal symptoms last from 48-72 hours to 7-10 days. This is followed by a longer term of opioid cravings.
- ➢ 85 % of Heroin users began with opiate prescription drugs found in Americas medicine cabinets.
- ➢ Drugs seem deadlier these days.
  - o Fentanyl, a dangerous synthetic opioid at least 50 times stronger than Heroin, is shipped from Mexico and China in small packages that are hard to detect by the USPS. It is mixed with Heroin and other drugs and is responsible for a vast majority of the overdoses. Carfentanil is even more potent.
- ➢ Only 12% of people with addictions in the United States

receive treatment.

➤ The crisis is now seen equally severe in rural and urban communities.

➤ Emergency rooms, morgues and child welfare programs are overflowing

➤ There is an increase in Hepatitis B and C and HIV/AIDS.

What are the Waves of this Perfect Storm

It seems to be a tsunami and we have missed the warnings. Until now. Several factors rode in on this wave.

➤ A lack of education about the dangers of opiate usage.

➤ 85% of Heroin use began with use of prescribed opiate medicines. Heroin was less expensive than prescribed drugs.

➤ Well-meaning doctors over prescribed opiates. A few have taken advantage Pain for Profit.

➤ One hundred million Americans claim chronic pain and doctors feel obligated to meet their request for pain alleviation.

➤ There has been difficulty in disposing of 'leftover' pills harmlessly. Pills remained in medicine cabinets

   o After a surgery I had, the hospital ordered 100 Oxycontin. I used one and came home with the leftover and unwanted 99. They were a challenge to dispose of safely and why did the facility order so many? It would have made more sense to order 5 or so, but I think it was a matter of profit for the facility. I did call the director about this.

➤ Pharmaceutical companies began to hire representatives to visit doctors' offices to promote the use of opiates and teaching that they were safe for long term usage. Long term usage is accepted in cases of cancer and other severe, intractable pain situations.

➤ The belief that opiates were the best for pain relief.

➢ The advent of manufactured Fentanyl and other synthetics and their addition to cocaine, methamphetamine, benzodiazapines and marijuana.

Current Trends and Events that Give Hope

As it is said, "It is not hopeless, but not easily solved."

➢ Increased funding and implementation of drug treatment in the jail and prison systems.

➢ Various states are implementing/expanding programs for prevention, education, support and treatment. There are large government grants available.

➢ Education is increasing for first responders, coaches, parents, the public, politicians, doctors. pharmacists, teachers

➢ The Center for Disease Control has issued National Guidelines for Opiate Prescriptions

➢ Several research projects are in process to find a non-opiate drug for pain relief and non-medical modalities to decrease pain.

➢ Drug company representatives in the United States can no longer visit doctors' offices to over promote opiate usage

➢ The DEA is monitoring opiate prescriptions

➢ There is increased attention and effort to get ally support to stop the stream of drugs from entering the United States.

➢ Drug deactivation kits are available in pharmacies and medicine drop-off location are available. Ask your local police/fire department.

➢ Television and media have offered many shows about the opiate crisis.

➢ More awareness of the need for affordable and high-quality treatment of adequate intensity and duration. This is needed for all addicted people.

There is a resultant and primary concern–doctors are frustrated with the regulations and patients and doctors are faced with the dilemma of dealing with legitimate and severe pain in chronic situations. In the case of post-surgery, the opiate usage needs to be short term and monitored.

Anyone can become addicted but not all are what we would classify as addict. Addiction is compulsive drug seeking and using despite negative consequences. Dependence is not the same as addiction. There are many stories about people who were prescribed opiates and never really wanted to take them. They will remark about the relief of being 'off the drugs' and will experience a few days of withdrawal discomfort. A person with a different brain reaction will find many reasons to want to continue using in their increasing dependency until it crosses a line into addiction. There is yet not clear understanding of what makes this difference, but the genetic predisposition plays a strong role.

The Drugs Used in the Treatment of Opiate Addiction
There are drugs used in treatment that:

> ➤ REDUCE the cravings and compulsion to use: Methadone, Buprenorpine, Suboxone, and Vivitrol. The concern of many is that their use often seems to be started without any discussion of treatment options. They can be misused and require a detoxification if eventually no longer wanted. Most addicts would prefer a drug free life. Stable recovery is possible. The program for physicians, which is substantial and not based on maintenance drug therapy, is highly effective. There are many arguments to their use. My own view is that they are second best. The person on them is only as stable as the assurance of their next dose, but maybe it is an improvement to be "better, but not fully well." And, of course, alive.

The above thoughts also reflect the experience and belief of Dawn Farm and other abstinence-preferred treatments. Expansion on these thoughts may be found in Addiction and Recovery news Position on Buprenorphine Maintenance, written by Jason Schwartz.

- ➢ BLOCK the re -uptake of opiates and block the effects of the drug: NARCAN
- ➢ EASE the withdrawal agony:
  - o A new drug, Lucemyra, has been approved by the FDA to reduce the furies of withdrawal. It is not an opioid. Its availability might encourage an addict to enter treatment or recovery if the agony of withdrawal could be alleviated.
- ➢ TREAT any underlying issues: For example
  - o Because the drug use has reduced Dopamine production in the brain (which is the neurotransmitter that produces pleasure) it is common to feel depressed in early recovery. This is an example of the temporary need for an anti-depressant to bridge the gap while the brain re balances and begins to wake up to Dopamine production again.

As I write this about opiate addiction, I keep thinking of the three most recent members of my group of parents. All three have adult children who are heavily into alcohol and marijuana and there is a long history of grief for everyone. Because of the popularity of alcohol, and now marijuana, there seems to be less shock and outrage from the public than we are seeing from the opiate crisis. The tragedies of their use are less dramatic and take longer, but the outcomes are no less worthy of weeping.

The Treatment of Addictions

We've come a long way, and we are not there yet. William White has researched and shares in his blog about the history. See blog@williamwhitepapers.com. Recovery support began in the 1800's. It was not pretty. Asylums and private institutions and 'home cures' led to a loss in cultural faith that recovery was ever possible. Next came Prohibition and criminalization and drunk tanks in jail, and large city wards in psychiatric asylums and 'drying out 'sanitariums for the rich. A.A. started in the 30's and there was hope again. New treatment methods appeared with in and out-patient programs and methadone maintenance clinics. The use of Heroin in our Vietnam vets created a tipping point in the 70's. Federal funding in 70-72 allowed for insurance coverage and public education led by recovering people. Rapid growth of addiction treatment grew to a current $35 billion-dollar industry. However, this rapid growth did not mean that quality of treatment kept pace. The focus was not on patient outcomes and wellness.

The 80's and 90's brought more criminalization as a moral failing rather than a medical disease. Restrictive insurance coverage and an aggressive system of managed care led to many closures of facilities and much shorter lengths of treatment. Since 2000, the opioid epidemic has influenced a shift in the treatment scene. Legislative and regulatory responses now require insurance coverage on a par with other medical conditions. White states, "There has been slow progress to integrate addiction treatment with mainstream healthcare and mandate modern best practices. Instead, addiction treatment is still largely delivered with diverse philosophies and methods stemming from its beginnings as a 'folk healing art'.

I know this to be true. Families in my group of parents have expressed constant frustration at their inability to find affordable facilities, frustrated with the inability to find quality care, frustration at the often promised days of treatment being drastically reduced by insurances once their child is in treatment, frustrated by a frequent lack of inclusion in the treatment process, frustrated by the difficulty in connecting with any therapists or having their calls returned, frustrated by lack of a link to substantial after care, frustrated by complete lack of any family education offered. It should not be so hard to find good help. In all fairness, some in the group have experienced excellent care for themselves and their son or daughter. All of these have been at high-end facilities. One set of parents spent $100,000 over an 8-month period. Others have a child in methadone treatment. Some have an incarcerated child. Some have an adult child still in residence. Some have no contact at all. Some have a child in a residential setting. Some are grateful for their child's recovery. Some have a son currently in treatment. All have hope.

The treatment field itself has some relatively new approaches. They describe themselves as being scientifically based, such as researched and evidence based, and have a focused on what they call a softer and kinder approach than the older traditional ones which they identify as "too harsh, confrontational, punitive, and/or shaming." I have read all of the books on this and do not agree with their assessment of the older way. Al-Anon calls it 'loving detachment,' Interventions are held in a loving sense, and the Tough Love that they allude to is mostly tough on families. I am certain that there are situations and individuals who have not been professional or "loving" at the moment, but the general approach has always been with high regard toward the vulnerable person with the addiction and it has never been the philosophy of the past approaches to be unkind.

I do like the newer thoughts that view the entire family as the client. The newer books, although still mostly focused on the addicted person, give examples of how to speak in a less angry and shaming way. For example, it is better to say, "I love to be with you when you are sober," than, "I hate being around you when you are drinking." This makes sense to me and, as always, my wishes are for the needs that families have on how to better communicate. This is hard to do when you are angry. There are family courses you can take to help you learn to put your anger aside and be positive in all your communication. This is when my roll of Golden Duct Tape comes in handy. Apply over mouth, chill out, and rephrase.

I see this as useful and effective and easily learned by those who attend any 12-Step family meeting. What I do not like are the inferences that what has worked for so long is no longer useful or effective. Surely, much needs to be improved in our treatment systems. At least there is more attention these days to that fact. There are layers of concern. However, you will often hear that almost any program will work if the person truly wants to be clean and sober. It pains me when I hear that a newly drug free person went to their first meeting and "it did not work for them." Of course not. You need to commit to 90 meetings in 90 days for any of it to make sense. The whole experience is new and uncomfortable until it becomes not only comfortable, but eagerly awaited.

William White, in his latest excerpt from Recovery Rising, presents a compelling view of how recovery evolves and can become a melding of early AA attendance and later discoveries through more holistic experiences. The early AA focus is on the fact that "self" is the problem (such as self-centered, selfish, self-absorbed, self-pity, etc.) and needs to be surrendered. Self-sacrifice and service to others is the program. Other pathways to recovery emphasize the positive value of self in the recovery process.

➤ Self-knowledge

- self-esteem
- self-confidence
- self-sufficiency
- self-discipline
- self-respect

White proposes this question: Does this person need to get into themselves or get out of themselves. Or do they need both at various points in their recovery? I think: Yes.

Many hundreds of people seem to age-out or simply decide to quit using. Many hundreds find some other way to focus their lives and find a path to recovery for themselves. Many are happy to simply stop using drugs. Others become interested in the fuller life that recovery can offer. What remains almost universal, however, is how little information and education and support the families find for themselves. Time is a healer, of course, but there is also the joy of coming to terms with the past in a deeper way.

There are two treatment programs that I would like to discuss with you. (No—I am not endorsing or benefitting in any way. I just have always admired them.) Both encourage the goal of drug free and abstinence living.

Dawn Farm, founded in 1973, is an actual pig farm in Michigan. The founder, Jim Balmer, and the current Director, Jason Schwartz, have been frequently quoted in this book. Both have worked with Ernie Kurtz and William White who are also quoted. Their philosophy stated, "We need to create a milieu of opportunity, choice and hope." That, in a nutshell, is how the Farm has evolved. Jason refers to a 'front door and a back door' which alludes to the full spectrum of help offered. Initial treatment and then an amazing aftercare. There is not acute medical detox offered, so the cost is managed. Clients must detox elsewhere and then transfer. After the initial few weeks, the client is in a system that encourages connections and opportunities for growth. The 12-Step programs are a vital part, of course, but the amazing situation is that they are heavily involved in a local community with an array of services and programs and support for long term recovery. School, employment, recreation, and housing are available. The community is called The Healing Forest. Random drug testing, immediate addressing of any relapse with an increase in treatment. Accountability reigns. Many of the residents and graduates are employed by the city and going to work is almost like going to a meeting with good friends daily. Even the city has healing attitudes about addiction and addicts.

William White tells this story: "A tree was in poor soil with no moisture, sun or nutrients. It was almost gone. But someone came along and picked it from that spot and replanted it in a tree nursery. Water and sun and kindness and care. It revived and was again ready to leave the nursery. Where should it go? What would become of it if it returned to its original soil?"

How often is that what happens when the addicted person 'graduates' from treatment? From detox on, there is no such thing as a neutral decision. A person needs to choose to continually plant themselves in the healthy soil where hope and support and monitoring and love abide. Someone once said that change for the addicted person is easy—you just need to change everything!

The Physicians Health Program (PHP) is the second program that seems to have the key to success. It is a 5-year program and is referred to as the Gold Standard of treatment. I realize that this is not available to all but medical personnel, but the factors and guidelines of this program need to be incorporated in all programs. It requires:

> ➢ abstinence

- ➢ frequent drug testing
- ➢ swift response to relapses
- ➢ 12-Step attendance
- ➢ completion of a treatment program
- ➢ inclusion of family

By the way, attendance at meetings is NOT the same as participation. The elements of hope and strong community support cannot be overemphasized.

Sharing the thoughts of William White once more, it is true that we must have hope for recovery. Usually, we only hear of the tragic and sad tales of addiction. Do you know there are millions of recovering people living happy lives? We do not hear their stories, so it is no wonder there is an attitude of no hope. NOT TRUE. Not true at all. It is a disease and the recovery is to be proud of and shared whatever diverse range of recovery method was successful.

Chapter 20: The Blogs

The following are blogs by the author previously available on a hospital blog site. They are reprinted here with permission. They contain mini versions of some thoughts found in *I Love You But Not Your Addiction*.

#1 We Need to Quit Taking it Personally that which is Personally Happening to Us

I suggest that everyone who loves and addict start carrying around a Q-tip in purse or pocket. This is to remind you that you need to **Q**uit **T**aking **I**t **P**ersonally.

Of course, it feels personal. The truth, however, is that none of the behaviors or actions or words or disappointments or unloving moments in the relationship with the addict are a reflection of you or your worth as a person. Addiction of someone else is not about you. Never has been, is not, and never will be. This is true regardless of the nature of the relationship. You are off the hook!

Whether you are a child, a spouse, a sibling, a friend, or a parent, you need to be clear in the knowledge that you are not the problem and did not cause the problem. It is only when we think that we are and then we try to help that we run the risk of the becoming a part of the problem. Later on, that is called enabling. Surely, we annoy others and hurt them and fail the and are less than perfect in our humanness. This is still not the reason that addiction develops. The addict sees chemicals as a solution and has little thought or knowledge that their solution shall become a problem.

Addiction has a life of its own.

I guess this is the good/bad news for families and friends. Because it if has nothing to do with us, then we also face the reality that there is nothing we can change that will fix the addict. We must then face our feelings of powerlessness and pain.

#2 When I Knew Better I Could Do Better

So, who knew?? Not many people have home or school preparation for how to live more effectively with an addict. It should be worth at least 100 credits. If you are the child of an alcoholic, you learned how to survive, nut not necessarily how to cope. As an adult, we need coping skills.

People always advise that one should take care of themselves. Sounds good, but what does it mean? In my years as a therapist with hospital-based family programs, there was a simple picture that people seemed to grasp. I drew a boxing ring and in it was a stick figure of the addict doing a wild dance with their addiction. Arms and legs flailing about. The other stick figure in the ring was the family member standing next to the addict doing all the well-meaning behaviors. Helping, rescuing, lecturing, saving, protecting and etc. Actually, all the family member got for their effort were several bruises as the arms and legs of the addict continued to swing about. Also, the anger grew and grew.

I then erased the family stick figure and simply placed it just outside of one of the ropes of the ring. Protection. Not abandonment, but a safe place from which to observe the ongoing dance of the addict. The rope symbolized all of the ways of taking care of yourself. They included educating yourself about addiction, attending your won support group (Alanon or Naranon) no longer taking it all personally, setting boundaries for yourself, returning to your own authentic life and the things that you have postponed doing, learning to be responsive and reactive, tending to healthier living.

You would be amazed what changing your perspective can lead to. And, as a bonus, when you finally see that the addict continues

303

the wild dance, you can really see how it is not about you.

#3 You Do not Need to Go to Every Argument You are Invited To

There is a great difference between reacting and responding. Someone once said (not sure who) that maturity is marked by the lack of reactivity. It means that you have stopped allowing others to pull your strings. You actually put the old brain in gear and think awhile before you answer.

This is a valuable thing to master in life. And imperative if you are struggling with someone who uses chemicals (alcohol is a chemical) to excess.

It is well known in recovery circles that the addict will create an argument as a 'set-up' to reach for the bottle. Creating distance is necessary for the addict, who prefers isolation and being in the company of other addicts. So, be careful that you do not take the bait. You feel better about yourself and retain personal power.

Many a spouse has been left behind, feeling that they said something wrong that upset the addict. Then, in their guilt, the whole system deepens as they try to make it all better by walking on eggshells. Please. You are not in a relationship any longer, but now in case management.

Please remember that these addict behaviors are common and as much a part of the disease as a cough is to a cold. The addict's brain is again trying to protect it from the reality of what a mess they are in. It is an unconscious defense mechanism.

One Alanon presenter once suggested that there are some neutral responses to a coming argument: Oh, Oohh, or Ooohhhh! She had the audience practice saying them.

#4 Is Your Own Self-Growth Abandoned in Favor of Waiting for Others to Change?

It is so common to become eclipsed by someone else's problems, and as addiction begins to take the relationship hostage, one easily begins to put their energy into trying to "fix" that other person. I remember a man who said he had purchased a bout for their entertainment, nut was afraid to take his wife out on the water for fear she might get drunk and fall overboard. When asked, he realized that he had not been on that boat for 6 years!

How common it is to postpone the dreams and plans in life waiting for the addict to stop using. Like, where did I go??

Ask yourself: What will I do if nothing ever changes?

The sad reality is that none of your sacrifices will change another person. Another example I have heard so many times is the wife quitting work because the addict complains that her being gone creates his need to drink. So, she then finds herself at home simply watching him drinking and nothing changes. Except her loss of a source of self-esteem and security.

#5 My Life Cannot be What You Have Figured Out!

Years ago, the man in my life and I came home from the video store with two choices. I had picked Jungle Book and he chose a John Wayne movie. Once home, I was going on and on about how all adults need to see Jungle Book with all of its great life lessons. He listened patiently from the chair as he held his Joh W. video. After I had exhausted by list of arguments, he simply looked at me and uttered the pondering for today.

Of course, we watched John Wayne.

This man had 30 years in AA and learned to keep it simple. And I have quoted his great line many times. It seems to make it all so clear.

#6 The Choice is Always Yours (Aldous Huxley)

There are so many dilemmas and questions and choices if you are in a relationship with someone who is addicted. There are not too many "rights" or "wrongs". The situations are all so different, even though they are so alike. It is like having a cat up a tree. We all know what that must be like, but there are different cats and different trees.

It occurred to me one day that I really was between two unpleasant choices for myself. If I said, "TES" to the person, I would feel resentment. If I said, "NO," to the person, I would feel guilt. (I used to even feel guilty about feeling guilty!)

Over the years and multiple opportunities to make such a decision, the choice of feeling guilt took priority over the choice of feeling resentment. The fact is that I got much better at shedding guilt rather rapidly and not so hot at letting go of resentments. So, No it was and Guilt it was. It felt like being kind to myself and, amazingly, the world still turns.

#7 Sometimes, The Only Thing You Can Do "To" an Alcoholic is the Only Thing That Will Help

The Ad Council once ran this as an ad. It surely recognized that the responses we need to follow in a relationship with an addict to seem, at times, cruel, unloving and harsh. It does indeed feel like a punishment or an angry decision. However, it is possible to say, "No," lovingly. That is the ultimate destination for a family member, and this attitude is learned in attendance at Alanon or Naranon. Family meetings are available in 157 countries). It is important to match our attitude to the facts. The fact is that none of our home remedy efforts to help the addict are effective if they are efforts to fix yet another mess made by the addict's use.

To refuse to be a part of the problem is, at first, very hard on the family or friend. We are delusional, however, if we feel that one more bail out of any kind is helpful. It is only a Band-aid on a gaping wound.

We will later explore the process of interventions, which is highly effective. Even this great tool feels as if we are doing something TO the alcoholic. That is, until everyone realizes that it is the most loving form of Tough Love. Tough on us and the addict.

#8 My Life is Crumbling Into Place

While facilitating a family and friends group at a hospital, there were several memorable moments. One of my favorites was a spouse group where 12 wives of 12 patients (sounds like On My Way to St. Ives) were exploring the weeks issues. The door opened and in flew a last arrival, exclaiming, "I am so happy today. I think my life is crumbling into place." We all knew exactly what she meant.

Like a jumbled puzzle where none of the pieces make sense, when you finally get an education about addiction and truly understand that it has nothing to do with you and when you finally begin to emotionally extract yourself from the chaos, it does begin to clear the picture. It does feel like the implosion of all your prior perspectives and conclusions and what rises from the dust is reality and a grip on yourself. All of which, ironically, is also the best thing ever to happen to the addict. The pieces begin to make sense.

We have been reactive, and our way of thinking had become our way of being. Now, at last, there is the freedom of responding and only then do thinking and acting become congruent. Whew!

#9 It Seems That I Just Keep Slamming Into My Limitations
We all have 'em. But what I want to talk about today is a limitation that I have observed mostly in men. Actually, men are socialized to "fix" things. Do we not give little boys a tool belt as a gift? Did we not ask Dad to fix the bicycle? Or toaster? (And I know that many women, at this point, are feeling a protest coming on)

However, we frequently look to a male to be a fixer. Thank heaven that so many of them are up to the tasks.

But it is a reality that you cannot fix an addict whether child o spouse or parent or sibling or friend. Here is where it gets rough for men because they have often agreed with me that their failure to "fix" the most important people in their lives has led them straight to feelings of anger because it creates feelings of inadequacy in them. And this anger is so detrimental to their health and relationships. It feels like a measure of their worth as a person.

The truth is that they need to know that it is not humanly possible to fix someone who does not wish it. It is a hard lesson in powerlessness and sadness. It is this sadness that they need to allow. It is hurtful, but far less damaging than anger. They then need to get support and education about addiction to discover what behaviors and actions just might have an effect on the addict's choices.

#10 I Cannot Save You From Your Darkness, But I Shall Not Close You Out of my Heart

This is a line from *The Ya Ya Sisterhood*. The oldest and responsible daughter of that Southern family with the charming and brutal alcoholic mother came to this realization after she returned home as an adult. She was attending a family reunion after many years away and she saw that not much had changed in the family dynamics. She had always tried to cheer up her father, stop her mother from drinking or being upset, rescue her siblings. It did not work. She had left home angry and bitter. As she returned North to her adult life, the thought for today was also her thought on the road. It is a bittersweet reality. On one hand, it is grievous to know you really cannot change someone else and, on the other hand, it is a great relief.

So often, we use anger to separate us from what upsets us. How profound that she was able to see that she could still funny act loving with her family. She realized that allowing the soft feeling toward others does not mean you are going to jump into the ring with them. It is the great lesson of Alanon and they call it Loving Detachment. Detachment does not mean abandonment.

#11 The Relationship Remains the Same But the Fellowship is Broken

This is not as confusing as it seems if you understand that once a person becomes addicted, they are really just not available to you. And, this can mean any addiction of any type. To the computer, to sex, to shopping, to busyness, to eating, to working, to volunteerism, to any excessive preoccupation.

The relationships remain, as in parent to child, spouse to spouse, child to parent, friend to friend, sibling to sibling. However, the connections are broken. Many, if not all, of the "used to's" are evaporated. The addiction slowly eclipses the ways we connect to others. I remember missing my son's great sense of humor when he was preoccupied with marijuana.

We have an initial vague sense of loss and cannot identify it. We make excuses. We try to make it OK and try to fix it, whatever "it" maybe. We settle for reduced contact. Even if the addict is sitting next to you, their focus is elsewhere. You can tell. Their addiction becomes increasingly the only game in town, and we do not have an invitation.

#12 If I am What I Do and Then I Don't, I'm Not

This little profound statement takes some explaining. It is often the feeling of lostness and emptiness that family members have once the addict reaches treatment, begins to change and the people in the relationship start a needed new way of relating to each other. In the case of the family member being a spouse, it may have involved some heavy-duty caretaking and controlling of the addict and this role, no longer desired in recover, sometimes leaves the spouse feeling unemployed or pink-slipped. The addict is struggling for self-reliance and confidence and the spouse needs support in no longer being the addict's answer to life. It can feel depressing and disorienting to the spouse who has wished for a partner, but now struggles with words and feelings on just how to not be the once with all the answers.

In the case of parents and an adult child in recovery, the same feelings occur. Just how do you come to grips that your parent days are over, even though you remain the parent?

Just how do you develop an adult to adult relationship with your child? Most mothers especially dislike this true statement" Mothers are not for leaning on, they are to make learning unnecessary. Ouch! My response to this daily pondering is that we are not roles, we are individuals. Roles change but relating as individuals is part of the richness of recovery for everyone.

13 Do You Chose to Become Less in Pain or More?

A friend of mine once said, "Nothing seems to be getting better except me!" And this is the wonderous feeling one can acquire if one chooses to do the hard work of turning lemons into lemonade. It is said that the only real disability in life is a bad attitude.

Loss and pain enter every life eventually, and in a myriad of forms. It is the choice of whether we want to have had a sad life, or a happy life with sadness in it. Maslow said, "Make growth choices, not fear choices." One question I ask myself is whether I would prefer to be better or bitter.

Pain is a great alarm clock. It can wake us up to the need to come to terms with whatever the pain is about. Alanon has always been a great help in this journey and helps one give perspective to life. We can stay attached to the pain or let go and risk that we shall not perish. The pain in my life has always led me to a path that offers growth and a whole new turn in the road. So, move on!

#14 Letting Go and Letting God is Not a Passport to Inertia

There is such wisdom in the Serenity of Prayer, which is recited at every 12 Step Meeting.

"God grant me the serenity to accept the things I cannot change, the courage to change the things I can and the wisdom to know the difference."

It is the final phrase that is the challenge. It is also said that God does not drive a parked car. We need to follow a dual path knowing full well that we do not control the outcome of others, but also knowing that there are some more effective attitudes and behaviors and actions that we might try when attempting to encourage or motivate the active addict toward wanting help.

It is imperative that we reach out to professionals, 12 Step literature, 12 Step family meetings, or the wealth of literature now available on the subject. We need to stop our reactions and start responding from a base of knowledge and facts.

A common uninformed family behavior is to react over and over. Why do we keep on repeating actions that have never worked?

As an Alanon member once said, "The addict is on drugs and we need to be on Alanon."

#15 Verities and Balderdash

Verities:

Chemical Dependency is Not:

> ➤ A Mental Illness
> ➤ A Bad Habit
> ➤ A Moral Weakness
> ➤ A Sign of Bad Character
> ➤ A result of Life's Pressures
> ➤ A Temporary Loss of Control

Balderdash:

> ➤ To Think That Any of the Above is True!

How many hours and years family members mull over all of the reasons they think that the addict they love is using alcohol and other drugs. We think reason after excuse after explanation.

The fact is that chemical dependency is its own entity. It has a lie of its own.

There is an old saying that the man takes a drink, the drink takes the drink and then the drink takes the man.

The first time the drug is used may well be just a social decision. It may be used in the hope that it will enhance an already fun time. The altered state of mind and feelings may also be sought as a solution to a problem. The then solution eventually becomes another problem.

The fact is that there are many people with a mental illness or life pressure or moral weaknesses who do not alter their minds with alcohol or other drugs.

It is important that family members learn to understand that addiction clouds and confuses the picture. Like cream in coffee.

For example, alcohol is a depressant. Many alcoholics are surprised to find that when they stop ingesting a depressant, they stop being depressed.

The first thing that needs to stop is the chemical use. It is only then that a clear picture can emerge of other issues that need to be addressed, if any.

#16 Feeling Whoa, Whoa, Whoa

With all due respect to what has been called the worst song ever written from 1975, I want to talk about these pesky little things that seem to pop up forever for family and friends of an active addict.

It was once researched (do not ask me when or by whom) that if a person was using chemicals during an event, such as alcohol, that the passage of time will obliterate any feeling memory of that event. Not so for the drug free family member who will register the even in their brain with all of the myriad of feelings that came with the happening.

The drug free brain will then hang on to the feeling memory until the end of time.

So, what's the problem?? It is found in the recovery. The addict may remember, however vaguely, the things that occurred, but not the feelings that registered at the time. Remember, that the addict is sedated, anesthetized, and numbed. For the other, however, the feelings will accompany the memory and reappear in full force— even years later.

That is a major difference in the recovery takes of both people.

In Al-Anon, no learns to be on guard against the unguarded moments. You need these skills when, out of the blue, some old feeling grabs you and you are in a painful place again. It is not unusual for your phone to ring at 3 am and your heart races even though your addict has been in recovery for 8 years and is asleep next to you. It is not unusual for the sober addict to be detained on some errand, and you start to clock-watch with increasing old dreads. Those feelings are like flashbacks and have a powerful pull. In a recovery program, you learn to quickly recognize what is probably irrational and are able to calm yourself back to reality.

#17 From an AA Member

As Pat says, "The good news is that as we recover, we have feelings again and the bad news is that as we recover, we have feelings again."

#18 It is Not That You Lied to Me, it is That I can No Longer Trust You

It is important for those who care for an active addict to not take it personally when they are on the receiving end of a lie. We need to understand that as the disease progresses, there are several defense mechanisms that begin to be in play by the addict. Most of these are unconscious and common to addiction. It is the brain of the addict finding ways to protect itself from the reality of the shape it is in. If I can lie to myself about what is happening to me, I can surely lie to you.

Once a person has lied, there is a loss of credibility. Much of the pain of the family is the loss of trust as a deceit is uncovered. Family and friends expend a great deal of energy now testing trust. It feels so unloving and unkind to admit that you no longer trust that person. We lie to ourselves about that. All of which drags us down the rabbit hole.

If recovery begins, the addict wants our trust and we lie again, saying that we do trust. We do not want to be emotionally honest for fear it will upset the recover person.

Well, let me suggest a better way.

It is OK to be honest and nicely tell the truth. "No, I do not trust yet. I trust you, but I do not trust addiction. Let us not talk about trust again for a year. Let us instead just focus on what we both need to do in our recovery. I want to trust you and I love you."

It is important to think of recovery as a Podiatrist program. We need to watch the feet and not the mouth. Are your feet and their feet where they need to be? Hint: meetings and in healthy places.

#19 Do You Listen to Learn or to Argue?

We have various degrees of listening skills. Some of us keep our earflaps open with comfort and others of us shut them quickly. Maybe some of this response to the words of others started way back in that childhood of ours. Maybe some of us needed to shut our flaps quickly as kids. Others of us may have felt safe enough to keep the channel open. Learning to listen well can be learned or re-learned at any age. It takes practice. One starts by becoming aware of their listening skills.

Do you pull thoughts over your ears? Do you feel a need to defend, fix, distract, or react, or run away when someone is talking to you? How comfortable are you in just simply being a sponge and absorbing the person's information? There is no need to do more than dimply listen to them (which is not the same as hearing them) if you wish to be a safe person in the relationship.

Have you turned on a talk show on TV or radio lately? It can become a cacophony of noise with all the heads out-yelling each other and none learning a thing. Including the audience.

Think about it. If you are talking, you are not listening.

The world could use more listeners. It is a gift if you have someone to help "listen to me into clarity."

#20 Does Your Adjustment to Life Require Suffering?

In the 12 Step Program, one of the healthy concepts often referred to is that we should never let yesterday use up too much today.

If you had a childhood which was imprinted b someone's addiction, there was a great chance that it created some suffering for you. Of any or every kind. You may have been robbed of trust, respect, fun that was safe, connection and loving behaviors from parent. Actually, even if the addict was your sibling, there was suffering for you in that home.

So, we build defense systems and survival skills. One of these may have been the conclusion that it was not safe or wise to feel good, be happy, or have fun. As a child, it makes sense that to never expect these things would at least not lead to yet another disappointment. It is not uncommon for children of alcoholics to not trust feelings of well-being because the next parental drink or drug would plunge the household or picnic into another bad memory.

Neither is it uncommon for these children, now grown and into their own live, to recognize that they are uncomfortable with sanity, consistency and pleasure and to trust that it is OK to feel good. Actually, they can sabotage the good times only from an unconscious need to return to what feels familiar. (Many relapses are thought to be based on this truth)

It is OK to be OK. It is OK to feel OK. Childhood conclusions can be reassessed in the light of today's realities.

#21 Facts Do Not Cease to Exist Just Because They Are Ignored

Mental health is said to be a dedication to reality at all costs. Denial and delusion are really great defense tools to keep us out of pain. The problem is that we tend to stay in pain in order to avoid pain.

Truth hurts, but at least you can deal with it. Trying to not face reality is like punching away at a fog. There are so many times when one has only a fugitive moment of perception. Here and then gone. We need to go from being ignorant of being ignorant to being aware of being aware.

So, what am I talking about? I am remembering how I thought my husband had sinus trouble because he was always sick (alcohol will do that). I often called his work and made the excuses. I am remembering how I thought my son had a bad cold when his nose kept running... (cocaine will do that). I am remembering how I believed the mouth of addiction.

Denial can be wonderful as it offers a temporary soothing of the heart. It seems to me that there is the denial that follows knowing and the denial of truly not knowing. Both are only a detour to truth. It is also a fact that when you do not know you are hanging onto something, such as a delusion, it is awfully hard to let go.

I think that denial is the biggest use for families. It is one of the biggest contributors to not being truly helpful to the addict. I want to say, "wake up," and try to see things as they really are and not as you would have them be.

#22 A First-Class Human Being Has Some Regard for Human Frailty

This often hard for a family member to swallow: I sometimes have said that there is nothing harder than living with an unrecovered family member.

Actually, in the perfect world, family members and friends would receive attention and help and education about addiction about two years before the addict starts recovery. That is about the time needed to deal family resentment, anger, blame, hurt, and a myriad of losses. The timing is awful–an addict goes into treatment or recovery and others are expected to have nothing to resolve about what has been happening. Families are expected to be supportive and caring. Well, good luck.

I like the analogy of everyone having an open wound on their heart. It needs to heal and repair itself. It is best to not keep ripping off the scab which is what happens when we keep bringing up the past as a weapon, when we keep reminding each other of all the hurts and relationship failures, when we do not tend to our own recoveries. Often, the family member simply wants the addict to heal, but has no grasp on the fact that they themselves harbor so much unfinished business. What is common to hear is, "Well, it was not my problem, it was theirs." Yes, this is true. It is also true that you have been deeply wounded and are in need of some help to mend that heart.

The addict has to stay sober long enough to learn how to be sober. As hard as it may seem, the others in their life need to not pull the rug out with angry words. I did not say that you are not going to have anger. I also did not say that you are in way responsible to someone's relapse. I have often suggested that we all put a 6-inch piece of duct tape over our mouths for several months and only release it when we have kind and supportive words. Then, everyone go to their meetings, remove the tape, open your ears and mouth and speak. Back to the car—tape in pace again until the day comes when your heart truly feels loving and has a new perspective.

#23 Maturity is About Trying to Come to Grips With Your Flaws

I have also seen it stated that maturity is nothing more or less than how one deals with their feelings. Or perhaps it is to spend your life trying to outrun lesser versions of yourself–which sounds like not wanting to face your flaws. This is no better program than the 12-Step meetings to encourage one to look at their own inventory. I knew one man who put a mirror in his home that had two words written on it. At the top, it said, "The Problem." At the bottom. it said, "The Solution."

I can remember the first time that I had a fleeting glimpse at myself. Married to a man with unrelenting alcoholism, I was full of unrelenting criticisms. I had pulled into our driveway with no kids in the car and no distractions when suddenly I had a full blast of how it must feel to him to come to me. Well, I naturally slammed the lid on that nauseous revelation and continued to be the whiner. In those days, I really had a doctorate degree in sniveling, whining, nagging, and pouting. All these years later, I can have some compassion for that former self and realize what a waste of energy it all was. It is so common to see that cycle of inebriated person and angry other. Which comes first?

In a recovery program, you learn that the only person under your guidance is yourself. It is amazing how much better you feel once you face your own flaws and refuse to be a part of that cycle of the decline. It feels so good to really have some power over something once you catch on that the only outcome you can impact is your won. Like Alka-Seltzer says, "Oh, what a relief it is!"[27]

---

[27] **D. Gergen** www.governing.com

#24 If You Remove Your Expectations From Me, You Are Free to Receive My Gifts

I once read that, depending on your expectations, you can spend your whole life being pleasantly surprised or sadly disappointed. Wow.

How wise was one man in the recovery program, after a few years of attendance, to utter that he had just about given up on what to expect and just lived to see what would happen next. Wow.

Often our expectations of a situation or person are based on what we need to have happen or see. Reality is to see what we see and to know what we know. Do we see what we want to see and not what we need to see? Do we need an "illusionectomy"? Wow.

I think one of the hardest parts of life is to see reality. Denial and delusion abound. They are really useful for keeping fear and pain at arm's length. So, we keep expectations alive and complain often when the person or life falls short. Wow.

Truth may be painful, but at least you can deal with it. Wow.

The wise man above was quite peaceful internally. He had hopes, but not expectations. He knew that having the latter would set himself up for resentment and anger and disappointments. He also knew that we can become so blinded by what we expect, that we fail to see what is truly available to us.

One lady in my group had a cried for years and said she just wanted to be happy. Who knows where she got that concept. I suggested that life was not always happy. It was possible to have a happy life with some unhappiness in it. A light went on for her. She later said that, even with her husband drinking, she now felt content. She had expected more and was missing the moments. Wow.

If you want all of your birthday presents wrapped in green paper and all you get is that darned blue paper, are you letting expectations destroy your day?

#25 Because We Need to Change What We Do Does Not Mean the Situation is Our Fault

A lot of us are guilt based. We react strongly when someone suggests that we might need to take a peek at our part in a relationship or a situation. Over conscientious people are especially hard to convince because they have tried so hard and so long to be helpful and to fix things. The very suggestion that change is needed in ones actions, thinking, or attitudes, feels threatening.

It is so easy to identify the person who needs to change. The addict. Plain, pure, and simple. They need get clean and sober and tend to their recovery. The family member, however, often reacts like a deer in the headlight to the very suggestion that some change is needed by them.

It needs to be made clear that the need to learn and alter our behaviors does not at all imply guilt. It is very true that many addicts continue their use regardless of how enlightened the family has become. It is conversely true that many addicts choose recovery in the most ineffective of environments.

There is a process to change. The first step is to become aware of what might need change. They you need to digest the thought. Next, you prepare for it and then you try it. The final step is to maintain it. This process is greatly evident in very 12-Step meeting. You go, you wake up, you think about it, you try it, and then you like it, and you keep on. All of this takes time and support and the information and ideas you can get from others in your shoes.

You learn that we are responsible to each other but does not mean that you are my fault!!

#26 One Potato, Two Potato, Three Potato, Four

There is a thing called projection. We are all good at it. It is an unconscious trick of the mid. It usually keeps us more comfortable. If you are an addict, you are highly likely to use this trick frequently. If you are the family member, you re highly likely to be the target.

Think of the childhood game of Hot Potato. Projection is like that game. You can wrap up a feeling and toss it into the lap of someone else. There are other little tricks of the mind that also keep us from facing what we really feel. Denial, rationalization, minimizing, etc. But this projection thing seems to be an unknowing favorite for the addict. One fact that families need to accept is that while the severity of the addiction increases, so also do the defense mechanisms. Thinking changes as a protection from reality. It serves a purpose. It keeps a person from facing the full reality of the mess they are in. On a positive note, it might even keep a person from suicide.

But the family and friends need to be aware when the potato comes their way. During my days in the family program, a family member who arrived slate was often greeted in the lobby by a patient with some guilt inducing comment. "Why are you so late?" "You forgot to bring me clean socks," or, "Why didn't you call last night?" What the patient cannot express yet, for whatever reason, is all of the guilt they feel having to be in treatment, guilt for the behaviors, guilt that the family member is spending a day in a family program. So, the guilt is now on the visitor, who, more than likely, catches the potato and begins to explain about the lateness, the socks, or the phone call. Mission accomplished!

A bucket of lead is easier to carry if two people have the handle. But the patient needs to slowly get hones, get in touch and begin to own their feelings. Such is necessary for recovery. And, the family member needs to stop catching the potato. We do so over function!

We tend to catch guilt, fear, shame, hurt, inadequacy, loneliness, and a whole host of negative feelings that really are not being tossed our way.

It is not easy to be aware of every spud that comes your way, but one gets better it. In general, if you are feeling OK and suddenly find yourself explaining at length, you probably should get ready to make one large potato salad for lunch.

#27 Since the House is On Fire, Let Us Warm Ourselves [28]

The first time I read this, I laughed. I was not sure of just why it was funny, but something inside of me recognized the truth of it and knew it to be wise. It also struck a chord of "Oh, darn, what is it that life is now asking me to deal with?" I am tired of needing to cope with life's stressors. I am tired of needed to do more emotional work. I am tired of the need to change perceptions. How about good old status quo?! But the fires in life come uninvited and surely. They can be started by others or by ourselves, or just by spontaneous combustion.

As Huxley said, "The choice is always ours. The fire is not always our choice, but how we respond is. Attitude is everything. Eventually, we decide whether to escape, to let the fire consume us, or to turn the tables and use the heat to our advantage.

The Good/Bad news is that every lie eventually has pain, loss, and grief. We can choose whether or not to find the opportunities for growth and. Insight in each struggle. The expression: Older but wiser" comes to mind.

Some of the gifts of struggle and loss and the warming factors are:

> Acceptance of powerlessness over most people and events
> The awareness that I can change things about myself that may have been part of the kindling
> The growing knowledge of and reliance on God in my life
> The ability to listen better
> The willingness to love others even if I would not choose to have lunch with them
> The focus on all the joys and blessings that remain
> The trust that the fire will be contained in time

---

[28] Italian Proverb

#28 The Choice is Always Ours (Huxley) Or Not!!???

Out of the mouth of an Al-Anon member came this jewel of a thought. We were discussing the dilemma of whether and why anyone would stay in residence with an active addict. He said he had been thinking about this and felt that he had gone through three stages.

The first was the stage of being a **Victim**. This was when his wife was actively drinking, and he was actively living his work life and not really focused on the situation beyond feeling annoyed and challenged and reactive to all of the situations which called for his management skills in the family. He had not identified the real enemy within and simply had not awakened to the source of any problem. He really did not clearly see that there was a problem. He was like that frog in the ever-increasing pan of water being heated on the stove. He just kept swimming faster.

The second stage was that of **Hostage**. It was a slow awakening to the fact that the bottle in the back of the closet was not normal social drinking. In this stage, he sought some help. Coming out of denial and into reality was a slow and shocking journey. He noticed more and more and learned more and more and hurt more and more and tried to control more and more. He recognized that he was losing himself and seemed to be operating in lesser versions of himself. After much time, he finally got it. But he still felt trapped. It was a great relief to not be taking things personally any longer and it felt wonderful to have the support of others who understood. He still could not see his way clear to leave the situation. For good reason actually.

He faced the great question of "what will you do if nothing ever changes?" and found that he needed to find his answer. There were so many compelling reasons to not leave the marriage. Money, children, extended family, the comfort of habit, the power of vows once taken. Staying felt wrong. Leaving felt wrong. He was a hostage to the dilemma This man slowly worked through all of the barriers. He stopped blaming his wife for her choices and illness and relapses and behaviors. He stopped his complaints. He stopped reactivity to her and began to accept the fact that his choice to remain was his and his alone. He developed compassion for her struggles and decided that this circumstance in his life had afforded him growth and self-awareness. He now felt that he was in the third stage of leaving (or not).

He saw himself now as a VOLUNTEER in residence. And he clearly understood that his choice to remain was in the interest of fulfilling needs of his own. The household became more peaceful and the days more pleasant.

There is a story about being a bird in a cage. If you now have an open door to your cage, you can fly out or remain. It is the feeling of being trapped that is so debilitating. If you choose to remain, you can decorate your cage to the max. Then, the choice is truly yours.

#29 See—Say—Do

The process of change is only easy if it relates to changing your socks. The process of changing what I might need to change to improve myself is less obvious and often hidden to me. In the 12 Step program, it is referred to as Step 4. It asks for "a searching and fearless moral inventory of ourselves." It is a new focus. We have been really riveted to the inventory of someone else and that has been easy. An addicted person has much of which to be critical.

How many hours and conversations with friends involved hoping that the other person would change? Get sober? Get loving? Get helpful? Get home? Get up? Get with it?

It is both the good news and the bad when we finally realize that the only person we can change is standing in our shoes. And, we need to. This both exhausting and freeing to finally see the amazing truth that we can feel better when we tend to our own growth.

Well, there is a process to change. We cannot change what we do not SEE needs changing. That is when some light bulbs can turn on at a meeting as the person across the table triggers a truth in self with their own story. Or, you have a moment of clarity. I can remember the day when I pulled into our driveway and suddenly had a full, stunning awareness of how HE must feel coming to home to ME. Not a pretty sight. The next step to change is to actually hear yourself take ownership and verbalize what needs to change. There is something about sharing it and hearing your own mouth express it all that makes it irretrievable and, surprisingly, less awful. Somehow it all seems less powerful and more manageable.

The big step of DO. Can I replace judgement with perception? Can I replace reaction with response? Can I replace impatience with patience? Can I replace resentful with forgiving? Can I replace disagreeable with agreeable? Unkind with kind? Indifference with loving? Not easy, but doable.

Addiction can bring out the worst or the best in us. Why let someone else's disease make us less? I love this quote:

"Our goal is to have a relationship with both men and women that does not diminish the other and a relationship with others that does not diminish self."[29]

---

[29] Favor Church - Our goal is to have a relationship with ....
https://www.facebook.com/favor.church/posts/2015331048729118

#30 The Day Came When the Risk to Remain Tight in a Bud Was More Painful than the Risk it Took to Blossom[30]

There is so much loss and grief in life. It is so difficult to allow grief. It hurts. It paralyzes. It is like standing in bubble gum. Sometimes for months or years, even forever. We distract ourselves and find ways to avoid facing the losses. We fall unto anger or depression or spend our days and energies on bargaining a way the loss (trying to make it not have happened with all of our 'what if' thinking and blaming and avoidance).

Unresolved grief can be like a cancer that eats away at our progress and recovery. Someone once stated that the hallmark of a true adult was one who could see reality, accept responsibility for their own behaviors, and could do their grief work.

The following is a good visual analogy for grieving. It is a myth, but very helpful.

When lions go on a hunt, they pick the oldest and biggest of the pride to sit in the middle of the clearing as they wait for the prey to appear in the circle. This old guy has no teeth and no claws and no clear eyesight, but he can surely roar the loudest of all. So, they wait; the prey appears; the roar is enormous; the prey runs into the surrounding brush. Guess what's in the brush?? The real danger. The lionesses and younger males.

The moral of the story is simple: GO for the roar.

You need to cry and allow the feelings and, indeed, lean into them. There is no right way to do this. Just do it. The danger in the brush for us is all of the ways we distract ourselves from the pain allow it to fester and settle in and contaminate our health and emotional life. Crying is OK. Crying is healthy. Crying is cathartic. Crying

---

[30] Anais Nin

is what the body wants us to do. Wherever did we get the idea that it was not dignified? Or, manly?

This emotional honesty uncorks us for progress and growth and moving on. I always remember that blossoming requires water.

Chapter 21: The One-Liners

Over the years, many people have requested a list of the multitude of 'one-liners' that I have quoted in lectures on a myriad of topics in the family program. They seem like an easy way to remember some main ideas. Often a short sentence can capture what an entire book might be talking about. This list has resided on many refrigerators and in many drawers and some purses/wallets. The difficulty is in finding all the sources. When possible, credit is gladly given. When not possible, the credit is seldom originally mine, but the source remains a mystery. Some are deeply moving; some are practical, some are humorous, some are even debatable. Many are found in prior chapters and are worthy of repeating here. Reading a few at a time and marinating in them slowly is best. How do you eat an elephant? One bite at a time. Enjoy.

- ❖ We need to **Q**uit **T**aking **I**t **P**ersonally that which Is so personally happening to us. (Q-TIP).
- ❖ *Even when a need exists, and we are well qualified to meet it, we are not necessarily called to respond to it. To be doing what is good can be the greatest obstacle to doing something even better.*

Suzanne Farham

- ❖ *The person with addiction is not doing anything to you-but in spite of you.*
- ❖ *We become less in our pain-or more.*
- ❖ *Sooner or later, we must give up all hope of a better yesterday.*
- ❖ *When I knew better, I could do better.*
- ❖ *Because we need to change what we do does not mean the situation is our fault!*

❖ *I cannot lead you out of darkness, but I shall not close you out of my heart.*

❖ *Do not prepare the path for the child. Prepare the child for the path.*

❖ *A mother is not a person to lean on, but a person to make leaning unnecessary.*

❖ *We all have issues in our tissues.*

❖ *You do not have to go to every argument you are invited to.*

❖ *Do you listen to learn -or to argue?*

❖ *He pulled his thoughts down over his ears. (Helen Hudson)*

❖ *My life is crumbling into place! (Linda. Family member1988)*

❖ *My life cannot be what you figured out. (Al Turoski)*

❖ *You cannot cross a chasm in two small jumps.*

❖ *What hurts us is not what we do not know. It is what we think we know is true and is not.*

❖ *Depending on your expectations, you can spend your whole life being pleasantly surprised or sadly disappointed.*

❖ *I had just about given up on what to expect. I just lived to see what would happen next.*

❖ *Is your own self-growth abandoned in favor of waiting for others to change?*

❖ *Sometimes, the only thing you can do to an alcoholic is the only thing that will help.*

❖ *We are responsible to each other, but that does not mean you are my fault.*

❖ *How do you make a man? You thinketh him so.*

❖ *When I do not know that I am hanging onto something, it is hard to let go.*

❖ *Families are the training ground for forgiveness.*

❖ *A bitter pill is better swallowed than chewed.*

❖ *You are not your story.*

- *When you remove your expectations from me, you are free to receive my gifts.*
- *About delusion and dental: mental health is a dedication to reality at all costs. Facts do not cease to be true just because they are ignored.*
- *Forgiveness is about letting go of past behaviors. Trust is about the future behaviors.*
- *We cannot assume, because things are not going the way we want, they are not following a better plan.*
- *Co-dependency is an erroneous perception of self and love.*
- *Co-dependency: a pattern of painful dependence on compulsive behaviors and approval from others in an attempt to find safety, self-worth and identity. (Early definition from founders of COA movement).*
- *Do you suffer from terminal niceness??*
- *Co-dependents put high value on self-sacrifice.*
- *Does anyone really want the fruits of somebody else's self-denial?*
- *"If I am what I do-then I don't-I'm not"(Edith Bunker)*
- *The false self in codependency makes the moment more comfortable and the future more difficult.*
- *Are you addicted to someone else's potential?*
- *If you become more it does not make me less.*
- *Addiction and codependency are outer reaches for inner security.*
- *Adapt your attitude to fit reality, not the opposite.*
- *Just because you say it is over does not mean it is over.*
- *To want everyone to like us is normal.*
- *To think this is possible is insane.*
- *To act as if you can make this happen is crippling. (Robert Handelsman)*
- *The only real disability in life is a bad attitude.*

- *Some victims just want sympathy for the plight. (Mary Spencer)*
- *No one can make you feel inferior without your consent. (Eleanor Roosevelt)*
- *Children's talent to endure stems from their ignorance of alternatives. (Maya Angelo)*
- *Denial: we go from being ignorant of being ignorant to being aware of being aware.*
- *We stay attached to the pain or let go and risk that we will not perish. (Anis Anin)*
- *Thank heaven he is charming otherwise I would stone him to death. (Family member)*
- *Does your defense system destroy your support system?*

- *I will come to the family program just as soon as he remembers where he left the car. (Family member)*
- *My commitments are going to get me committed.*
- *The problem with life is that it is so daily*
- *Detachment: I do not get mad and I do not get had.*
- *A first-class human being needs some regard for human frailty.*
- *The only thing worse than being an alcoholic is to see one at your dinner table.*
- *My mouth has a life of its own. It keeps dieseling.*
- *Going to a meeting and expecting to be sober is like sitting around a barn and expecting to be a cow. It takes about 5 years to reach emotional maturity in AA----until you can be in a frame of mind that is not intrinsically your own. (AA wisdom)*
- *It is ironic that those of us who most want a solution, become involved and slowly become a part of the problem. (author)*
- *"The tragedy of her life is not that he left---it is that she never showed up."*

- *Reality is to see what you see and know what you know. I may see what I want to see and may not see what I need to see. Do we need an "illusionectomy"?*
- *The solution to my life occurred to me one evening while I was ironing a shirt. (Family member)*
- *We are all in the same boat on a stormy sea, and we owe each other a terrible loyalty.*
- *Edison found 467 elements that did not work.*
- *Do we use our talents and characteristics to try to control the lives of others? (I kissed him to make him a prince, and I turned into a frog).*
- *Does your adjustment to life require suffering? (Mary Spencer)*
- *Are we so open-minded that our brains fall out?*
- *Not everything that is faced can be changed, but nothing can be changed until it is faced.*
- *Let go and let god is not a passport to inertia.*
- *I do not detach from you, but I do detach from the agony of involvement in your problem. (Little Alters Everywhere).*
- *Please do not judge how lovable you are by some else's inability to love.*
- *We need not be responsible for another person's irresponsible behavior. It makes us irresponsible to do so.*
- *At meetings you learn to be on guard against the unguarded moments.*
- *It is easier to get your way if you have more than one way.*
- *Ask yourself: what will I do if nothing ever changes??*
- *The person with addiction needs to stay clean long enough to learn how to stay clean.*
- *Eventually, we must learn to stop being eternally furious with whom we picked to fail us.*
- *Are we too devalued to act in our own behalf with no motive except self-interest?*

- *Do you let someone climb their ladder of self-esteem by stepping on your rungs?*
- *Make growth choices – not fear choices.*
- *The care of others and 'subordination of self' are not synonymous.*
- *Codependency is really good at maintaining what probably should be allowed to collapse.*
- *A funny thing happened on the way to 'my way.'*
- *Never let yesterday use up too much of today.*
- *Advice-I listen to.   Pain- I obey!*

From AA:

- *If you do not change, you will use. If you do not use, you will change.*
- *A person may have many excuses, but the person with addiction uses*
- *For only one reason: they are addicted.*
- *Our dilemma is that we hate change but would love it if things could remain the same but get better.*
- *We need to come to terms with two things: our pain and our powerlessness*
- *Detach: don't---even---think---about---changing---him/her.*
- *We have fugitive moments of perception. And gauzy memories*
- *The condition of being human is to accept the truth that things do not last.*
- *One of our great losses is the preciousness of routine.*
- *"if you do not change direction, you may end up where you are heading" Laotzt1 (604-531 BC)*
- *"if you can't be content with what you have received, be thankful for what you have Unknown*

- There is great power in a made -up mind
- 12-step attendance is not the same as involvement.
- You are not defined by your circumstances.
- If you are ready, nobody can say anything wrong. If you are not ready, nobody can say anything right.
- Every trail has some puddles.
- You are more likely to get your way if you have more than one way.
- Something may be necessary but not sufficient.
- "why do you sit there looking like an envelope with no address on it?" Mark Twain
- The 12-step programs need to be used as a vitamin, not an antibiotic.
- "Well-sometimes I use them as an antibiotic": (Lee— Recovering Alcoholic)
- Parents who tolerate abuse and continue to fund their adult addicted person: this is like underwriting your own elder abuse. (Dr. Phil)
- God-in his wisdom-has given us opportunities brilliantly designed as difficulties.
- Sometimes the hardest things to do are the things we have to quit doing.
- Be supportive-----not custodial!
- Doing less may be doing more.
- There are two kinds of business: my business and not my business.
- We do not see people as they are. We see them as we are. (The Talmud)
- The art of wisdom is knowing what to overlook. (Anais Nin)
- Trust leaves on a fast horse and returns on a slow turtle.
- Hope is a wonderful companion and a very poor guide.
- Being ignorant of ourselves, we often beg our own harm. (Shakespeare)

- *Change is messy.*
- *If I cannot change the people around me, I need to change the people around me.*
- *What do you wear when you walk down the aisle to marry a chemical?*
- *When you are hurt and angry, you are in it. When you are sad, you are watching it.*
- *He is R and R. Retired and relapsed. He is lost in the sauce*

- *Some family members are amnesiacs and revisionists*
- *'It is good to start the 12-step programs in the summer. You will stick to the chairs.*
- *"You know you are doing something right when you stop feeling like a creep." Mary s. (family member)*
- *Expectations are pre-arranged resentments*
- *I will come to understand my pain and find its value in my life.*
- *Misery is to be overcome. It is not to be used as a marinade.*
- *Good parenting is a guarantee of nothing*
- *A parent's love does not mean a child's success.*
- *When the horse is dead---get off.*
- There is no problem so big and complicated that it cannot be run away from. My brother
- *What does your guilt keep you from doing?*
- *That which hinders the problem becomes the problem.*
- *) A family in recovery needs to look at their habits of avoidance and independence.*
- *Are you being nibbled to death by ducks?*
- *What upsets me is not that you, lied to me, but that I can no longer trust you.*
- *The glory of time is that it keeps everything from happening all at once!*
- *It is OK to let others be responsible to you.*

❖ *Sobriety allows growth to happen. It does not make it happen.*

A final quote from Jeff Jay (author of Wits End and other books). I had called him for support in the seemingly endless task of writing a book. He gave me this quote:

❖ "Someone has said that a book is never finished. It is just finally abandoned."

OOOOOOPPPPPS.... Just One More Thing...

Ten Great Things About Recovering From Someone Else's Addiction

By Stephanie Abbott

1. The sun manages to come up without your help.
2. Therapy finally kicks in.
3. You can stop apologizing for what someone else did.
4. Other people can solve their own problems-or not.
5. You <u>really</u> know you didn't cause it.
6. The statute of limitations has expired on your old mistakes.
7. You let other people be wrong even though you could improve things given a chance.
8. It's okay when other people can see that you and your life aren't perfect.
9. Worry is no longer a virtue.
10. You don't believe that only selfish people enjoy themselves.

Stephanie Abbott, MA, is the editor of NACoA NETWORK.

Resources Referred to in Text

Before it's too Late: Working with Substance Abuse in the Family

David C. Treadway

ISBN:13-978-0393700688

The Dance of Anger: A Woman's Guide to Changing the Patterns of Intimate Relationships

Harriet Lerner, Ph.D.

ISBN: 978-06-231904-3

Unspoken Legacy: Addressing the Imapct of Trauma and Addiction within the Family

Claudia Black, Ph.D.

ISBN: 978-19-209457-9

My Dad Loves Me, My Dad has a Disease

Claudia Black, Ph.D.

It Will Never Happen to Me

Claudia Black, Ph.D.

ISBN: 0-345-34594-0

It Takes a Family

Debra Jay

ISBN: 978-1-61649-534-3

Love First: A family's Guide to Intervention

Jeff Jay and Debra Jay

ISBN: 978-1-59285-661-9

At Wit's End: What You Need to Know When a Loved One is Diagnosed with Addiction and Mental Illness

Jeff Jay

Jerry A. Boriskin, Ph.D.

ISBN: 978-1-59285-373-1

Recovery Rising

William L. White

ISBN: 12-978-1976051869

Beyond Addiction: How Science and Kindness Help People Change

Jeffrey Foote, Ph.D., Carrie Wilkens, Ph.D., Nicole Kosanke, Ph.D., with Stephanie Higgs

ISBN: 978-1-4767-0948-2

Beautiful Boy; A Father's Journey Through His Son's Addiciton

David Sheff

ISBN: 978-0-547-20388-1

Clean: Overcoming Addiction and Ending America's Greatest Tragedy

David Sheff

ISBN: 978-0-547-84865-5

The Resilient Self: Now Survivors of Troubled Families Rise Above Adversity

Steven Wolin, MD, Sybil Wolin, Ph.D.

ISBN: 0-8129-9176-1

Grandchildren of Alcoholics: Another Generation of Co-dependency

Ann W. Smith

ISBN: 978-0932194558

Another Chance: Hope and Health for the Alcoholic Family

Sharon Wegscheider Cruse

ISBN: 978-0831400729

Addict in the Family: Stories of Loss, Hope, and Recovery

Beverly Conyers

ISBN: 978-156839998

Everything Changes: Help for Families of Newly Recovering Addicts

Beverly Conyers

ISBN: 978-2592856978

The Prison with No Bars: A Book for Families Dealing with Addict Lovd Ones

Clint Crawford

ISBN: 978-0692979150

The Natural History of Alcoholism Revisited

George E. Vaillant

ISBN: 978-0674603783

Addict in the House: A no-Nonsense Family Guide Through Addiction and Recovery

Robin Barnett, EdD, LCSW

ISBN: 978-1626252608

Opening Our Hearts: Transforming Our Losses

Al-anon Family Groups

ISBN: 978-0910034470

Not — God: A History of Alcoholics Anonymous

Ernest Kurtz

ISBN: 978-0894860652

On Death and Dying: What the Dying Have to Teach Doctors, Nurses, Clergy & Their Own Families

Elisabeth Kubler-Ross, M.D.

ISBN: 978-176775548

The Road Less Traveled: A New Psychology of Love, Traditional Values, and Spiritual Growth

Scott Peck, MD

ISBN: 978-0743243155

Slaying the Dragon: The History of Addiction Treatment and Recovery in America

William L. White

ISBN: 978-069221365

The Spirituality of Imperfection: Storytelling and the Search for Meaning

Ernest Kurtz and Katherine Ketcham

ISBN: 9780553371321

The Gifts of Imperfection: Let Go of Who You Think You're Supposed to Be and Embrace Who You Are; A Guide to Wholehearted Life

Brene Brown, Ph.D., L.M.S.W.

ISBN: 978-1592858491

Stage II Recovery: Life Beyond Addiction

Earnie Larsen

ISBN: 978-0866834605

Recovery 2.0: Move Beyond Addiction and Upgrade Your Life

Tommy Rosen

ISBN: 978-1401944483

Making Peace with You Past: The Six Essential Steps to Enjoying a Great Future

Harold Bloomfield, M.D.

ISBN: 978-006-933142

Intimacy, Change, and Other Therapeutic Mysteries: Stories of Clinicians and Clients

David C. Treadway

ISBN: 978-159380746

Pleasure Unwoven

Dr. Kevin McCauley

https://www.youtube.com/playlist?list=PLA8F89537FD4C3FD1

Codependent No More: How to Stop Controlling Others and Start Caring for Yourself

Melody Beattie

ISBN: 978-0894864025

Selfish Brain: Learning from Addiction

Robert L. DuPont, M.D.

ISBN: 978-1568383637

Recommendations

https://learn.genetics.utah.edu/content/addiction/mouse/

For Information on Drugs, Resources, and Current Thoughts on Addiction

http://www.williamwhitepapers.com

https://addictionandrecoverynews.wordpress.com

www.lovefirst.net

www.al-anon.alateen.org

ncadi.samhsa.gov/

www.nmha-----national mental health assoc.

www.nami./ ---mental health

www.al-anon, alateen.org/

www.nida.nih.gov

31008524R00226

Made in the USA
Lexington, KY
14 February 2019